Architectural Guide
Chisinau

Architectural Guide
Chisinau

Stefan Rusu

With additional contributions by Vlada Ciobanu, Irina Dubinschi,
Anastasia Felcher, and Vitalie Sprinceana

DOM
publishers

View of the Rascani district from the Centre district

Contents

Top: View of the Residential Complex on Mazarache Hill designed by Y. Skvortsova,
A. Kurovsky, A. Spasov, G. Rodidyal, E. Fedchenko, S. Nedler, 1984.
Left: View of the industrial area and Ciocana district from the city centre.
Right: View of Government Hall from the city centre, designed by Semyon Fridlin, 1964.

The Unknown City

Stefan Rusu

For almost half a century, the city of Chisinau, incorporated into the Soviet project of the USSR, was modernised according to socialist principles and standards. The capital of Moldova (the Moldavian Soviet Socialist Republic; MSSR) was perceived as a peripheral city and compared negatively to other capitals, whether in the Baltic States (Tallinn, Riga, Vilnius) or in Central Asia (Bishkek, Almaty, Tashkent).

Sporadic mentions of Chisinau in any literature (Архитектура СССР) were especially critical, addressing inconsistencies in the city planning and development, while only occasionally presenting notable public or residential architectural projects. [1] Perhaps due to its marginal position at the Western extremity of the Soviet Empire, Chisinau was fresh and fertile ground for the experiments and creative formulae that have shaped the current urban structure, which remains in perpetual transformation.

A dramatic scenery has dominated the urban landscape over the past several decades. Although it has undergone complex modernisation, the urban landscape and its management methods seem to present the viewer with scenes from a grotesque play, characterised by a general degradation of architectural heritage and dysfunctional urbanism. Many are attracted to the city; others are repelled by it. Poised between attachment and aversion, there is an unexplored space, which we would like to explore from a conceptual and stylistic point of view.

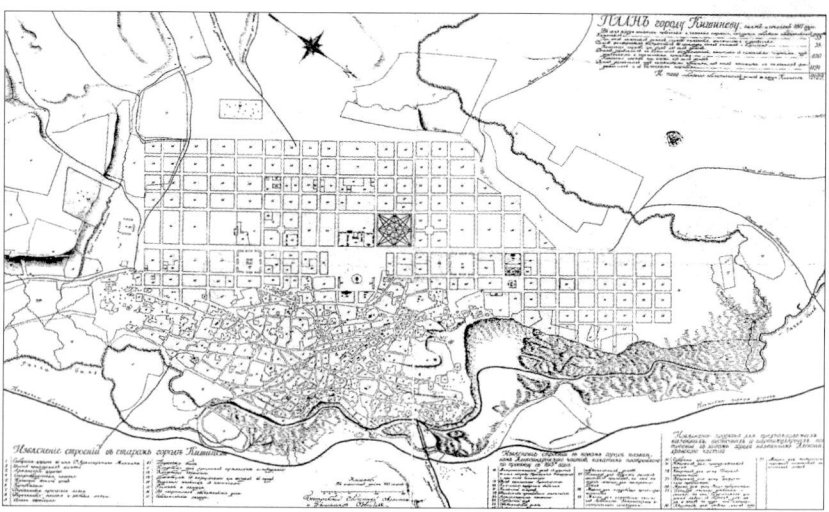

Structure of the eighteenth century: the medieval town (below) and the grid plan developed during the Russian Empire (above), 1817. *Source: National Archive of the Republic of Moldova*

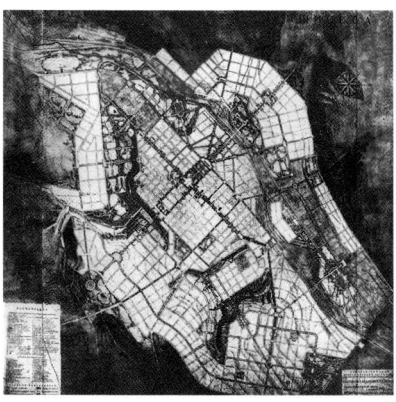

The master plan for the reconstruction of Chisinau.
Designed by the Aleksey Shchusev studio, 1947.
Source: Archive of Aleksey Shchusev Museum, Chisinau

Functional zoning scheme for Chisinau.
Designed by the Aleksey Shchusev studio, 1947.
Image source: forum oldchisinau.com

Building the New City

Chisinau underwent radical modernisation in social and political terms after 1940, with the annexation and co-
optation of the region into the USSR political project. The urban structure was
thoroughly rebuilt in the first phase after the Second World War and was later
developed in stages synchronised with
the five-year plans. Several factors contributed to the condition of the city after the war. Retreating Red Army troops
(the engineering battalion and the NKVD
troops) blew up a number of buildings in
1940. The city was then bombarded by
the German air force in 1941, and later in
1944 it was subjected to intense bomb-
ing raids by Allied aircraft (both Soviet
and American) at the time of the counter-
offensive by Soviet troops, which left the
city in ruins. [2]

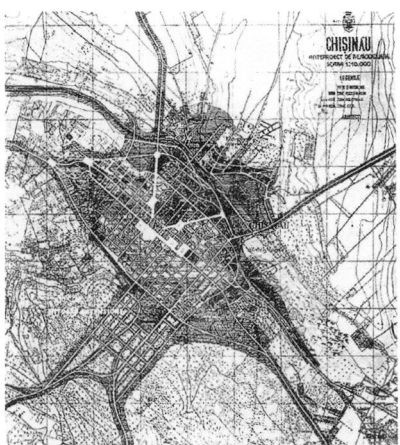

Sketch of a city redevelopment plan designed by
O. Doicescu and D. Ghiulamila, 1942.
*Image source: Technics and Life magazine, no. 1,
1943, pp.25-26, Archive of A. Vatamaniuc*

The buildings that were most affected
were in the historical core of the city,
made of interspersed stylistic and ideological elements such as the structure of
the medieval city in the eighteenth century, the grid plan with the neoclassical
architecture of the Russian Empire from
the nineteenth century, and the art deco
and Bauhaus architecture from the period
of the Romanian Kingdom from the twentieth century. Apart from the fact that
the urban structure was in ruins, society
was disintegrating due to the forced dis-
location of the local population and the
segregation and genocide of the Jewish
population from the ghetto in the lower
part of the city, instrumented during the
Romanian administration. [3] Social engineering was continued by the Soviet
administration after the end of the war
with famine (1946–1947) and the de-
portation of the native population in
1941, 1949 (Operation South), and 1951
(Operation North).
The revival of the city required a substantial effort from the newly installed administration, which had woefully inade-
quate material and human resources. The
Union of Architects of the MSSR was established in 1945 in Chisinau in order to
consolidate the profession. The first assembly, comprising 20 members, elected Piotr Ragulin as chairman. [4] The rehabilitation and reconstruction of the
city, which also involved the elaboration

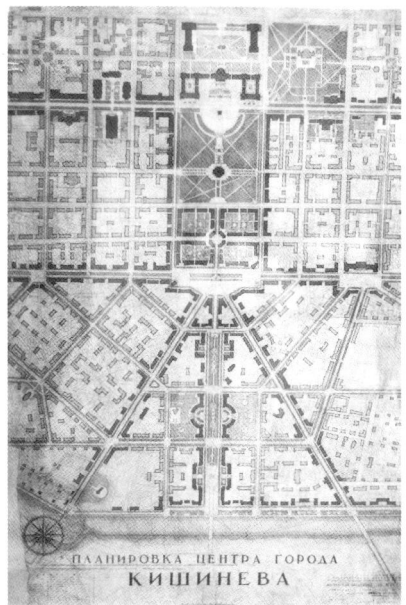

Systematisation of Chisinau city centre.
Designed by Aleksey Shchusev's studio, 1947.
Image source: forum oldchisinau.com

of a city master plan, involved the academic Alexey Shchusev, who was also in charge of the rehabilitation of the cities of Stalingrad (Volgograd), Novgorod, and Kyiv. [5] Shchusev's concept was developed in his Moscow atelier and guided by a neoclassical typology inspired by the Russian architecture of the nineteenth century. Chisinau's grid structure with radial-concentric elements is very similar to that of the city of Novgorod. A possible source of inspiration was the plan developed by Octav Doicescu during the

Romanian administration (1943), which included a radial-concentric solution for the lower part of the city, as well as other ideas that were later found in the systematisation of the city. [6]

The city master plan initially developed in 1945–1947 by the team led by Shchusev was approved in a revised format as late as 1951. After the death of Shchusev in 1949, completion of the master plan was managed by Robert Kurtz (chief architect of the city) and Piotr Ragulin, with the participation of architects from Moscow and Leningrad as well as locals (V. Voitsekhovsky, A. Ambartsumyan etc.). The master plan entailed the restoration of old buildings, the construction of new buildings, and the creation of industrial areas, highways, public squares, and green spaces. According to this plan, the main boulevard (V. Lenin) was maintained as a thoroughfare connected by the C. Negruzzi and the Y. Gagarin Boulevards (Muncesti Street) with the Station Square. The main sites, besides the centre, were to be the districts of Rascani, Botanica, and Buiucani. From 1955 onwards, new districts with standard apartment blocks made of locally sourced limestone and reinforced concrete panels started appearing on the outskirts of the city. In the early 1960s, spatial solutions became more diverse, and the appearance of the façades became more elaborate, including balconies and loggias, and was complemented with chromatic accents. [7]

Reconstruction of Chisinau's university complex. Sketch by Aleksey Shchusev, 1945–1946
Image source: Archive of Aleksey Shchusev Museum

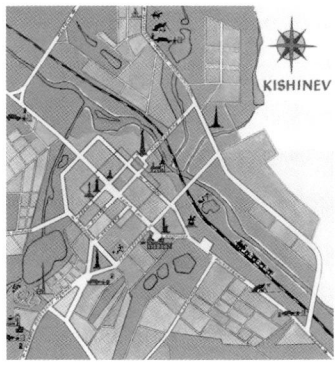

Mock-up of the city centre based on proposals made by the teams of Moldgiprostroy (Robert Kurtz, Shoikhet et al.) and LenNIIP (A. Tarantul, S. Sokolov et al.), 1968

Tourism booklet depicting the city centre and adjacent districts (raions). Vneshtorgizdat, USSR, 1970

In the 1960s, specialised design institutes were created, the main objective of which was to accelerate and reduce construction costs by using standard designs. The standardised designs were not developed only for residential buildings, but also for the public centres of cities and villages. The first public buildings of this type were designed by R. Kurtz, V. Voitsekhovsky, V. Mednek, A. Kolotovkin, and others. With the transition to the production of prefabricated blocks and the emergence of regulations and state standards, architecture became subordinated to the construction industry. Only particularly important buildings were erected according to individual designs. Chisinau was one of the first cities in the USSR to lay the foundations for the industrial production of residential buildings. [8]

With the increase in population, the Moldgiprostroy Institute (R. Kurtz, S. Shoichet, and A. Kolotovkin), in collaboration with the Institute of Urban Research and Development in Kyiv, developed a feasibility study between 1963 and 1965 for the development of the city until 1980, based on which a city master plan that was approved in 1969.

In 1966, a competition was organised by the USSR Gosstroy and the MSSR Gosstroy, the USSR Union of Architects, and the Executive Committee of the city of Chisinau. The projects presented by Moldgiprostroy (R. Kurtz, S. Shoichet, and others) and the Leningrad Institute of Development (A. Tarantul, S. Sokolov) were selected for the development of the

detailed plan. According to the recommendations, the detailed plan was approved in 1971. It involved the reconstruction of the city centre and the complex development of the new residential districts. The ensuing avalanche of funds that financed the development of the city is explained by Leonid Brezhnev's special concern for Moldova, which he associated with the beginning of his political career. In 1973, on the foundations of Moldgiprostroy, the Chisinau GorProiect institute was created, with an exclusive focus on the development of the capital. In 1983, the Chisinau GorProiect institute, together with the Central Institute for Scientific Research for Urban Planning, developed a new feasibility study for the period up to 2000. The city was supposed to expand in two directions: first towards Sireti-Ghidighici Lake, nicknamed the 'Chisinau Sea', and secondly towards the airport. The projected growth in population was expected to reach 800,000. In 1985, a new city master plan was drawn up at the Chisinau GorProiect Institute (Y. Tumanyan, A. Kogan, B. Bendersky, and others); after a long hiatus, it was finally updated in 2007. [9]

The Faces of Socialist Realism

In the central area of the city, it is possible to distinguish stylistically distinct areas that have been inserted into the urban texture formed at the end of the nineteenth century and the beginning of the twentieth century. These insertions were directly influenced by the political influences that dominated society. They took shape under the guidance of the political leaders of the time (Stalin, Khrushchev, Brezhnev) and can be found in the design of buildings and urban infrastructure in most cities of the Soviet Union.

The architecture of socialist realism was established as a state ideology in 1933 with the official approval of the Palace of the Soviets (Boris Iofan) project in Moscow. Later, during the First Congress of Soviet Writers (1934), socialist realism gained legitimacy and became mandatory in all fields. As an ideological programme, it was the forerunner of the most important landmarks of the Soviet Union. On the one hand, it aligned with the main goal of the Bolsheviks – to create a New Soviet Man. On the other hand, it pursued the advanced ideal of the constructivists, who strove to build an urban utopia in which this New Man could live. But Stalin had other plans, and he ended the utopian project of the constructivists (Ginzburg, Milinis, and the Vesnin brothers etc.). The evolution of constructivism in the USSR was interrupted; the architects lost their creative freedom, and under pressure from the authorities, returned to classical architecture.

The period 1933–1955 was marked by tutelage, as socialist realism became an ideological programme, which eventually included the Republic of Moldova (the then MSSR) after the annexation of the region in 1940. Some buildings, architectural ensembles, and public squares realised on the threshold between the two stages and ideological narratives of Soviet architecture are certainly part of the utopian project stylistically framed by theorists using the term the 'Stalinist Empire'. In the local context, it would be more appropriate to call this 'Stalinist eclecticism', since such structures echoed the architecture promoted in Moscow and other capital cities.

Rebuilding the city was a difficult task, and military personnel were first enlisted to help in the process. In a short period of time, the centrally appointed government played a decisive role in reconfiguring the city according to the socialist model. One of its members, Leonid

Brezhnev (1950–1952), who became the First Secretary of the MSSR CP, had the mission of defusing the precarious situation and reindustrialising the republic. For his part, Alexey Shchusev guided local professionals during his visits to Chisinau, insisting on the specifics of Soviet architecture, which shunned bourgeois decorations and harmonised well the proportions and architectural forms. In his vision, based on the Stalinist formula 'socialist in content and national in form', the architecture of socialist realism in the MSSR was to be a synthesis of classicism, features specific to Chisinau, and traditional folk elements.

After Shchusev's death, the reformation of the city according to the socialist canons continued thanks to the perseverance of local architects. Robert Kurtz, Valentin Mednek, and Valentin Voitsekhovski, known as the 'Kumevo' group (an acronym drawn from the first letters of each of their names), hailed from a European school (the Ion Mincu Institute in Bucharest and the Brno Faculty of Architecture). In addition, Serghei Vassiliev and Victor Smirnov, as well as Fiodor Naumov and Agasi Ambartsumian implemented the stylistics and principles of the Soviet school of architecture (exemplified, among others, by the Moscow MARKHI and the Tashkent Institute of Construction).

Thus, two trends emerged, promoting socialist realism and interpreting the spirit of the Stalinist era in different manners: one represented by local architects, endowed with a universal language (Kumevo), and another with more

MSSR Pavilion at the Exhibition of Economic Achievements of the USSR (VDNH). S. Vasiliev, Fiodor Naumov, (official version: Fiodor Naumov, A. Zakharov, V. Tukanov, S. Vasiliev) 1952–1954
Image source: Archive Velichko

Decoration of the window, side façade of the pavilion of the Moldavian SSR. (VDNH). Photo 1954
Image source: Archive Velichko

conservative visions (Vassiliev, Smirnov et al.). Smirnov came to the MSSR with solid experience, having assisted Shchusev in the construction of the Alisher Navoi Theatre building in Tashkent. He acted in the same spirit in Chisinau, designing the Pushkin Theatre (the Mihai Eminescu Theatre) in 1956. Likewise, Vassiliev authored a number of landmark buildings with a characteristic individual style. One of them was the MSSR Pavilion at the Exhibition of Economic Achievements of the USSR (VDNH), completed in December 1954 in Moscow. Together with Agasi Ambartsumyan, he designed the Republican Library (Krupskaya), built in 1953–1957, and, in collaboration with Iosif Eltman, the Dinamo Stadium (1950–1955). The meeting room of the Supreme Council of the CP of the MSSR, rebuilt in 1953–1956 on the basis of an existing building (the Rascanu-Derojinschi Urban Mansion, built by Alexander Bernardazzi), can be considered the major work of the architect.

During the same period, members of the 'Kumevo' group were equally productive, creating a distinct and balanced style based on Renaissance architecture and building iconic structures in the central area of the city (the Trade Union Headquarters, the Central Post Office, the Ministry of Food Industry), in a style best described as a pared-down expression of neoclassicism. Voitsekhovski proved to be the most faithful successor of the canon of national architecture defined by Shchusev, and the most consistent in combining neoclassicism with traditional motifs. Another reference design is the EREN Pavilion (the Republican Exhibition of National Economic Achievements). The distinctive elements of this building are the monumental exterior reliefs on the pediment and the counter-reliefs on the side, to the left and to the right of the main entrance. Thus, the 'Kumevo' group, in addition to the conservative protagonists, faithfully completed the programme of socialist realism.

Other areas that exemplify the Stalinist Empire style are the Republican Stadium, Valea Morilor Park, and the Dinamo Stadium, all aimed to educate and maintain the New Man in a competitive physical shape with a well-built body. In the MSSR, the programme of creating the New Man and a new society by building the utopia represented by festive and triumphalist architecture lasted a relatively short period from 1944 to 1955. It came to an end during the transition from the Stalinist regime to the new policies initiated by Nikita Khrushchev. There were also exceptions that delayed the effects of the decree, as well as the ongoing fight against excesses in architecture and construction. Some buildings were completed after the shift in official discourse (such as the Chisinau Hotel and the Central Post Office). It is obvious that the gap between the compositional endeavours of the architects and the acute social needs of society forced drastic changes both in the organisation of the construction industry and in the evolution of designs. [10]

The Origins of Soviet Modernism in Moldova

Ilya Ehrenburg's novel, *The Thaw*, become the moniker for the détente period that occurred after Stalin's death in 1953. Khrushchev's rule brought relative relaxation. Ideological control weakened and was marked by ambiguity, and change and

The National Palace (initially the 'October Hall') designed by Semyon Fridlin, 1974

continuity coexisted. On the one hand, a certain ideological relaxation was allowed; on the other, intellectuals had to remain regimented and work in the service of the communist state.

It was against this backdrop in 1955 that Decree No. 1871 of the USSR Council of Ministers 'On Excesses in Architecture' was issued, marking the beginning of Soviet modernism. In the middle of the night of 24–25 February 1956, Nikita Khrushchev presented one of the most influential political documents of the twentieth century: 'On the Cult of Personality and its Consequences'.

Soviet modernism reached Chisinau via Ukraine. Semyon Fridlin's team from Kyiv came up with the third version for the Government Hall, which was accepted, and later with the October Hall project (the 'Nicolae Sulac' National Palace). [11] At the same time, Victor Dubok of Kyiv designed the Intercity Telephone Station (1967), which was similar to the Kyiv and Kharkov projects. In terms of style, the façade of the Government Hall is indebted to the spirit of the Kremlin Palace of Congress (Mikhail Posokhin, Ashot Mndoyants et al.), which had a strange fate but also a special symbolism. The project of the Palace of the Soviets (Boris Iofan) started in 1937, but it was abandoned in 1957. A new building was built, not in the place chosen by Stalin but in the Kremlin. Its construction was kept secret and it was inaugurated in 1961. In

Parliament of the Republic of Moldova (former Central Committee of the Communist Party of Moldova) designed by Alexander Cherdantsev, Grigore Bosenko, 1976

a symbolic gesture, Khrushchev criticised the cult of Stalin right from the rostrum of the Palace of Congress, designed in the style of Soviet modernism. Naturally, the decree on excesses in architecture and the report on the cult of Stalin had an impact on the MSSR.

In 1961, Ivan Bodiul was appointed First Secretary of the MSSR CP. He was to dominate the political scene until 1983, and many important urban projects were developed precisely during this period. Apart from necessary urban development, there were also excesses; for example, the symbolic reconfiguration of the main axis of the Government House resulted in the demolition of the bell tower of the cathedral (1962), while the cathedral was transformed into an exhibition centre affiliated with the Artists' Union. Another attempt to symbolically reconfigure public space resulted in clashes with those in power. The attempt to move the statue of Stefan cel Mare from the centre of Chisinau and exile it in the city of Vadul lui Voda sparked a protest in 1964. At the initiative of Mihai Morosanu, a group of students collected signatures (approx. 3,000) and protested against the relocation of the monument. Eventually the authorities gave up on the idea, but Mihai Moroşanu was persecuted and convicted for his actions according to article 71 of the penal code for 'crimes of nationalism'.

As hard as it may be to believe it nowadays, it was in this environment that the landmarks of this period appeared: the Press House (Semyon Shoikhet, Abram Vaisbein, 1967), the Noroc restaurant (Vladislav Kudinov, Victor Zaharov, 1967), the Tennis Hall (Semyon Shoikhet, Alla Kirichenko, 1968), the Writers' House (David Palatnik, Victor Iavorskii, 1974), and the Parliament Garage (Anatolyi Dubrovsky, 1978). Following the same style, the Republican Clinical Hospital was designed by another team from Kyiv (KievZNIIEP) led by V. Baklanov.

A number of standard designs were taken over and adapted to the local context. For instance, the design of the new airport was developed by the team at the Lenaeroproekt Institute in Leningrad led by A. Eksner. Another imported design was used for the MEZON plant complex (1969), subordinated to the Ministry of the Electronics Industry of the USSR, which was similar to the MICRON plant in Zelenograd. [12]

Despite the internationalism and the democratic spirit embodied by modernism, Bodiul managed urban policies in an authoritarian manner, and therefore decisions on reconfiguring the city and placing important landmarks rested with him. So did certain excesses, such as the demolition of specific neighbourhoods to make way for the administrative urban centre. This resulted in the annihilation of the heritage of the Jewish community (e.g., the Choral Synagogue). Retaliation and the erasure of the memory of the Jewish community had began in the 1940s with the nationalisation of synagogues in Chisinau. The radical change in the demographic composition of the city and its architecture were amplified by the advancement of the Soviet project and its accompanying societal transformation.

The Late Effects of Soviet Brutalism

Under the auspices of modernism, many new styles appeared, including brutalism, represented by virile concrete structures with rough textures and a bold geometry of volumes. Brutalism emerged as a phenomenon in the 1950s in Britain due to a lack of resources to maintain and continue refined styles in architecture and design. Most supporters of this style held socialist positions, highlighting the merits of brutalism as not only a low price of construction (which was a key advantage in the post-war period), but also an uncompromising anti-bourgeois attitude and stylistic 'honesty'.

The brutalist style also manifested itself in Soviet architecture. This trend most clearly reflected the political and social ideas that were to be embodied not only in words, but also in visual representations. Each building was to have its own individuality, to be different from all the others, and to differ radically from the principles of early modernism. The lightness and clarity of the modernist style were sacrificed for the weight of structures and the roughness of monochrome surfaces. Reinforced concrete became the favourite building material, and stylistically these buildings sent a message about relinquishing excesses. In essence, rendering was abandoned as an element of modern architecture, and instead the rough surface of the concrete was showcased. In the case of Chisinau, finishing did not disappear completely, as it was re-introduced in order to mask the imperfections of technological processes.

Buildings that can be associated with this style include the Oncology Institute (1992), the Moldtelecom Company headquarters (Alexandr Kireev, Nicolai Dorofeev, Vladimir Shalaghinov, 1983), the ALFA Joint Stock Company complex (1976–1985), and the ACVAPROIECT Institute (Molgiprovodkhoz, Anatoly Kolotovkin, Tatiana Lomova, 1980). Brutalism as a style defies clichés. Given their use of volume, such buildings could include the Joint Stock Company 'Apă-Canal Chişinău'/S.A. MoldovaGaz, the headquarters of the Botanica Council (Leonid Voronin, Nadejda Malitseva, 1987), and the 'toothed wheel block' (Isaak Schvartzev, 1987). Political factors played a decisive role in the emergence of the 'toothed wheel block' residential complex when Bodiul decided to demolish the Hutzulevka neighbourhood. [13] The 'residential complex of four tower blocks with social infrastructure' (G. Solominov, O. Vronsky, 1974) on Dacia Boulevard can also be considered an architectural ensemble that decisively combines modernist ideals together with brutalism.

Postmodernism with Local Colour

According to American theorist Fredric Jameson, 'the emergence of postmodernism can be traced to the post-war boom in the United States in the late 1940s and early 1950s, and in France since the founding of the Fifth Republic in 1958'. A completely different situation is characteristic of Soviet architecture: here there is a substantial time lag between the development of ideas and their application. Postmodernism as a modern perception of the world is a protest against reality, a controversy with modernism, and at the same time a summary and a rethinking. While modernism sought to find certainty and an unshakable foundation, postmodernism was concerned with everyday life, radical pluralism, and uncertainty.

In the early 1960s, there were no Bessarabians in leadership positions, with the top political elite being imported mainly from Ukraine. The persecution of intellectuals intensified towards the end of the 1960s. After a brief ideological thaw and a position expressed at the Third Congress of Moldovan Writers (1965) by A. Busuioc, V. Besleaga, V. Vasilache and others, I. Druta was forced to move to Moscow, where the democratic aspirations of the Moldovan writer were seen as progressive, while locally, Bodiul regarded him as a nationalist. [14] The same fate befell theatre director I. Ungureanu, who worked at the 'Luceafărul' Theatre as artistic director between 1964 and 1971 and was then accused of nationalism. Subjected to similar accusations, writers A. Busuioc, V. Besleaga, and V. Vasilache were all persecuted and left the cultural stage.

The twilight of Soviet modernism came with the tightening of controls and the ever more drastic limitation of citizens' rights to free speech. The end of the 'thaw' coincided with the Prague Spring

The ACVAPROIECT Institute designed by Anatoly Kolotovkin and Tatiana Lomova, 1980

in 1968, suppressed on the orders of the CP of the USSR (the Politburo). The leaders of the Czechoslovak Communist Party sought to reform of the communist system from within by relying on 'socialism with a human face'. At the same time, the pressures inside the USSR intensified with the student protests in France (the 'Red May' of 1968). [15]

The ideology of postmodernism took shape in the architecture of the USSR in the second half of the 1960s, but the stylistic instrumentation of this new direction did not come into practice until the second half of the 1970s. The reasons for this delay can be found not only in the infamous bureaucratisation of the design and production process, but also in the

The Palace of the Republic designed by Ivan Zagoretsky, Alexander Shevtsov, Mikhail Orlov, and Stanislav Makarchuk, 1984

'Guguta' Café ('Noroc' restaurant), redesigned by S. Lebedev and N. Zaporojan, 1976

'Noroc' restaurant, designed by V. Kudinov and V. Zakharov, 1967. *Image source: National Archive of Republic of Moldova*

sluggishness of the technological complex. To an even greater extent, they lie in the traditions of the national culture and in the mental habits and behavioural stereotypes of the local population.

Through the efforts of Bodiul, who was a Brezhnev protégé, the situation of the party staff gradually changed in the late 1970s, when rapid nationalisation of the local political elite took place. The staff policy in architecture and construction was based not only on the flow of graduate students from institutions in Moscow, Tashkent, and Kyiv, but also of architects with proven experience invited from other republics (Gennady Solominov, Yuri Tumanyan etc.). The first generation of native architects from the Polytechnic Institute graduated only in 1967, and since then the design teams have been formed using local specialists. [16]

It should be noted that architects and the technical staff were not persecuted. On the contrary, they were encouraged and stimulated by the political elite, while the disobedience of the other intellectuals (writers, poets, theatre directors etc.) was not tolerated. This attitude remained unchanged until the disintegration of the USSR. Contrary to the nationalisation tendencies of the local elites, in the sphere of culture the persecutions continued with the banning of the band Noroc, which had created quite a stir in the Soviet world with a number of hits that appeared on the Western song charts. The group was disbanded and lost the right to operate in Moldova by order No. 477 of 16 September 1970 signed by Minister Leonid Culiuc while he was visiting Ukraine, just as the band was preparing to tour South America.

The persecutions against Noroc coincided with the twilight of modernism, at a point when postmodernist tendencies had barely taken root on local architecture. In the wake of these events, and under the influence of the reprisals against both the westernisation of musical culture and against the liberal spirit that dominated society, expressed by long hair and 'cloche trousers' (flares), the

'Noroc' restaurant was transformed into a café for children ('The Fairytale', later renamed 'Guguta'). The restaurant did not fit into the logic of increasingly tighter control over the public space.

It was under the leadership of Bodiul that the headquarters of the Central Committee of the Communist Party of RSSM (Alexander Cherdantsev, Grigore Bosenko, 1976), the Ministry of Foreign Affairs (G. Solominov, 1977), and the Institute of History of the Party (A. Cherdantsev, 1978) were built, and Bodiul closely followed the construction process.

The next period, after 1980 and marked by the Moscow Olympics, can be identified as a period of stagnation. The development of the city took place according to previously drawn up plans and less generous budgets. Thanks to Brezhnev, still in charge of the SUCP, the first Moldovan native, Semyon Grossu, was able to become first secretary of the MSSR, during which time the pressure and ideological control of the centre weakened somewhat.

In the second half of the 1980s, the construction industry as well as the political sphere fell into decline, and this included a number of large-scale projects, such as the State University, supported by S. Grossu, for which the technical documentation had already been prepared (Moldgiprostroy). The project failed due

The modernist glass façade of Cinema Moscova designed by N. Kurennoy, 1965
Image source: Wikimedia Commons

to the massive demolition works that were necessary but difficult to achieve in the upper part of the city. Besides, at that stage neither the MSSR Gosplan nor the MSSR Gosstroi had the necessary resources. This is essentially when the construction sites and the large-scale projects in the historical core of the city came to a halt. Postmodernism lasted and extended as a period from the 1970s to the mid-1980s. Among the representative buildings of the period are the Palace of the Republic (1984) and the Faculty of Journalism of the State University (1987).

Amnesia and Architectural Heritage

During the Soviet period, ordinary citizens did not care about preserving the city's buildings. The state institutions were supposed to look after them, as evidenced by the deliberate attention to certain historical layers, highlighted by informational plaques placed on buildings in the historic centre of the city. At the same time, the historical layer represented by the buildings and synagogues of the Jewish community was ignored by the authorities, being marginalised and even excluded from public discourse. [17] During the transition to the late 1990s but also after 2000, another negative factor arose: the lack of resources for the restoration of the built heritage, the maintenance of which was left to the owners. This was the period when certain buildings from the interwar period were refurbished. The target of the privatisations during the transition period were several public buildings, such as houses of culture and youth centres, which were given another designation after 1992. The most visible indicator of urban transformations were the cinemas and the houses (palaces) of culture. On the one hand, the changes were natural, occurring at the same time as the decline of the analogue format, but on the other hand, they were easy solutions pursued by real estate developers. Thus, privatisation affected all the cinemas, which were transformed into casinos (Flacara), Baptist churches (Sipca and Mir), or malls (Iskra). Others, already privatised, were adapted to duplex technology and continued to be

Choral Synagogue, Chisinau, 1913–1940 (refurbished into A. Chekhov Russian Drama Theatre)
Image source: Wikimedia Commons

it was decided to expand and modernise it as a whole. During the process of rehabilitation, the wall mosaics disappeared and the original façades were altered. This is also the case of the Moscova Cinema, where the modernist elements – the façade and the foyer – were irreversibly transformed.

After the war, some public buildings were refurbished, such as Biruinta Cinema, the Philharmonic, and Chekhov Theatre. The Philharmonic and Chekhov Theatre were built using part of the structures of previous buildings – the Circus in the case of the Philharmonic and the Choral Synagogue (1913–1940) in the case of Chekhov Theatre. [18] The decision to place the Russian Theatre on the foundations of the most important synagogue in the city, perfectly functional before 1940, meant the resumption of a policy of social engineering. Responsibility for the disappearance of the city's most important synagogue lay with the authorities, while the architects took a neutral position as executors of orders and supervisors of the construction process.

used as cinemas (Patria, Biruinta). An exception is the defunctionalisation of the Moscova Cinema and its transformation into a cultural centre (Nicolay Iskimji, 2000) and later the E. Ionesco theatre.

The youth centre in the Ciocana district was handed over to the Guguta theatre, while the Gagarin youth centre was used as a leisure space (nightclub, disco) and later abandoned and left to decay. In some cases, it was decided to keep the building (Moscova Cinema), but to add a new façade. In other cases, the buildings have been adapted and expanded according to the will of the new investors (Chisinau airport). In no case were these buildings considered heritage objects. On the contrary, preservation of the original architecture was never taken into account. In the case of the airport,

The reconversion of the interwar buildings, sometimes implemented with abuses, had a meaning and a logic conditioned by the austerity and the acute lack of resources characterising the period immediately after the war. During the transition period, however, the approach to urban planning was based on

The A. Chekhov Russian Drama Theater, Roman Bekesevich, 1966
'Planeta' publishing house, USSR. *Photo: B. Krutsko*

the annihilation of structures associated with the modernisation period with the clear intention to break with the communist period. Gradually, a new urban and social structure was formed – a new city for a new type of society. The city's multicultural heritage remains an insufficiently explored cultural resource, and the architectural heritage has been allowed to decay.

A Predictable Ending

The events associated with the depoliticisation of the public space in Moldova followed in the wake of the disintegration of the USSR with the signing of the Belovezh Accords in December 1991. The decree issued by the Presidium of the Parliament of 25 August 1991 'On the Liquidation of the Consequences of Communist Propaganda' marked the beginning of the campaign of revising the communist symbolism in Chisinau – a process that has also extended to smaller cities and rural areas. The names of cities and villages (streets, boulevards, districts, etc.) were changed, while the monuments and the symbols from façades associated with the communist ideology were torn down.

These events did not influence only the architecture by stigmatising buildings and public spaces, but also the urban policies, which were categorised as totalitarian at a time when society and the political class were looking towards other horizons in the anticipation of a democratic order. Public buildings, obsolete and left to decay, as well as the urban infrastructure, outdated but still efficient, can be blamed today for a number of deficiencies. However, they remain a heritage that was produced with a level of effort and resources that are impossible to reproduce today on a similar scale.

Now, several decades after the fall of the USSR and after a period of economic and social collapse, a significant part of society still looks back with nostalgia. In such a context, the general state of amnesia that has enveloped society and the abandoned state of much of the architectural heritage of the post-war period are completely inexplicable.

Bibliography:

[1] V. Sokolov, 'Oportunităti utilizate şi neutilizate', Arhitectura SSSR, January 1981.

[2] Dinu Postarencu, 'Chisinaul in 1941', Editura Museum, 1996.

[3] Paul A. Shapiro, Ghetoul din Chisinau 1941–1942, Bucuresti, Curtea Veche, 2016.

[4] V. Smirnov, Gradostroitelistvo Moldavii XIX–XX vekov. Editura Kartea Moldoveneasca, Kishinev, 1975.

[5] K. Afanasiyev, 'A. Shchusev', Moskva: Izdatelistvo Stroyizdat, 1978.

[6] Tamara Nesterov, Andrei Vatamaniuc. Istoria deschisa a planului de sistematizare postbelica a Chisinaului, Revista Arta, 2019.

[7] A. Kolotovkin, I. Eltman, G. Peldash. Arhitectura Sovetskoi Moldavii, Moskva: Izdatelistvo Stroyizdat, 1987.

[8] Ibidem.

[9] Martin Klimke, Jacco Pekelder, Joachim Scharloth, Between Prague Spring and French May: Opposition and Revolt in Europe, 1960–1980, Published by Berghahn Books, 2011.

[10] V. Smirnov, Gradostroitelistvo Moldavii XIX–XX vekov. Editura Kartea Moldoveneasca, Kishinev, 1975.

[11] Tamara Nesterov, Implementarea realismului socialist in Chisinaul postbelic. Proiecte si realizari, Chisinau-Arta, Cercetare in Sfera Publica, Centrul KSAK, 2011.

[12] The centre of high technologies JSC 'MEZON'. <http://www.mezon.md/en/index.html>

[13] Anatol Eremia, Hutuleuca – veche mahala in partea de jos a Chisinaului. Chisinau, Encilopedie, 1997.

[14] Vasile BAHNARU, Gheorghe E. COJOCARU. Congresul al III-lea al Uniunii Scriitorilor din RSS Moldovenească (14–15 octombrie 1965). Studiu şi materiale. Chisinau: Editura 'Tehnica-Info', 2016.

[15] V. Smirnov, Gradostroitelistvo Moldavii XIX–XX vekov. Editura Kartea Moldoveneasca, Kishinev, 1975.

[16] A. Kolotovkin, I. Eltman, G. Peldash. Arhitectura Sovetskoi Moldavii, Moskva: Izdatelistvo Stroyizdat, 1978.

[17] Anastasia Moscaliuc, 'Jewish Contribution to Architecture in Chisinau', The Journal of Ethnology and Culturology 15 (2014).

[18] Anastasia Felcher, Chisinaul evreiesc pe care l-am pierdut. <https://www.platzforma.md/arhive/37472> accessed 10 December 2017.

The Soviet 'Microraion' – A New Lifestyle

Vlada Ciobanu

The extent of apartment block construction during the Soviet era – a symbol of urbanisation, rapid industrialisation, and massive societal change – has been reflected in novels, movies, and even in the works of classical music composers. Not many people remember that Shostakovich wrote an operetta, and what is more interesting, its title was *Cheryomushki* – the name of a district built in Moscow in 1956.

'Is this really our apartment?' wonders Lida cheerily, one of the protagonists of the movie made based on the operetta. Flirtatiously, Boris replies: 'The typical abode of the second half of the twentieth century. The era of reinforced concrete. The era of standard elements.' The two sing and dance and their costumes and movements change to reflect the passing eras. In the middle of a dance, the pair unexpectedly jump out the window straight onto suspended prefabricated elements. They continue to dance frenetically as they glide over many multi-storey apartment blocks. The camera pans to reveal a huge construction site. The entire scene reflects the joy of having finally been assigned an apartment for private use. The movie was made in 1962 (Lenfilm) based on the operetta composed by Dmitry Shostakovich in 1959, the libretto being authored by Soviet comedy writers Vladimir Mass and Mikhail Chervinsky.

This is Shostakovich's only operetta, and it is a humorous take on the massive migration of Soviet people from 'kommunalkas' and barracks into private apartments. It presents the lives of several characters of various ages and professions as well as their first experiences with – finally! – their own private living space. This migration towards private apartments and the boom in construction meant a new life for many.

The Soviet 'Microraion' – A New lifestyle

After the Russian Revolution*, urbanisation and industrialisation resulted in cities becoming increasingly crowded and the demand for housing increased greatly. Besides, the authorities were supposed to provide not just a roof above citizens' heads, but also a new type of city for a new man – the Soviet man. Egalitarianism – one of the essential principles of society – also had to be reflected in the way cities were built. This meant uniform districts for all social strata and identical living quarters for all people, with the same reasonable distances between home and shops, schools, and parks. Everyone had to have equal access to the same public facilities and services. At the same time, it was necessary to bridge the deep gap between the urban and rural environment and create a common living standard. Houses belonging to the rich were seized; living space was redistributed in order to avoid overcrowding; tenants' committees with elected membership were established; and renting was abolished[1].

After the daring ideas and the grandiose designs of the 1920s and the decorativist and monumentalist architecture of the Stalin era came the era of mass development: plain five-floor apartment blocks made of cheap panels, easily assembled. It was the era of 'standard elements', as the protagonist of the *Cheryomushki* movie states.

[1] Andrusz, Gregory D., *Housing and Urban Development in the USSR* (State University of New York Press, 1984).

* The Russian Revolution began on 8 March 1917 when the monarchy was overthrown and ended in 1923 when the Bolshevik party, led by Lenin, came to power.

When Khrushchev took power in the Soviet Union in 1955, Moscow had twice as many inhabitants as it could accommodate.[2] There were a variety of causes for this housing crisis: a shortage of materials caused by two World Wars, Stalin's preference for grandiose architecture lacking cost-effectiveness, and an emphasis on heavy industry rather than housing development.[3] In the mid-1950s and early 1960s, it became clear that cities could no longer be developed the way they had been up to that point and that perimetral buildings could not provide appropriate orientation for the apartments in order for them to be insulated from noise and receive the proper amounts of light.[4] Meanwhile, the administration faced the task of providing decent housing for city dwellers. This marked the beginning of the construction of the 'Khrushchyovkas'. They were relatively cheap to build, had simple, prefabricated standard elements, featured small rooms, and did not require an elevator.

Жилищное строительство was a technical and scientific journal published by the architecture and construction committee and targeting constructors, architects, designers, and construction workers. Issue no. 1 of 1964 opens with Nikita Khrushchev's report detailing the colossal effort being made in the housing domain. He states that between 1954 and 1963, over 17 million housing units were built in cities and workers' townships, as well as over six million houses in the countryside. 'These houses welcomed 108 million citizens – almost half the population of the Soviet Union.'[5] The Soviet city had several levels: the city itself, the 'raion', and the 'microraion'. A microraion was a complex of residential buildings combined with a range of services and shops that would meet the everyday needs of its inhabitants. Several microraions together formed a raion.

The basic idea of the microraion was that it combined the housing role with a whole range of services. Such services were distributed according to the function of an urban area, that is, residential, retail, and socialisation space. They were designed in such a manner as to reduce the time spent outside the microraion by its inhabitants. The microraion was self-sufficient.

The planning of microraions borrowed principles from the so-called 'New Towns' in Great Britain that were built after the Second World War. These, too, intended to mitigate the housing crisis. They also borrowed from the planned unit developments in the United States of America – themselves appearing after the war on the outskirts of cities. The travel reports presented by the Soviet architects who played a major role in the development of housing in Estonia suggest that the Soviet architects had connections with their European colleagues.[6]

The microraions had very clearly stated standards and rules. Their populations should be housed in five-floor blocks of 6,000 to 12,000 residents – or 16,000 to 18,000 in the case of nine-floor blocks. As a rule, they covered an area of approximately 25–35 hectares.[7]

2 'The Disappearing Mass Housing of the Soviet Union'. <https://www.bloomberg.com/news/articles/2017-03-08/the-disappearing-mass-housing-of-the-soviet-union>.

3 Gentile, M., 'The Rise and Demise of the Soviet-Made Housing Shortage in the Baltic Countries'. <https://link.springer.com/chapter/10.1007/978-3-030-23392-1_3>.

4 Основные градостроительные концепции и современные проблемы реконструкции жилой среды середины 1950-х - 1960-х годов. <https://cih.ru/k4/p1f.html>.

5 Жилищное строительство, nr. 1, 1964. <https://books.google.md/books?id>.

6 Leetmaa, K., Hess, D. B., 'Incomplete Service Networks in Enduring Socialist Housing Estates: Retrospective Evidence from Local Centers in Estonia'. <https://link.springer.com/chapter/10.1007/978-3-030-23392-1_13>.

7 Сапрыкина Н.С. Этапы и закономерности развития архитектуры, 2007. <https://archi.ru/lib/e_publication.html?id=1850569776>.

Still image from the movie *Cheryomushki* produced by Lenfilm Studio in 1962

Steel structure bearing the inscription 'peace' in several languages on Dacia Boulevard (formerly Peace Boulevard), 1990s

which were located outside the cities (holiday homes, pioneer camps, sports training facilities, sanatoria etc.)[8]

Issue no. 10/1964 of *Жилищное строительство* features a detailed description of a microraion structure, including a concise layout.

Another important element of the cities were the massive plants producing standard panels and prefabricated elements. Each larger town had one, and mobile plants were sometimes installed in some microraions, producing standard panels for building homes. They were able to build around 300–600 apartments each year, making the process cheaper and more efficient.

Pedestrian-Friendly, Green, and Free of the Tyranny of the Streets

The microraions were in fact designed as pedestrian areas, with great emphasis placed on the use of public transport. They were also very green – close to today's ideals! This model meant that the cost of building and maintaining roads was greatly reduced. Although people did own cars, they were not used on a large scale, especially since the Soviet Union did not have the capacity to produce that many cars, and the population did not have the necessary funds to buy them. In fact, the Soviet Union's intention was to promote walking, urban mobility, and the functional diversity of each raion, so that any citizen could have his/her needs met within its bounds. The microraions had no room for motorways, and heavy vehicle transport was forbidden. Temporary parking spaces for cars were provided, as were comfortable pedestrian walkways, separate from the streets.[9]

The short distance between work and home was in fact one of the essential elements in the planning of microraions. In the Soviet era, it was acknowledged that commuting reduces productivity, as well

The microraion was designed as an area that would serve citizens. The term 'step service system' (*ступенчатая система обслуживания*) was used in the 1960s. According to the description in the book written by architect N. S. Saprykina, the first step was covering the day-to-day needs of the microraion, meaning kindergartens, *домовая кухня* ('Soviet canteens'), communal leisure areas, and playgrounds – all of these had to be within 200 m of any of the blocks. Schools, grocery and industrial goods shops, and canteens were within 400 m.

The second step concerned the raion. This included workers' clubs, cinemas, the raion retail centres, sports complexes, libraries, *univermags* ('universal' department stores), specialised shops, and the raion health centres. They served the population of several microraions and had to be located within a radius of 800–1500 m of the housing units. The third step concerned services for the entire city. This included government/administration offices, theatres, concert halls, museums, large sports complexes, restaurants, hotels, research institution facilities, etc..

The fourth step concerned mass leisure facilities and medical/health centres,

8   Сапрыкина Н.С. 'Этапы и закономерности развития архитектуры', 2007. <https://archi.ru/lib/e_publication.html?id=1850569776>.

9   Основные градостроительные концепции и современные проблемы реконструкции жилой среды середины 1950-х - 1960-х годов. <https://cih.ru/k4/p1f.html>.

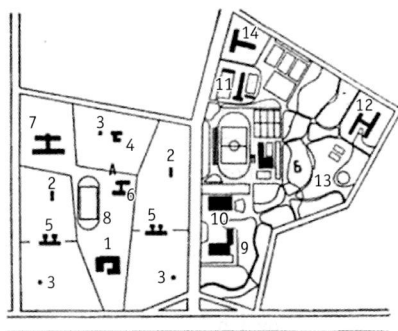

Layout of the organisation of the raion cultural and administrative services: 1 – social centre; 2 and 3 – service units; 4 and 5 – kindergartens; 6 – day-care centres; 7 – elementary school; 8 – the microraion garden; 9 – retail centre; 10 – cultural centre; 11 – sports centre; 12 – primary school; 13 – raion park; 14 – health centre.

as cutting short free time allotted for social activities. However, public transport was not necessarily sufficient. Soviet citizens believed the streets to be unsafe, and the housing blocks and the entire organisation of the microraion were supposed to protect citizens from the 'tyranny of the streets'.[10]

Another innovation lies in the fact that the buildings were not placed along the streets, but rather in a staggered manner, thereby preventing the formation of a solid wall of buildings. The blocks faced into the inner yards, towards the green and common spaces.[11]

As a rule, the microraions were built on the outskirts on large unused plots of land. Green spaces thereby worked to insulate the microraions from the roads and the rest of the city. An interconnected system of landscaping the blocks, the roads, and the common spaces was thus created.[12] A defining element of all microraions was the fact that they were built taking into account the local

climate characteristics in order to create the most favourable health and hygiene conditions. They were often located near plants specialising in the manufacture of prefabricated components, but it is probably more important that these green spaces conformed to the modernist vision according to which an attractive living environment must be located away from the crowded city centres.[13]

'Chisinau has become Younger, Wider, Taller'

'The liberators saw a horrible picture of ruins and fires. It seemed no force was able to revive the city and rebuild its buildings, streets, factories, and schools. [...] Much more was built in the city in the post-war years than during its 500-year history. Before the war, Kishinev had 760,000 square metres of space, while after the war this figure increased fivefold. The city grew younger and became wider and taller. The wastelands gave way to big residential districts: Botanika, Ryshkanovka, and Boyukany.' This is how Chisinau is described in *Around Kishinev without a Guide*[14], a small tourist guide printed in 1979 in Russian and English found by chance at the flea market near the train station.

'Heat and power engineering, tractor building, electric machine building, chemistry, and the food and light industries are the leading economic branches.' The guidebook takes the readers along the main streets of the city, presents the most important buildings, parks, and tourist attractions, and informs them that: 'The will of the Party, selfless work of the Kishinev dwellers, and fraternal assistance of the Soviet peoples raised the city from ruins and ashes to turn it into a big industrial centre.' Despite what the guidebook says, the train station building was not the first reconstruction carried out by the Soviets in Chisinau. The

10 Hess, B. D., *Transport in Mikrorayons: Accessibility and Proximity to Centrally Planned Residential Districts during the Socialist Era, 1957-1989*, 2017. <https://journals.sagepub.com/doi/abs/10.1177/1538513217707082>.

11 Hess, B. D., *Transport in Mikrorayons: Accessibility and Proximity to Centrally Planned Residential Districts during the Socialist Era, 1957-1989*, 2017. <https://journals.sagepub.com/doi/abs/10.1177/1538513217707082>.

12 Основные градостроительные концепции и современные проблемы реконструкции жилой среды середины 1950-х - 1960-х годов. <https://cih.ru/k4/p1f.html>.

13 Leetmaa, K., Hess, D. B., *Incomplete Service Networks in Enduring Socialist Housing Estates: Retrospective Evidence from Local Centers in Estonia*. <https://link.springer.com/chapter/10.1007/978-3-030-23392-1_13>.

14 Gabuniya, E., *Around Kishinev Without a Guide* (Timpul Publishing, 1979).

Around Kishinev without a Guide
По Кишиневу без экскурсовода

The cover of the *Around Kishinev without a Guide* guidebook printed in 1979

reconstruction used the ruins of the old building, of which the foundations and the walls remained. This information can be found in a book by the chief architect of Chisinau from the late 1950s and early 1960s, Victor Smirnov, titled *Urbanismul în Moldova* ('Urbanism in Moldova') and published in 1975. The architect reviews Moldova's architecture starting in 1812, with greater emphasis on the reconstruction of the city after the Second World War. The first reconstruction works took place in 1944–1945, mainly in industrialised cities such as Chisinau, Tiraspol, Bender, and Balti. Although construction capacities were limited, 75 industrial facilities were renovated over two years in Chisinau. A car factory had already been established by 1945 (although it was more of an automobile repair plant).

Slowly, the construction of housing blocks for the workers began. In 1946, two buildings with four apartments in each were built for the factory's technical and engineering staff. The buildings were of poor quality, according to Smirnov, due to the lack of trained construction workers. In January 1946, the first three-storey block appeared on the central Lenin Boulevard, its façade recalling the two-storey hotel that previously occupied the plot. Built with the advice

of architect Aleksey Shchusev, the building became a sample of the extent construction development grew at the time. This was also the time when the two-storey buildings near the train station and the two four-storey buildings in Buiucani and Gorkii Street were built.[15] In the book *Arhitectura Moldovei Sovietice* ('The Architecture of Soviet Moldova'), written by Kolotovkin, Eltman, and Shoikhet and published in 1987, the authors identify three stages in the development of the city:

The first is the period immediately following the Second World War, which meant rebuilding the city and designing plans for its development. Around the same time, Alexei Shchusev developed the first master plan for Chisinau in 1951; it was supposed to be a roadmap for the development of the city until 1970 and up to a population of 250,000. In that particular period, single-storey stand-alone homes were still being built. However, as the land crisis deepened, such constructions were banned and replaced with two- and three-storey blocks.

The second period began roughly in 1955 and it was influenced by the housing shortage at the time. Building apartments became a priority. The city of Chisinau was developing at an increasingly faster pace; business sites appeared and the transport network was growing. The master plan was no longer up to date. In 1963, the team at Moldgiprostroy, led by architects Robert Kurtz and Semyon Shoikhet and supported by specialists in Kyiv, developed a new one, approved for use until 1980.[16]

The third period began approximately in 1971, and it is characterised by massive construction work taking place both in the capital and on its outskirts. This stage was guided by the decisions made by the Communist Party Central Committee and by the USSR's Ministers' Council, as reflected in the document 'On the actions to develop the city of Chisinau'. It is in this period that various versions of

15 Смирнов В., 'Градостроительство Молдавии', 1975, pp. 31–35.
16 Колотовкин А.В., Шойхет С.М., Эльтман И.С., 'Архитектура Советской Молдавии', 1987, p. 78.

apartment blocks were tested, and some buildings were as tall as 20 floors.

These three periods followed the general directions decided in Moscow and implemented in the rest of the Soviet republics. For example, at the 12th convention of the Union of Soviet Architects of the MSSR, it was stated that: 'Obviously, in Chisinau as well, from the first days, the Soviet power was beginning to establish itself; the activity to transform it into a Soviet city had begun.'[17] The article 'Rehabilitating the historical heritage of Chisinau in the post-war period and starting the construction of a Soviet-type urban identity (the 1940s and 1950s)' gives an overview of the discussions of the era referring, among others, to the preservation of the existing assets and showcasing the specific national elements on the one hand, and following Moscow's directives on the other. Articles and books about the construction of Soviet raions and microraions on the territory of today's Republic of Moldova are scarce (almost impossible to find, in fact), and most of them are in Russian. A great number of the references to the city's historical buildings concern those in the old centre, and the *monuments of national architecture* were now considered to be those dating from the late nineteenth and early twentieth centuries. The reconstruction of Chisinau after the war, however, had been a colossal effort, and the new raions were the site of many premieres and experiments. Let us follow the birth and development of the Botanica raion, based to a great extent on the information found in the two books mentioned above.

From Sovetskii to Botanica

In the 1990s, in the middle of Dacia Boulevard close to the intersection with Cuza-Vodă, there used to be a heavy steel structure bearing the inscription 'peace' in several languages. For the generation that had grown up in independent Moldova, this was a kind of monument dedicated to world peace rather than a last memento of the former name of that boulevard, *Prospekt Mira* ('Peace Boulevard'), the main thoroughfare of the Botanica district connecting the city centre with the airport. Botanica did not grow out of an empty lot. In 1842, this was the place where the Ministry of State Property of the Russian Imperial Government opened the first school of horticulturists and winemakers. Nearby, the first dendrological park was established, called 'the English garden'. However, locals called it 'the botanical garden'. Hence the name of the district, 'Botanica' (formerly 'Sovetskii'), established following decree no. 1494–IX of 23 March 1977 of the Presidium of the Supreme Soviet of the Moldovian Soviet Socialist Republic of the 9th legislature.[18] Botanica, together with Rascani, are the districts where construction work was very intense in the second stage of the city's development. The first microraion with blocks made of large panels (prefabricated and assembled on site) appeared here on Zelinski Street in 1960. This type of construction was first applied in Botanica specifically due to the stable soils in the area, a prerequisite at the time (starting in 1965, blocks like this began being built in other districts as well).[19] The materials were supplied by the house building shops within the prefabricated concrete plant.[20] Microraion no 1 had three sections: one on Zelinski Street, another next to Trandafirilor Street (opening onto V. I. Lenin Park, currently Valea Trandafirilor/'Rose Valley'), and a third that hosted the School of Workforce Management and was somewhat set apart from the rest.

The appearance of the microraion was, however, criticised by architect Smirnov, who was of the opinion that setting the blocks in parallel rows and lines was uninteresting. The authors of the book *Arhitectura Moldovei socialiste* ('The Architecture of Socialist Moldova')

17 Ursu V., Reabilitarea patrimoniului istoric al Chisinaului în perioada postbelică şi initierea constructiei unei identităti urbane de tip sovietic (anii '40–'50 ai sec. XX). <https://www.slideshare.net/ghenador/identitile-chiinului>.

18 <http://www.botanica.md/sectorul-botanica>
19 Смирнов В., 'Градостроительство Молдавии', 1975, p. 84.
20 Смирнов В., 'Градостроительство Молдавии', 1975, p. 90.

Overview of Dacia Boulevard (former Peace Boulevard) from the Botanica district, 1985

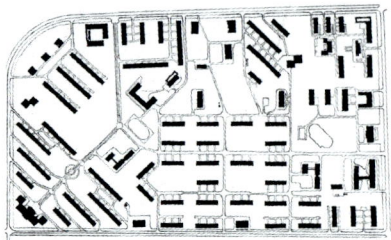

Microraion N1 from the Botanica district, designed by Valentin Voitsehovski, 1960–1966

also said that, due to the fact that several blocks were built at once using a single crane, the resulting buildings were aligned and without enough space between them (author's note: and also lacking any other buildings with social functions). The authors hastened to add, however, that the neighbourhood did have cultural and retail facilities.[21]

Building Botanica took longer than building Rascani. The microraions were planned before the entire raion was planned in detail as a whole, and the new master plan had to include a much-needed thoroughfare that would connect the city with the airport. Originally, Timoshenko Street (currently Decebal Boulevard) was the central street, determining the structure of the entire raion, the microraions, and the blocks, as well as the location of schools and kindergartens. Later on, *Prospect Mira* ('Peace Boulevard') was designed and built – it subsequently became Botanica's main street.[22] In an interview conducted for this article, Ala Kirichenko, the architect who designed the Botanica district, remembered that in the 1960s when she arrived in Chisinau, she would travel to Moscow very often. Returning from the airport, she would take the bus on Muncesti Street. The architect described this as being a rural road, with the bus having to avoid horse-drawn carriages, and if it rained, it filled with mud. This was what prompted her to design a great boulevard that would connect the district with the city centre.[23]

Microraion number three in Botanica was built along Peace Boulevard. The density of construction was 3080 square metres, but the microraion territory covered 25.2 hectares. In the south, land was set aside for the commercial and logistics centre serving the entire raion, i.e., three microraions. Smirnov says that a centre that could serve the population of an entire raion was an interesting and promising experiment. This despite the fact that its construction had not yet begun (in 1975: author's note), which had created inconveniences for the local inhabitants.[24] Building microraion four was a difficult decision due to the existence of free-standing homes. In the end, it came to be seen more or less as a part of microraion three but separated from it by the railway. 1966 saw active construction work take place on Muncești Street, as this was the exit road towards Odessa. Instead of one-storey houses, blocks of five-to-nine floors were being built, changing the landscape towards the railway.[25] Together with the construction of Peace Boulevard, Muncești would lose some of its importance. The authors were of the opinion that a second exit from the city would be required very soon.

In 1970, the third period in the construction of Chisinau began, coinciding with the ninth five-year plan. Construction of microraions three, four, and five was finished and work had begun on the sixth. The prognoses showed that so many microraions ought to cover housing demand until the end of the five-year plan.[26]

21 Колотовкин А.В., Шойхет С.М., Эльтман И.С., 'Архитектура Советской Молдавии', 1987, p. 86.
22 Колотовкин А.В., Шойхет С.М., Эльтман И.С., 'Архитектура Советской Молдавии', 1987, pp. 79–80.
23 Interviu realizat de autoare, în data de 1 July 2020.

24 Смирнов В., 'Градостроительство Молдавии', 1975, p. 89.
25 Колотовкин А.В., Шойхет С.М., Эльтман И.С., 'Архитектура Советской Молдавии', 1987, p. 83.
26 Смирнов В., 'Градостроительство Молдавии', 1975, p. 117.

Microraions six and seven were built in 1972. Smirnov believed this period to have a high level of both planning and architecture. The author states: 'the density is higher, the green areas have increased. They are more modern spaces.' Orgstroi, Moldgiprostroy, and Odesstransproiect worked on designs for buildings made entirely from sliding and mobile forms. Many of the 12–16 floor blocks were on Prospekt Mira and on Sovetskoi Armii Boulevard (currently Traian Boulevard). At the same time, the construction of five-storey apartment buildings continued, and their quality improved. In the early 1980s, a decision was made to accelerate construction on the city's thoroughfares. Several six-storey blocks appeared on Peace Boulevard (Prospect Mira Boulevard) at the junction with Hristo Botev, while on Sovetskoi Armii, blocks with 15–20 floors were built, with retail spaces included, and tall apartment blocks were erected at the entrance from the airport side of the city.

The period in which the microraions were built was a time of constant experimentation. The number of floors changed, and so did the room proportions and the apartment structure as a whole. The work involved teams of architects, engineers, and technicians, sometimes with support from colleagues in Odessa or Kyiv. A solution would be tested on one building, then replicated in other regions. Development on the vertical as high as possible was always praised, especially because it saved land, even though this increased costs per square metre. Of course, we cannot talk about microraions without mentioning the structures with social functions.

Residential building on Trandafirilor Street designed by Roman Bekesevich

There were standard schoolhouses, with a compact layout on three floors, built from soft chalk. School construction was another field for experimentation. Kindergartens, too, had standardised layouts, all with two floors. Of course, there was room for experimentation here, too. For instance, on Timoshenko Street in Botanica, builders constructed a pavilion-type kindergarten with a slate roof (architect: D. Palatnik). This model was picked up and replicated in other districts as well. Increased attention was paid to the construction of healthcare facilities in each district. Around the same period, Iskra cinema was built in Botanica by architect R. Bekesevich. It had a lobby and a hallway and was roomy and comfortable for the audience.

Conclusion

The Soviet microraions were the product of the minds of architects, technicians, and engineers. There was room for experimentation, improvements, and apparent improvements. Over three decades, the microraions changed in appearance, mainly becoming taller. They were designed in such a way that their inhabitants would have equal access to public services while enjoying a comfortable lifestyle with easy access to green areas and without long commutes to their jobs. Of course, taller did not necessarily mean better – Western countries gave up on building tall apartment blocks that had the potential to develop into ghettos. Moreover, rigid planning caused, for example, the 'New Towns' in Great Britain to no longer be seen as attractive among the population. Currently, the deserted cinemas, the interventions of the green spaces on the playgrounds and on the sports grounds between the blocks, the unkempt buildings, and the new residential developments built in parks cause these districts, which were formerly symbols of development and progress, to now be viewed as symbols of chaotic and corrupt decisions.

Chisinau's Industrial Environment

Irina Dubinschi

To begin, we need to understand how the city's industrial environment came into being. For that, we need to define the industrial environment, which appeared as a phenomenon after the industrial revolution. The industrial revolution went through stages of developing and experimenting with new machines, technologies, and inventions capable of increasing production potential.[1] Production potential depended on the working class. The latter became disadvantaged, in Engels' opinion; Engels, together with Marx, put out the *Communist Manifesto*, which glorified the modern worker that was capable of increasing the productivity of factories and mills owned by the bourgeoisie, but stating that the latter had to be replaced by the state in the position of owner. The USSR was established in 1922 and its economic development was based on five-year plans, collectivisation, and intensive industrialisation. Collectivisation was introduced by force, in contradiction with the basic tenets of proletariat politics. Meanwhile, the de facto industrialisation of the USSR differed from that described by the *Communist Manifesto* in two regards. Firstly, according to Engels and Marx[2], workers were assumed to have a certain level of training and culture, being elevated and knowledgeable professionals; in the first 30 years of the USSR's existence, however, the workers were not trained to work in factories; they were farmers raised in rural areas without professional traditions passed down through the generations, and with a limited level of culture. Secondly, the manifesto proposed the idea of giving power to the elevated proletariat, who were knowledgeable about the production process and about the factory in general and capable of contributing their own opinions about the work process and innovation; however, the Soviet proletariat lacked the ability to manage an entire industrial production system; consequently, the British and later the American management model was adopted.

Urbanisation in the USSR member countries started together with the development of industry, and this is how the industrial environments of cities were formed. Therefore, the notion of an 'industrial environment' meant the totality of economic processes taking place in an urban space equipped with all the elements required for the operation of the industrial structure. In Chisinau, the industrial environment was poorly developed[3] during the period of the Russian Empire; the Jewish community owned 29 out of the existing 38 factories, the most famous one being the brewery located on land that used to belong to the parents of the architect Bernardazzi. In the interval following the pogroms of 1903 and 1905[4], the capacity of Chisinau's industrial environment dropped dramatically, as industrial development stagnated. The period between the two World Wars brought a focus on the city's cultural, rather than industrial development. We can thus conclude that in the inter-war period, industry remained in the development stage it was in after the pogrom period. After 1944, Chisinau's industrial environment was devastated by war; in 1947 Robert Kurtz (a protégée of Aleksey Shchusev) presented a development plan that also included the development of the industrial area, involving 35 industrial plants.[5]

1 Sennett, Richard, 'The Craftsman'," Strelka Press, pp. 118–120.
2 <https://www.marxists.org/romana/m-e/1848/manifest/c01.htm>.
3 <https://dbs.bh.org.il/place/kishinev>.
4 Identitătile Chisinaului – 5th edition, Aliona Gratii – Mitopoetica oraşului Chisinau , Arc, pp 90.
5 Identitătile Chisinaului – 5th edition, Andrei Vatamaniuc – Aşteptându-l pe... Doicescu, Arc, pp 135.

The development of the industrial environment in the capital of the Moldavian SSR was also a result of the desire of the central leadership to accelerate the massive industrialisation of the entire territory; the unintended consequences were social, demographic, and economic crises. Nevertheless, once mass collectivisation was achieved and the centres of the countries included in the USSR were urbanised[6], the USSR's process of industrialisation began to develop and the state rose to prominent positions on the international political stage. However, this process was different from that described by Raymond Aron[7]: in his theory, industrialisation is hindered by the importance of the family for the individual proletarian; in the case of the USSR, Soviet industrial society positioned itself as the family of each worker. In its desire to perform globally as an economic and industrial power, the USSR's main goal was to industrialise the urban centres of its member countries. In order to speed up the process, it was necessary to establish institutions that were competent in the design of industrial areas and buildings. Thus, the Soviet Union Architect's Union was established in 1932,[8] allowing the five-year plans to proceed and to apply the Secretary General's orders concerning reform in the economies of the Union's member countries. At the time, the architects' function was merely to create functional buildings that met production requirements and that were planned in such a manner as to allow for the increase of production quotas per factory. For the time being, the union

could not produce a rapid design system, and therefore the German-born American architect Albert Kahn was brought in. Together with his team, Albert Kahn developed a new methodology for designing industrial ensembles. Later on, his name was concealed by the Soviet nomenklatura, and the main designer signing the engineering documentation was the 'Госпроектстрой' engineering institute.[9] The American architect developed a revolutionary technique of designing and producing documentation, allowing the final project to be delivered in very short timelines. For example, the construction of a plant that would normally take 1.5 or two years, could last just two or two and a half months when using the engineering documentation developed by the 'Albert Kahn Associates Incorporated' company. The process of building the industrial estates in the 1920s and 1930s did not have any particular standards or regulations for industrial sites, but these were definitely present in Kahn's innovative technology. He was Henry Ford's favourite architect, having built many factories for the automobile magnate[10]. These innovative engineering technologies resulted in the creation of an industrial environment across the territory of the Soviet Union (such as the Kharkiv tractor

6 Aron, Raymond, '18 lectii despre societatea industrială' pp. 79.
7 In his teachings, Raymond Aron presents the industrialisation process as a separation from one's family.
8 Ostapov, Alina, 'Activitatea Uniunii Arhitectilor din Republica Sovietică Socialistă Moldovenească' pp. 1.
9 Меерович М.Г 'АЛЬБЕРТ КАН В ИСТОРИИ СОВЕТСКОЙ ИНДУСТРИАЛИЗАЦИИ', pp. 1–9.
10 <https://www.archdaily.com/783103/spotlight-albert-kahn>

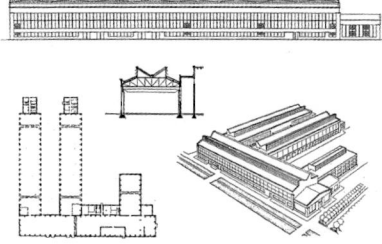

The engineering documentation developed by Albert Kahn Associates Incorporated

The blocks of the Mezon microelectronics factory established in 1969, Rascani district

The main entrance of the Steaua Rosie (Red Star) knitwear factory. Post card set, 'Planeta' publishing house, 1970

factory, 1929). This also means that the 'borrowed' industrial architecture was also present in Chisinau's industrial environment. For instance, the Автодеталь tractor factory (later renamed Tracom) was designed by specialists from Kharkiv, who, in turn, had borrowed the technical documentation from their American colleagues. During construction of the tractor plant in Chisinau[11], some issues appeared when applying the technical documentation in practice, as the latter did not take into account the existing groundwater, and this led to commissioning delays.

An engine repair plant was built in Chisinau in 1945. It was transformed into the tractor plant 16 years later and one year after that, production began on the T-50B model.[12] From 1962 to 2008, the tractor plant produced 257,635 units.[13] The plant's layout follows the industrial model proposed by Albert Kahn – the production halls were built according to the distribution of the manufacture of the various components for the tractors. By analysing the maps from 1930, we can see that the territory of the current Tracom industrial estate used to be dedicated to production shops. Later in 1940, they were transformed into military workshops and included in the site of the tractor factory as we know it today. The plant was reorganised as an industrial park, offering spaces for rent to small production units manufacturing windows and doors, furniture, and other wood products, for example, as well as larger companies specialising in telecommunications and internet provision services.

Those in charge of designing and building Chisinau's industrial and urban environment were largely trained outside the MSSR. For example, Robert Kurtz studied architecture in Bucharest, and the Ukrainian Chuprin (who designed the railway station) studied in Kyiv. Nevertheless, in 1944, the union of Moldovan architects was registered in the Moldovan SSR and counted just four members. Its name was changed to the MSSR Architects' Union in 1955.[2]

After the 1970s, the architects working in the MSSR had greater choice regarding the artistic form of their creations. In other words, during the period between 1945 and 1960, the strictness of the control exercised by the state apparatus on industrial architecture was clearly visible: all the buildings and facilities were built according to the style dictated by Moscow's central power. After the 1970s, we can already see elements of decor on the façades of both production and administration buildings, sometimes mere highlights of architectural features added by the authors, but showing, nevertheless, that control was less intense and more flexible in terms of artistic realisation. The capital of the Moldavian SSR has several examples of façade decor, including concrete columns and coloured glass at the Mezon, Alfa, Topaz, and Bucuria factories. For example, the Mezon factory has similarities in volume use and shapes

11 Журнал 'Техника молодёжи', №3 1972. Т. МАРИН 'ТРАКТОР РОЖДАЕТСЯ В КИШИНЕВЕ,' pp 26.

12 <https://tracom.md/pi-tracom/history/>

13 <https://www.prospect.md/ru/gallery/tehnika/kishinevskiy-traktornyy-zavodao-traktornyy-zavod-tracom.html>

with the Chicago Dodge plant, designed by Albert Kahn, but the cubical shapes covered with blue stained-glass windows show the building's clear identity.

Chisinau's industrialisation process began together with the development of the zone plan[14] mentioned previously; this was the time when the reconstruction of the city began. The entire city was being reorganised and replanned. Later on it would be divided into industrial areas (with a total of 559 plants as of late 1986[15]) and mixed-use areas, where factories with a minimum impact on the aesthetic of the city would be located (such as the Ionel and Steaua Roşie knitwear factories), the exceptions being the Alfa (1976), Bucuria (1946), and Sigma (1963) factories placed on the front line of Alba Iulia, Mihai Viteazul, and Decebal Boulevards, showcasing the Soviet industrial architecture while being an integral part of residential areas. In Chisinau, while the city and industry underwent reorganisation, an industrial society was formed; the term is taken from Raymond Aron (Aron, 2003), who states that every industrial society is based on the creation of new technologies and on technical progress. Technical progress relies on engineering innovation, which in turn results from scientific progress. However, in the USSR, science was tightly controlled by the state – any invention could be blocked for fear it could end up in the hands of supposed spies or conspirators who would then transmit it to the Union's competitors or foes. This reduced the motivation of scientists, as well as trained professional and vocational workers in producing innovation and applying inventions in practice.

In the interval between 1960 and 1990, billions of roubles were invested in the MSSR in order to develop heavy industry, which only took off in earnest in the mid-1980s. The export of circuit boards increased, as did the export of micro-wire and glass-insulated current dividers – invented in 1969 by Ion Drabenco,[16] originally from Cuhureştii de Sus in the county of Soroca. Due to this invention, once the Microprovod production association came on board, the export of dividers and other micro-wire products expanded to countries such as the UK, Finland, and Austria.[17]

14 'КИШИНЕВ – ГОРОД БУДУЩЕГО': СТАТЬЯ ИЗ ГАЗЕТЫ 'МОЛОДЕЖЬ МОЛДАВИИ', №3 1972 ГОД, taken from the article <https://locals.md/2016/kishinev-gorod-budushhego-statya-iz-gazetyi-molodezh-moldavii-3-1972-god/> accessed 5 June 2020.

15 <https://www.youtube.com/watch?v=iqUAsX-j9hI min.30> accessed 18 September 2020.

16 <https://ro.wikipedia.org/wiki/Ion_Drabenco> accessed 12 June 2020.

17 <www.razboiulpentrutrecut.wordpress.com> КАКОЙ БЫЛА ЭКОНОМИКА СОВЕТСКОЙ МОЛДАВИИ В 1985 ГОДУ, accessed 12 June 2020

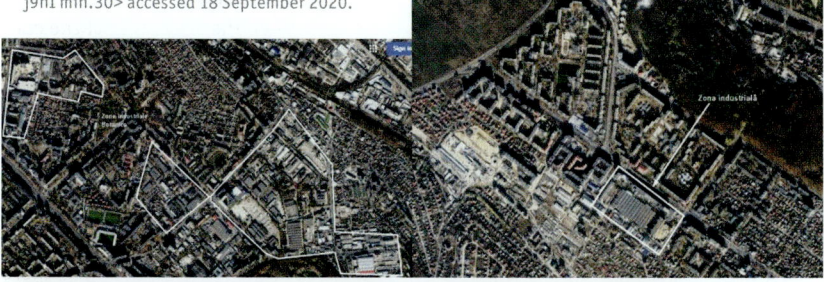

Industrial areas located in Ciocana Noua, Botanica de Sus, Buiucani, and Telecentru

However, substantial growth in Chisinau's industrial capacity occurred only after the investment granted by the Secretary General of the Soviet Union, L. Brezhnev, in 1972, based on the directive *'О мерах по дальнейшему развитию г. Кишинёва'.* This was a result of his personal relationship with the MSSR – between 1950 and 1952 he had been First Secretary of the MSSR Communist Party. After the development of the industrial areas of Sculeni and Ciocana between 1950 and 1960, new factories and production plants appeared, focusing on technical and scientific development and producing cutting-edge technologies for developing ever more innovative products. Examples include the Alfa television set factory (1976); the Topaz plant (1978) for manufacturing parts for reaction engines (for military aircraft such as Sukhoi and MiG) delivered to the Moscow Saliut aviation engine plant; the 'Giuvaier' jewellery factory (1972); the 'Avtodetal' tractor plant ('Tracom'[18] as of 1961); Moldelectromontazh (1972); and the Mezon[19] plant (1969) for manufacturing microelectronic products – one of the five top enterprises for microelectronics on the territory of the Soviet Union.

	1940	1960	1975
M SSR	5.8	52	226

Table 1. Growth pace of industrial capacity[20]

The Soviet Union's goal to exceed the production levels of capitalist countries was reached in heavy industry in the 1950s. Later on, light industry followed this trend, despite the fact that it had not been the focus of Soviet planners' attention, according to Raymond Aron (Aron, 2003). After the appointment of Brezhnev as Chairman of the Supreme Soviet Presidium, light industry in the MSSR developed even further. After the 1970s, light industry in the MSSR increased its exports of tobacco, wine, cognac, vegetables, and other foodstuffs. The food

processing industry of the MSSR is also credited with innovations in the area of food supplies for cosmonauts. According to the manager of the former institute for food processing research in Chisinau, Anatoly Sidorenco, the MSSR produced juices, sauces, and dried fruit pastes for use on space flights. Light industry in the MSSR focused on exports to capitalist countries such as the Netherlands, Spain, and Italy. According to the USSR Communist Party policies of industrial development, as the production capacity of factories in the MSSR soared, so did the number of workers in this sector, from 51,400 in 1950 to 293,000 and in 1973.[21] As an industrial city in the 1980s, Chisinau had the capability to produce approximately six times more than it did in the 1960s (see Table 1). This was possible not only due to the massive development in construction in the industrial and residential sectors, but also due to the massive migration of the workforce from the countryside to the city, a topic that is extremely visible in the film *Talpile verzi* ('Green Soles'), made by the 'Phoenix-M' Experimental Association and produced by the Moldova-Film studios.[22] The new inhabitants of the capital were accommodated for training in Техникум[23] ('Tehnicum') outfits and later sent to work in factory and plant jobs in both the heavy and light industries.

Meanwhile, starting in the 1960s, some factory workers were assigned housing; the apartment buildings allotted for housing the workers were later nicknamed *Khrushchevki*[24] and *Brezhnevki*. A

---

18 'Regarding actions required for the future development of the city of Chisinau'.

19 <https://www.youtube.com/watch?time_continue=13&v=WS4TXMNdsUg&feature=emb_logo>

20 <www.mezon.md> accessed 12 June 2020.

21 Макеенко М., Специализация Молдавской ССР в общесоюзном разделении труда, Киш., 1966

22 Talpile verzi <http://www.cinema.art.md/movie/798/index.html> accessed 6 June 2020.

23 A form of vocational school that used to rapidly train specialists for a specific job in which the trainee would be subsequently employed.

24 These forms of housing were adapted according to the requirements, satisfying the plan sent by Moscow and based on the slogan 'housing for every worker'. The nicknames originate in the periods and projects approved by the State General Secretariat led by Khrushchev and later by Brezhnev. 'Stalinki' was the housing assigned to the nomenklatura and to the intelligentsia of the Stalin era. Stalinka was considered to be the most expensive type of housing; it differed form other types of housing in terms of amenities, a higher number of rooms, more spacious interiors, and high (3.5 m) ceilings.

series of propaganda films dedicated to the assignation of housing to the working class was made. The films presented workers taking possession of their new residences.[25] One example is that of a family of workers employed by the Codru furniture factory. The story is about a couple, Maria and Vasile Morari. Parents to young Natalia, they were trained by the City Vocational Technical School No. 1 as technologists in wood manufacturing. In the 1970s, the couple was assigned a two-room apartment in a *Khrushchevka*-type building. As their family grew (they had three children), the couple were assigned additional space – part of a duplex-type house. As far as the *Khrushchevka*-type constructions are concerned, they had to be built with maximum savings in construction materials due to the recession. Margareta Lyubimova (head of the mass housing construction sector) spoke in an interview about the fact that the leadership mandated the saving of construction materials. The 22 kilograms of metal used for the construction of one square metre of building were strictly regulated.[26] This resulted in the development of a new technology for the production of construction materials and of new specifications and calculations for the production of concrete panels and other elements that would meet the standards of living required in the Soviet era.

The current enterprise Monolit was in charge of supplying construction materials to Chisinau.[27] The location of the former production branch is now occupied by the transnational group JLC Group[28] (specialising in the processing of dairy products sourced from the entire country). As the urban and the industrial environments were developing, the Ciocana Nouă, Botanica de Sus, Buiucani, and Telecentru microraions also developed;

they were interconnected through thoroughfares. Each of these microraions hosted a factory or a plant in order to facilitate the increase of productivity. The microraions facilitated the citizens' access to their workplace, while at the same time providing the infrastructure required for living: kindergartens, schools, shops, post offices, and multifunctional centres for trades. Industrial sites were placed near green zones or near the outskirts of the microraions if they emitted harmful emissions. Those that posed no health risks to the population were placed in the residential areas. The heavy industry plants were massed in the industrial estate of Sculeni in the immediate vicinity of the green area of the estate, organised by Soviet landscape architects (this area was a public garden between the wars). Other production and heating plant areas were located at the periphery of residential areas, and housing complexes were built near them in order to ensure quick access to the workplace. A few examples of factories and plants located in the heart of residential areas include the Alfa factory (producing colour television sets), Moldovakhidromash (producing vacuum pumps), Sigma (specialising in the production of special computing technology, it manufactured some of the computers used aboard the MIR space station),[29] Bucuria (sweets manufacturer), and Mezon (producing electronic goods such as cassette recorders). The establishment of these industrial areas shaped the city in space. The production facilities and complexes located in residential areas were designed according to a more refined aesthetic rather than as buildings with a merely functional architecture. During the period when the control of the central oversight committee for civil construction and architecture (*Государственный комитет по гражданскому строительству и*

25 Among these films were also Пора большого новоселья ('It's time for a big housewarming party') and Черёмушки ('Cherry Town').

26 Советская империя. Хрущёвки | Телеканал 'История' <https://www.youtube.com/watch?v=LyideCu4LFk> accessed 6 June 2020.

27 <http://wikimapia.org/#lang=ro&lat=46.984908&lon=28.924084&z=14&m=w&show=/15013366/ro/S-A-Monolit-Filiala-de-Producere-%C5%9Fi-Completare-Tehnologic%C4%83-(F-P-C-T-)-(1948)>

28 <http://jlc-group.com/en/history.php>

29 Ion Preasca, FOTO De la fabrici şi uzine la malluri şi ruine. Care este soarta foştilor giganti industriali din Chisinau, 7 November 2013, photo Tudor Iovu, creator: Iovu Tudor, copyright: +37379440490. <https://adevarul.ro/moldova/economie/de-fabrici-uzine-malluri-ruine-1_527b1cb4c7b855ff56c79092/index.html> accessed 17 June 2020.

архитектуре при Госстрое СССР) was more relaxed, architects began self-imposing aesthetic standards, so they would not negatively affect the general appearance of the areas they were working in. Some neighbourhoods, for example, were of special importance, as they included buildings representing the value of Soviet power, and in such cases, the architecture had higher prominence. For instance, the administrative building of the former Sigma plant is strategically located in a highly visible spot, with a square in front featuring elaborated symmetrical landscape architecture. As far as industrial aesthetic is concerned, it maintained a certain rigour, but we can distinguish specific variations from one factory to another in the case of the Alpha television set plant, the Sigma plant, and Topaz. All these buildings share several architectural principles. Firstly, the administrative buildings are separated from the production facilities in such a way that the frontal architectural complex is optimally highlighted. Naturally, the façades conform to the rigidity of an industrial aesthetic, but they do contain added decorative elements that underline the architects' personalised style. Looking at the Alfa television factory, we can see decorative columns placed on the top floor across the entire top outline of the façade, thus forming an ensemble of architectural elements that is visible from any angle. The façade is divided into three levels, the bottom one being the landscape line. Therefore, no matter the angle, the viewer can take in and admire the entire building because the latter does not conflict with the line of the boulevard and of the apartment buildings on the opposite side. The production halls were built according to the engineering standards developed in 1962,[30] when the area of production halls in the case of multi-storey buildings could not exceed 3,500 m². The upper floor could not exceed the dimensions of 18 × 24 m, and the height had to be lower than 3.5 metres from the current floor to the attic floor. An example

is the Steaua Rosie factory, which produced 37 million items of hosiery per year during the Soviet era.[31] The architecture of the production facility, with an area of 1,359 m², is representative of the Stalinist neoclassical style. The aim had been for the building to match the architecture of the city centre in post-war Chisinau.

The façade of the Topaz factory features a structure made from decorative aluminium elements placed symmetrically across the entire building, thereby dividing the strips of windows into equal and symmetrical parts. All the windows have aluminium brise-soleils, but on one part of the building, this solar protection grid consists of four aluminium ribs on each window, while on the other part, the grid consists of only two ribs on each window. This pattern difference splits the symmetry and the repeatability of the façade's exterior elements. The construction is executed in a Soviet modernist style, built from reinforced concrete. It is somewhat related to a brutalist style, but the lack of brute exposure of construction material on the main façade makes the building match the rest of the architecture in present day Dimitrie Cantemir Square.

The Mezon microelectronics factory specialised in the production of the main classes of integrated circuits: logic bipolar ICs from the series 133, 133, 533, and 1533; series 561 and 1561 ICOS; analogue bipolar ICs from the series 1092; 565 series RAM memory; series 585, 1802, 1596, 1828, and 1854 microcontrollers; and EEPROM ASIC series with 1.5 μ technology.[32] In terms of architecture, the complex consists of three buildings, plus a central administrative building. It is finished with glazed panels framed in aluminium, inspired by the international style. The production halls have a reinforced concrete structure, and the building of the main entrance to the factory is also made of reinforced concrete elements framed with a metal structure. The Ionel knitwear factory (established in 1945 as 'Knitwear Factory No. 1' and

30 <https://files.stroyinf.ru/ Data2/1/4293787/4293787377.pdf>

31 <https://www.youtube.com/watch?v=_ pdZPo4mAQc> minute 8:12.
32 <http://mezon.md/index.html> – about the history of the factory.

The Ionel Knitwear Factory ('Knitwear Factory No. 1', later renamed 'The 23rd Congress of the Soviet Union Communist Party') located in the city centre. Post card set, 'Planeta' publishing house, 1970

later renamed 'The 23rd Congress of the Soviet Union Communist Party') is located in the centre of Chisinau. The first building was made in a Soviet art deco style. It had an entrance portal that tended towards neoclassicism and it was finished in local stone. Overall, we can conclude that the industrialisation process was more active in the period after the 1970s – the period in which Leonid Brezhnev was the Secretary General of the Soviet Union Communist Party. At the same time, these investments were, of course, part of a strategy to prove to capitalist countries that the Soviet Union could look after the inhabitants of all its component socialist countries as well as it looked after those in the capital. The development of a great part of the industrial sectors was related to the growth of farming production: the manufacture of tractors, implements for combines, and the other machines required in order to support the agricultural development of the country. The housing construction sector also became more active in the country after the 1970s. This is when the establishment of the new microraions of Chisinau was in full swing. There was intense construction work in Botanica de Sus, Buiucani, Sculeni, Poşta Veche, and Ciocana Nouă. The rise in the quality of urban life started only after the beginning of massive investments in the development of housing, as well as in the construction of new factories and plants in the areas of food processing and the lighting industry. The strategy for the active development of heavy industry was supposed to be included in the coming five-year plan, but *perestroika*

intervened and effectively ended the era of development in industry and urban industrial infrastructure both in the city of Chisinau and in the rest of the country. To conclude, a new approach is required for the former Soviet industrial built assets. It is necessary to put their potential to good use. They have the capacity to attract investment both for production (in the industrial areas on the outskirts) and for the creation of hubs with social, economic, and cultural functions (in the industrial areas within the residential neighbourhoods). In order to achieve this, it is important to maintain the original (that is Soviet) architecture of these buildings, as well as to reorganise the adjacent spaces with the help of professional landscape architects.

Bibliography:

[1] Aron, Raymond, '18 Lessons about Industrial Society', pp. 79.

[2] Ostapov, Alina, 'Activitatea Uniunii Arhitectilor din Republica Sovietică Socialistă Moldovenească', pp. 1.

[3] Меерович М.Г 'АЛЬБЕРТ КАН В ИСТОРИИ СОВЕТСКОЙ ИНДУСТРИАЛИЗАЦИИ', pp. 1–9.

[4] Макеенко М., Специализация Молдавской ССР в общесоюзном разделении труда, Киш., 1966.

[5] Пищевая промышленность Молдавии и перспективы ее развития, Киш., 1969.

[6] Развитие и размещение производительных сил Молдавской ССР, М., 1972.

[7] Гильман Ф. М., Голенко Т. Н., Гудым А. А., Развитие и размещение производительных сил Молдавской ССР, М., 1972.

[8] Флориан Урбан, Башня и Коробка – Краткая история массового жилья; Strelka Press, 2019, pp. 195.

[9] Choay, Francoise, 'Pentru o antropologie a spatiului', Bucharest, 2011.

[10] Журнал 'Техника молодёжи', №3 1972. Т. МАРИН 'ТРАКТОР РОЖДАЕТСЯ В КИШИНЕВЕ', pp. 26.

[11] Sennett, Richard, 'The Craftsman', Strelka Press, pp. 118–120.

[12] Identitătile Chisinaului – 5th edition, Aliona Gratii – MITOPOETICA ORAŞULUI Chisinau , Arc, pp. 90.

[13] Identitătile Chisinaului – 5th edition, Andrei Vatamaniuc – AŞTEPTÂNDU-L PE... DOICESCU, Arc, pp. 135.

Inventing the Garden City. Recreation Areas and Public Leisure Architecture in Post-war Chisinau

Anastasia Felcher

The large-scale destruction the city of Chisinau (Kishinev) suffered due to the events of 1940–1944 was one of the reasons for the drastic difference in appearance between the pre-war city and the city immediately after the Second World War ended. Like many other besieged European cities that were bombed or successively served as outposts for troops and army units, Chisinau was in ruins by the time the war ended. Post-war reconstruction, planned and carried out by officials under the Soviet administration, radically changed not only the appearance of the city, but also its character. Industrial enterprises settled in former pre-war suburbs. In official Soviet historiography, the period between 1945 and 1955 was labelled as 'post-war reconstruction'.

In comparison to the pre-war city, architects paid quite a lot of attention to public institutions and spaces while developing urban plans for post-war Chisinau. Public areas were designed by architects despite the fact that the main priority was to construct residential buildings and institutions related to the economy and everyday life – manufacturing, administrative, medical, and educational institutions. At the same time, building cultural institutions (theatres and cinemas) and designing leisure areas and spaces (parks and recreational areas) were quite important from an ideological point of view. First, this emphasised the extent to which the city gained progressive and modern facilities (from the point of view of the Soviet administration) compared to the interwar period. This, in turn, emphasised the narrative surrounding the Soviet government's concern for the welfare, education, and leisure of ordinary people – again

compared to the interwar Romanian national state. This was often illustrated by comparative statistics on the number of cinemas built in Chisinau after 1944, which were regularly published in post-war Soviet periodicals. The same applied to parks and green areas. Secondly, creating recreational areas made it possible to actively involve the population in the process of urban development, to encourage them to take part in restoration work, and to assert that workers voluntarily seek to contribute to the restoration of the city from ruins. As we know from other cities where significant efforts were required to restore infrastructure after the war (Minsk in particular), the population took part in the latter rather forcibly. On the other hand, the example of Leningrad – where palaces and parks occupied for years during the war were restored – demonstrates that participation in restoring park areas was potentially perceived by the population as a symbolic act of victory in the war. A return to 'former greatness' and everyday routine was perhaps viewed as a sign of victory over the enemy, which had ravaged what were once beautiful monuments of culture and nature. Restoring the former beauty of parks meant overcoming the destructive presence of the enemy and neutralising this damage.

The situation in Chisinau differed from Leningrad and other cities behind and beyond the Iron Curtain. For the city that became the capital Soviet Moldova (or Moldavia as it was called back then), after the Second World War, architects and urban planners engaged in a completely different task: not restoring former recreation and leisure spaces but creating them anew. Soviet architects and urban planners designed recreational

The central entrance to Valea Morilor Park (formerly 'Central Culture and Leisure Park of the Leninist Komsomol') designed by Robert Kurtz and David Palatnik, 1954

39

Inventing the Garden City. Recreation Areas and Public Leisure Architecture in Post-war Chisinau

areas – designated by landscape architecture – outside the limits of the historical city centre. Despite this, the construction of parks and recreation areas caused considerable damage to the given urban fabric of historical buildings and cultural heritage. In some cases, new parks were built on top of cemeteries that had not been in use for some time. In such cases, these were levelled to the ground, and a park would be placed on the site of the cemetery. As a result, the majority of parks and recreation areas were established a good distance from the central areas of the city. This expansion of green areas to new residential neighbourhoods began in the early 1950s and lasted three decades, with the last park built in the Sculeni district in the late 1970s. Urban planners working on Chisinau avoided interfering in the city centre, as the latter had two major parks established in the nineteenth century. Those parks were

Alexander Pushkin Park (given this name in 1949; originally the Public Garden or Alexander Garden; currently Stefan cel Mare [Stephen the Great] Public Park) and Victory Park (given this name after the war; originally and now once again Cathedral Square – the name was re-established after the dissolution of the USSR). These parks were not only recreational areas, but also extremely important symbolic spaces with religious buildings and monuments to state and cultural figures. Like any symbolically rich space, these parks consequently held monuments of historical figures important to competing historical narratives. Under the Soviet administration, which added several monuments to these parks, the latter symbolised continuity, at least from an architectural point of view, from the period of Russian Imperial administration in Bessarabia (1812–1918), eliminating any mention of the interwar years. In contrast to these historical parks, recreational areas created after the war were much larger in size and somewhat different in function. Due to the relatively small size of the historical centre, new recreational areas were easily reachable by public transport and created an alternation of dense urban fabric with fully-fledged natural recreational areas. A distinctive feature of the new Soviet parks in Chisinau was a sense of natural

Summer Theatre for 7,000 spectators, designed by A. Kolotovkin and T. Lomova, 1957

origin despite purposeful design. The only park where this principle was ignored was the Botanical Garden of the Academy of Sciences of the MSSR, which opened in 1950. The park was placed in the Buiucani district. The Botanical Garden reproduced in miniature the natural landscape typical of the region. It therefore served research purposes more than the recreational needs of the general public. Overall, spacious green areas within the city limits contributed to the image of Chisinau as a garden city, a green southern place with a favourable climate and agreeable and welcoming local residents. This image was repeatedly reproduced in multiple tourist-oriented descriptions of the city, a series of postcards as well as video essays and programmes encouraging Soviet citizens to visit the southern regions of the country, and that expanded significantly after the war. The earliest initiative for developing new recreational areas after the war focused on Komsomol Lake (currently the Valley of Mills). Creating this lake on what was then the southern outskirts of the city involved the mass participation of Chisinau residents – primarily in digging the pit for the reservoir. The park project was developed under the direct supervision of the then chief architect of the city, Robert Kurtz, and at the initiative of Leonid Brezhnev. The latter was then the Secretary of the Central Committee of the MSSR Communist Party. In 1950, Brezhnev participated in the ceremonial ground-breaking of the park near the future lake, a site marked for visitors by a commemorative stone. Over the next two years, with a collective effort (including manual labour by Komsomol members) the pit was completed and filled with water from the inflow of the Byk River. Opened in 1952, the lake with its encompassing road (built slightly later) became the centre of the new park. The park received its official name – the Central Park of Culture and Recreation, named after the Lenin Komsomol (CPKiO). In addition to the lake, the park had well developed recreational infrastructure, which has consistently expanded over time. There was a summer theatre for 7,000 spectators

The Casa Mare pavilion designed by Valentin Voitsehovski in the frame of the Republican Agricultural Exhibition opened in 1956

(designed by A. Kolotovkin and T. Lomova and opened in 1957) – a popular venue for various events and concerts, hosting famous musicians, a daytime cinema, a playground for children, a restaurant, a beach, and a boat station (opened in 1953). Several architectural structures served decorative purposes and formed a coherent ensemble with the above-listed objects. A rotunda was installed next to one of the entrances to the park, with a fountain and a cascading staircase leading from it to the lake. Later, a second entrance to the park was added, from which a large granite staircase led to the lake. This further integrated the lake and park into the urban landscape and made them more accessible to citizens. This new granite staircase led to the lake from the main campus of Chisinau State University (founded in 1946), thereby significantly increasing the number of people visiting the park.

Official Soviet historiography labelled the period starting in 1955 as the 'Period of Urban Reconstruction and the Industrialisation of the Construction Industry'. It generally reflected the way the territory of the Central Park (CPKiO) district further developed. In 1956, the area next to the park was converted into an exhibition space and hosted a permanent Republican Agricultural Exhibition. Three years later, as in other cities across the USSR, it was renamed the Moldavian SSR Exhibition of Achievements of the National Economy (VDNKh MSSR). In accordance with this name, the exhibition halls boasted of achievements in agriculture, such as crop growth indicators, new crops, sowing and harvesting equipment, etc. The exhibition aimed 'to promote science, technology,

41

Inventing the Garden City. Recreation Areas and Public Leisure Architecture in Post-war Chisinau

culture, and best practices, training employees in all branches of the national economy to use new production methods'. Just like VDNKh in many large cities in other Soviet republics (Moscow, Kyiv, Minsk, Riga, Tallinn, Kaliningrad, Kazan, etc.), exhibition pavilions were devoted to specific industrial sectors ('Energy and Engineering', 'Consumer Goods', 'Construction', 'Agricultural-Industrial Complex', 'Machinery by the State Committee of Agriculture', and 'Science and Culture'). In addition, there were four thematic pavilions, including 'Casa Mare' (literally 'big house', a traditional ceremonial room used as a living room, smartly decorated and prepared to receive guests; used to celebrate family rituals and holidays). This pavilion reflected how professionals of the 1950s collectively imagined the traditional Moldavian estate and architecture. Having an example of housing that referred to indigenous local culture also promoted the concept of Moldovan ethnicity as entirely separate from Romanian. Arguing in public discourse and on the pages of academic journals for having two separate nations, supporters of this idea were making a political statement, for which arguments were sought in the fields of ethnology and ethnography. The problematic Bessarabian question, a stumbling block among politicians, diplomats, and researchers on both sides of the Prut River, thus found its way into newly built public architectural structures. The Casa Mare pavilion housed a folk group and a training centre for Moldovan folk dances, songs, and crafts. This again was an example of a modern state inventing a tradition with the help of conventional folk culture. Temporary exhibitions and events also took place on the territory of the VDNKh. The exhibition area included extensive gardens, vineyards, a forest park, and greenhouses. By the 1980s, the total area of the CPKiO park, including the VDNKh, amounted to more than 100 hectares. This met the challenges of introducing vast newly-designed green areas for Chisinau. As stated in an encyclopaedia published in 1979, the architects of Moldova paid special attention to designing green spaces, since they saw gardening as an important aspect of improvement applicable to all cities – and to Chisinau in particular.

One of the principles behind the design and urban planning practices in Chisinau since the late 1950s was to prevent the dominant presence of individual construction in central areas of the city. Urban planners saw the accumulation and concentration of individual development in the central zones as a possible obstacle to growth and the harmonious development of cities. Therefore, professionals invested effort in making the city expand and creating so-called areas of individual construction. These were Posta Veche (lit. 'old postal office'), Buiucani, Sculeni, and other neighbourhoods suitable for implementing large-scale urban development projects. In these newly developed neighbourhoods, one could build almost freely, with no need to demolish existing housing or other built objects. This meant, however, that like many European cities, Chisinau expanded at the expense of its former suburbs, and construction targeted the sites of defunct cemeteries. The latter were inevitably sacrificed for urban development.

This was the case in the construction of Alunelul Park (literally 'nut'; also the current name of the location) in the Sculeni neighbourhood between 1958 and 1961. This neighbourhood's location in proximity to the city centre proved to be the reason for targeting it for development purposes. This predetermined the expansion and infrastructure development to connect this area to the city. Like other areas, Sculeni required an area designated for public leisure. In order to create new facilities for public use, authorities decided to raze part of a Jewish cemetery. The cemetery dated back to the nineteenth century. After one part of it was demolished to free up space for new architectural projects, visual traces of the cemetery were erased. The rest of the cemetery was preserved and remained intact. Today, this cemetery is the only historical Jewish cemetery in Chisinau. Back in 1958, the cemetery was divided into two parts, one of which was originally supposed to become a market square. In 1960, the gravestones were broken into pieces and used as building material for a fence that was supposed to separate the area reserved for the market and the part of the cemetery left intact. Eventually, instead of the market, Alunelul Park (initially Kuibyshev Park) was created on the cleared territory, and the gravestones were used for paving the paths of its walkways. The park area occupied 10 hectares, had several pathways, and like other leisure areas in the city, hosted carousels and cafes.

All subsequent major parks and green areas in Chisinau reflected the same logic in their making – creating parks for newly built neighbourhoods. In the 1970s, three iconic parks were launched in Chisinau: the 'Park of People's Friendship' (1972), the arboretum (1973), and the most important one of this period, known today as the 'Valley of Roses' (founded in 1968 and completed in the 1970s). With the growth of new neighbourhoods with apartment buildings rather than individual houses, parks within walking distance became commodities of high importance for apartment residents. Currently known as the 'Valley of Roses', in the 1970s the spacious park in the Botanica district was named after Vladimir Lenin (city park of culture and leisure named after V. Lenin). In 1968, the park was founded in the southeastern part of the city on the territory of a natural green area of 145 hectares and a rose plantation. Similar to the Komsomol Lake project, city residents were engaged on a voluntary basis to carry out work on clearing territory for the future park. This emphasised the inclusive nature of city improvement initiatives. The centre of the park had a cascade of three ponds covering an area of nine hectares. Later on, the dams were reinforced and concreted. The park included green spaces and developed infrastructure – a stage, a playground, a sports zone, a concert and dance hall, a centre for technical creativity, beaches, and restaurants ('Doina', 'Old Cellar' and ship-cafe 'Neptune'). In the early 1970s, a Museum of Landscape Sculpture was launched on the territory of the park with works by sculptors from across the USSR. The museum was in fact an open-air collection of sculptures on both sides

of the park in honour of the 50th anniversary of the MSSR and the Communist Party of Moldavia. Thus, the authorities aimed to identify the territory of the region as Soviet. In the early 1970s, Iskra cinema (literally 'The Spark', also the title of an underground political newspaper of Russian socialist emigrants founded in 1900 by Lenin) was built at the entrance to the park in honour of the 100th anniversary of Lenin's birth. The cinema was located close to the park, creating a comprehensive area for public leisure.

The 1980s were marked by modern architecture in Chisinau. A number of iconic public buildings, including the circus, opera and ballet theatre, press house, and – in the immediate vicinity to the park in the Botanica district described above – the Palace of the Road Trade Union of Railway Workers (which later changed its name to the Palace of Culture for Railway Workers). Designed and constructed through an architectural project by Semyon Shoikhet and Abram Vaysbein, this palace hosted various public events (art exhibitions, competitions, lectures, sports competitions, etc.). Geographically, the palace connected the railway station located nearby with the Botanica district, while the park was located almost immediately next to the palace. As a result, the entire nearby territory was known as an area for public leisure, with the cinema, park, and the Youth Centre named after Yuri Gagarin (opened in 1972; named after the astronaut, who visited Chisinau in 1966; built using funds earned by Komsomol members) all further strengthened by the palace. Within a single area, Chisinau residents were offered cultural, gastronomic, sports events, and pathways for long walks in the park so large that it was not easy to spot the meticulous design and urban planning behind it.

Yet another park was launched to mark the 50th anniversary of the Communist Party of Moldavia, this time in the Sculeni district. Friendship of Peoples' Park (now 'La Izvor' or 'At the Source') was founded in 1972 in relative proximity to Alunelul Park. The name of the park referred to a broadly promoted idea of fruitful interaction and multi-level relations between the 15 Soviet republics. This cooperation

The 'Yuri Gagarin' Republican Youth Centre opened in 1972 in the City Park of Culture and Leisure named after V. Lenin (now 'Valley of Roses'), designed by Nikolay Klyushnikov

43

Inventing the Garden City. Recreation Areas and Public Leisure Architecture in Post-war Chisinau

was intended to be visualised through infrastructure and sculpture in the new park. The latter was not fully implemented, but the name remained. One of the main attractions of the new park were lakes formed by a cascade of ponds connected by channels. In addition to the given infrastructure for public leisure, which was in many ways similar to other parks in the city, this park also had an island, beaches, bridges, a 'Fairy Town' for children, the 'La Izvor' restaurant, a cafe, a boat station, and sports grounds. The park became a family holiday destination. For this purpose, the fairy-tale themed island was built for International Children's Day (it remained open until the mid-1980s). This island had many characters and fairy-tale themed compositions next to a miniature imitation of a castle. For a short time, the island was the most popular destination for leisure activities with children. The programmatic friendship between the peoples of the Soviet republics defined the choice of specialists who made sculptures for the island: the 'Guslar with Children' sculpture was designed by Lithuanian sculptor A. Roberertas, while the 'Flying' sculpture was by R. Peter from Estonia, and the 'Youth' sculpture was by G. Japaridze from Georgia. The island was visible from a suspension bridge, accessible from the main entrance by a paved walkway.

Similar to the park in the Botanica district, the park in the Sculeni district, founded in the 1970s, became the central

attraction for a large number of residents in a relatively new area. The area did not yet have a public transport network at this time. This spurred the development of infrastructure in the immediate vicinity of the park in the 1980s. Then, a project for off-street transport (a suspended cable car) was launched. In 1983, the Tbilisi-based 'Gruzgiprosakht' Institute started working on the cable car project. The project was supposed to be completed by the 60th anniversary of the MSSR in 1994, yet in reality, only one section of the cableway was initiated and used by 1990, and it connected the Sculeni and Buiucani districts. The lower station of the cable car was located opposite the 'Friendship of Peoples' Park, and the route ran from the park through a forest park to the Buiucani district.

Located in relative proximity to the 'Friendship of Peoples' Park, the Botanical Garden was reclassified in 1973 as an arboretum due to the transfer of the Botanical Garden to the outskirts of the city to the area located near the new airport (opened in 1960). The territory for the new Botanical Garden was chosen in the 1960s, and in 1975 the new Botanical Garden (104 hectares) was designated a research institute of the MSSR Academy of Sciences. With the help of the garden, researchers aimed to preserve the diversity of the region's flora. The arboretum, in turn, became more oriented towards public leisure. Not only the status of the park that became an arboretum changed, so too did its landscape. Instead of reproducing local flora, experts at the arboretum began to give preference to tropical and exotic plants. The scientific component of the arboretum also remained, and its employees actively promoted knowledge in the field of botany.

In general, the landscape architecture of Chisinau was a direct consequence of urban planning and the architectural transformation of the given urban structure. In the 1980s, specialists used professional magazines dedicated to the theory of urban planning to start drawing attention to the old Chisinau, its buildings and street design, which according to the emerging discourse were destroyed by Soviet architects. The authors argued for measures to protect historical buildings. In this context, the disregard for historical architectural structures in the layout of highways or parks was interpreted as the insensitivity of the authorities to the rich cultural heritage of the city and traces of its historical development. However, by that time, such parks and highways had already been in place for several decades.

The intentional greening of the city and development of the park system were integrated into the development strategy of Chisinau and met a number of aims that architects and planners had been working on for several decades. These tasks were both practical (the need for post-war reconstruction and public space suitable for leisure) and ideological (the glorification of the Communist Party and symbolic consolidation of the city with the USSR). Looking at both the 'post-war reconstruction' and the period of 'construction industrialisation' enables us to reflect on the specific aspects of landscape architecture in Chisinau. In the 1950s, the park near Komsomol Lake was adjoined to the historical centre, yet in the 1970s architects designed and launched parks outside the city centre. City life also moved to these new neighbourhoods. With these neighbourhoods put to use, new parks in Chisinau became part of expanding the city beyond the historical centre. Launching public leisure infrastructure within these new districts was an important component of urban development, which meant that newly built neighbourhoods were supposed to be self-sufficient. Their residents were spared the need to leave the area of residence for leisure, recreation, or walks in green areas. At the same time, increasing the number of residents and the development of infrastructure required modernising the transport system. As the example of the cable car transportation system shows, parks were the starting points for such projects. Chisinau as a garden city, southern city, and resort city – notions of exceptional importance in the post-war years – were gradually joined by an image of a technically equipped, industrially developed, but, nevertheless, consistently green city.

Sources and secondary literature:

[1]   Belkin, A.N., Landshaftnaia arkhitektura Moldavii [Landscape Architecture of Moldavia]. Kishinev: Cartea Moldoveneasca, 1976.

[2]   Kiktenko, V.K., Kishinev — gorod, ustremlennyi v budushcheie [Kishinev – City that Looks into the Future]. Kishinev: Cartea Moldovenească, 1982.

[3]   Kishinev: Entsiklopediia: A-Ia [Kishinev: Encyclopedia: A-Z] (ed. Timush, A.Ia. et al.). Kishinev: Soviet Moldavian Encyclopedia, 1984.

[4]   Kolotovkin, A.V., Pedash, G.A., Eltman, I.S., Arkhitektura Sovetskoi Moldavii [Architecture of Soviet Moldavia]. Moscow: Stroizdat, 1987.

[5]   Krupenikov, I.A., Dorogaia priroda Moldavii [Dear Nature of Moldavia]. Kishinev: Cartea Moldoveneasca, 1982.

[6]   Levit, S.E., Mokhov N.A., Odud A.L., Moldavskaia SSR [Moldavian SSR]. Moscow: Publishing House of the USSR Academy of Sciences, 1959.

[7]   Moldavskaia SSR [Moldavian SSR] (ed. by I.K. Vartichan). Kishinev: Publishing House of Moldavian Soviet Encyclopedia, 1979.

[8]   Odud, A.L., Kishinev: putevoditel' [Kishinev: Guidebook]. Kishinev: Stinta, 1961.

[9]   Podolian, A., Kishinev: fotoal'bom [Kishinev: Photo Album]. Kishinev: Cartea Moldoveneasca, 1966.

[10]   Slepchenko, E.V., Pafos sozidaniia [Pathos of Creation]. Kishinev: Cartea Moldoveneasca, 1967.

[11]   Smirnov, V.F., Gradostroitel'stvo Moldavii XIX–XX vekov ['Urban Planning of Moldova in the XIX-XX centuries']. Kishinev: Cartea Moldovenească, 1967.

[12]   Tuleanu, V.L., Tsvetushchii krai, Moldaviia [Blooming Land, Moldova]. Kishinev: Cartea Moldoveneasca, 1963.

[13]   Axenti, M., 'Urban Transformations as an Ideological Tool of Political Regimes: the Case of the Chisinau City Centre'.

[14]   Ritualizing the City. Collective Performances as Aspects of Urban Construction from Constantine to Mao, edited by Ivan Foletti and Adrien Palladino. Roma: Viella, 2017, 121-137.

[15]   Ursu, V., 'Reabilitarea patrimoniului istoric al Chisinaului in perioada postbelica si initierea constructiei unei identitati urbane de tip sovietic (anii 1940–1950 ai sec. XX)'/Identitatile Chisinaului, editat de S. Musteata, A. Corduneanu. Chisinau: Pontos, 2012, 89-94.

[16]   Gordeev, A., 'Gradostroitel'stvo Kishineva so dnia osnovaniia i do nashikh dney' ['Urban Planning of Chisinau from the Day of its Foundation to Present Day']/Identitatile Chisinaului: editia a IV-a, editat de S. Musteata, A. Corduneanu. Chisinau: Pontos, 2018, 106–113.

[17]   Lupascu, V., 'Istoricheskii park Kishineva «Gradina publika Stefan cel Mare»' ['Historical Park in Chisinau «Gradina Publica Stefan cel Mare»' /Buletinul INCERCOM (Nr. 7) 2015: 110–138.

[18]   For this publication the author referred to information available at <www.oldchisinau.com> and <www.locals.md>

Lower station of the cable car project from Buiucanii de Jos ('Lower Buiucani'), designed by Manana Kariauli, Vidjen Abovyan, Vakhtang Lezhava (engineer), 'Gruzgiprosakht', 1980s

Culture and State in Chisinau: The City's Cinemas

Vitalie Sprinceana

'The cultural revolution is ... a crucial turn, a direction of cultural development of the masses.' (V. I. Lenin)[1]

'Due to the fact that it has exceptional abilities for spiritually influencing the masses, cinematography helps the working class and its party to educate workers in the spirit of socialism, to organise the masses in the struggle for socialism, to elevate the masses' cultural level and their level of vigilance.'[2]

I shall attempt to present in this text a subjective and very general history of certain cultural institutions in Chisinau built during the Soviet period (1944–1994). I am interested both in the concrete history of these buildings and organisations and in their institutional history. By far, cinemas seem to me to be the most interesting and I will focus on them the most. They are not only architectural landmarks, but also instruments of cultural and social policies (institutions designed to contribute to the cultural and political education of the masses, to their mobilisation for the construction of socialism). These two aspects of cinemas allow us to tell a story about the Soviet state as the author of a massive and ambitious project of educating and mobilising the masses and of creating the Soviet citizen through urban planning and cultural policies. The magnifying glass of research, used in this text, focuses on an intermediate area located between a micro level (the actual cinemas in

Chisinau) and a macro level (cultural policies of the MSSR and USSR, radical policy changes in the field of architecture, etc.).

Architecture and Culture in the MSSR (1944–1991)

a) Culture and Cultural Policies in the USSR

Culture was a crucial aspect of the construction of the Soviet regime. The ideas of modernity and the European enlightenment, affirming the superiority of the rational organisation of society in relation to the scientific communities, and from which the Bolsheviks got their inspiration, were based on the anthropological model according to which human nature (individuals, society) as well as natural conditions have an outstanding plasticity – they can be shaped and reshaped indefinitely[3]. The Bolsheviks understood that radical cultural change (what Lenin called the 'cultural revolution') must take place at all levels of culture: from popular culture, everyday culture (rituals, common holidays, mass culture) to high culture (literature, theatre, film, visual arts). As the contradictions and class relations of the old world had 'permeated' every cultural genre – film, literature, rituals – creating various tastes and class distinctions (which amplified and strengthened class inequality), each of these genres was seen as a potential 'battlefront' and each became important in the war to liquidate the remnants of the old order[4]. The new

1 'Культурная революция — это... целый переворот, целая полоса культурного развития всей народной массы' in Ленин В.И. О кооперации // Поли. собр. соч. (5-е изд.). Т. 45, М.: Изд-во полит, лит-ры, 1965–1975. С. 372.
2 Директивы XIX съезда партии по пятому пятилетнему плану развития СССР на 1951–55 гг. Госполитиздат. 1952, p. 29.

3 Куренной В.А, СОВЕТСКИЙ ЭКСПЕРИМЕНТ СТРОИТЕЛЬСТВА ИНСТИТУТОВ. In Время, вперед! Культурная политика в СССР. М.: Издательский дом Высшей школы экономики, 2013.
4 Idem, pp. 8–9.

power would create different cultural fronts, close or reopen some of them later, improvise, propose something, then cancel that and propose something else, and create specialised institutions to manage the cultural field (the USSR established its first-ever Ministry of Culture). The Soviet state was an active cultural agent. It was the sole sponsor and creator of cultural policies in the territory that it managed, having a monopoly on cultural production until the late 1980s. The Soviet state mobilised, educated, and organised vigorously. The political cost of culture (the re-education of the masses and their engagement in the effort to build socialism) dominated economic calculations and notions of economic profitability.

b) The Socialist City. Socialist Urbanism in the USSR and the MSSR

Soviet architecture, as an art genre but also as a tool for creating the new man, was no less dependent on the political factor than other spheres of activity in the USSR. Urban planning and zoning policies always depended more on decisions taken at the central level than on discussions in the architectural milieu. The evolution of the design of the socialist city had a separate trajectory from the fertile debates in the architectural milieu (the discussion on urbanisation and de-urbanisation, the discussion on the territorial principles of industrialisation, etc.). The sinuous history of the socialist city is the history of a process in which the architectural and urban planning solutions represent more or less the architectural answer to the political requirements of the time.[5] The Soviet city is a political project reflecting the ambition to build a new urban space – a socialist urban space that would educate (or create) citizens who actively participate in building socialism. In practice, things were a little different. Soviet urban planners were able to seek to build a city that followed the party line only in the new territories where cities were built from scratch.[6] In cities that predated the revolution (or that existed before joining the USSR) such as Chisinau, urban interventions had to take into account, at least in part, the particularities of local history and the urban planning solutions (the historical and administrative centre, the subordination and class relationship between centre and periphery, etc.). Largely due to the victory of the followers of industrialisation over those who saw another way of developing the USSR (agriculturalisation, for example), the socialist city was an exclusively industrial city. It was an artificial, rational, and technical organisation of processes that must produce two kinds of results – economic and political.[7]

5 Меерович М. Г., Конышева Е. В., Хмельницкий Д. С. Кладбище соцгородов: градостроительная политика в СССР (1928–1932 гг.). – Российская политическая энциклопедия (РОССПЭН); Фонд 'Президентский центр Б. Н. Ельцина', 2011, pp. 9–10.

6 See also Stephen Kotkin's above-mentioned monograph, which documents, in outstanding manner, the construction process for the city of Magnitogorsk.

7 To support the assertion that urbanisation and industrialisation were not inevitable as means of developing the USSR, we point to a document resulting from the debate on urbanity and rurality, Aleksandr Chayanov's utopian writing (Чаянов Александр, Путешествие моего брата Алексея в страну крестьянской утопии). Source: <http://az.lib.ru/c/chajanow_a_w/text_0020.shtml>

The functions of the socialist city were closely connected with the political aims of the system. As a result, the cities were designed to 'contain a certain socio-professional component, a certain number of inhabitants calculated according to the indicators of distribution for material assets and for the supply of products. The city included types of homes mandated by the leadership, a concrete list of service objectives, etc.'[8] 'Work', 'daily life', and 'rest' were deliberately organised according to scientific (and political) calculations whose purpose was to exclude uncontrollable or undesirable social processes, but also, on the constructive side, to stimulate the emergence of new social relationships.[9] The socialist city was based on the principle of the development of an infrastructure of social and cultural service that would include 100 per cent of the population and the territory of the city. This infrastructure was organised according to hierarchical and territorial principles on several levels: urban infrastructure (at the level of the entire city), raion (district) infrastructure, neighbourhood infrastructure, block (building) infrastructure. The territorial hierarchy did not translate, as it did in capitalist cities, into territorial differences and inequalities, all the more so into exclusions. The basic principle of urban planning of the socialist city was that the Soviet citizen had to have in the immediate vicinity institutions and centres that would satisfy their basic cultural, economic, and leisure needs. In other words, the Soviet urban periphery is equipped, at least to a minimum, with all the necessary economic, cultural, and leisure infrastructure. By the time Moldova was included in the Soviet Union (1944), Soviet architecture and urbanism had already gone through a complex history. The nearly 30 years of Soviet urbanism had also acquired important experience. As we saw above, by 1944, the controversy between urbanists and dis-urbanists had long been forgotten. The Communist Party was in the process of standardising the urbanisation process and infrastructure construction, including cultural infrastructure. However, the reality in Chisinau was not at all simple: 70 to 80 per cent of the buildings in the historic centre had been destroyed during the Second World War[10]. Additionally, the city had lost much of its industrial and transportation infrastructure. The development priorities of the city were, in the first years, related to the reconstruction of the destroyed infrastructure. The housing issue was another problem. Before deciding to build a socialist city in Chisinau, the authorities in the first post-war years had to ensure the basic economic functionality of the city. The construction process took on an emergency turn. The first site rebuilt was the Railway Station (architect: L. Chuprin, 1948)[11]. At the same time, planning and reconstruction schemes were developed for Moldovan cities affected by the war.[12]. With the participation of Shchusev (and with the active involvement of the office of the architect Robert Kurtz), the first general plan of the city of Chisinau was developed. It was approved by the Government of the Republic in 1947, together with the urban planning schemes of the other cities of the Republic.[13] By 1950, the reconstruction stage was over in the city: all or part of the buildings that could be rebuilt had been rebuilt, including some cultural sites – the Republican Stadium, the Pushkin Theatre (now Mihai Eminescu National Theatre), and the Biruinta and Patria cinemas.[14]

8 Меерович, р.10.

9 Idem, р.50.

10 Virgil Pâslariuc. Cine a devastat Chisinaul în iulie 1941?. Source: https://www.historia.ro/sectiune/general/articol/cine-a-devastat-chisinaul-in-iulie-1941. See also T. Nesterova. Arhitectura din perioada postbelică a Moldovei sovietice. Arta, Nr. 1(AV)/2016, p. 96. Source: https://ibn.idsi.md/sites/default/files/imag_file/96_103_Arhitectura%20din%20perioada%20postbelica%20a%20Moldovei%20sovietice.pdf

11 There was a debate on the feasibility of moving the railway station building to another part of the city in order to accelerate the construction and development of industrial sites, but the technical capabilities and the limited resources did not allow this (see Смирнов, В. Ф., Градостроительство Молдавии. Кишинев: Картя Молдовеняскэ, 1975, р.34).

12 Смирнов, р.36.

13 Смирнов, р.36.

14 Смирнов, р. 47.

c) Socialist Cinemas. Architecture and Cultural Policies

The architecture of Soviet cinemas evolved over time. Lenin, and after him Stalin, Khrushchev, and the other general secretaries, realised the importance of cinemas and cinematography as a means of propaganda in favour of the Soviet way of life and a tool for mobilising the masses in the construction of socialism. In the first Soviet decades, the authorities used both the cinematographic infrastructure that existed before the revolution (obtained through nationalisation) and also innovated – mobile cinemas (Russian: *кинопередвижки*), etc. Mobile cinemas became necessary as a result of two factors: on the one hand, the dramatic increase in the importance of cinema in the politico-cultural projects of the new Soviet state (the elimination of illiteracy, the struggle against religion, educating and mobilising the masses) and on the other hand, the obvious inadequacy of the cinematographic infrastructure inherited from the old regime (in which cinematography was an art accessible only to a small category of the population) for the needs of the new state (in which cinematography had to be a mass art and had to reach everywhere, both socially – to all groups – and spatially – in all the corners of the Union)[15]. For objective reasons – the civil war, technological capabilities, controversies and battles between the various projects of the 'first workers' and peasants' state' that followed Lenin's death in 1924 – the construction of new cinemas became possible only after the 1930s. The various discussions within the architectural community and at the party level on the ways in which cinema can reach the masses converged, by 1930, on the idea of building large cinemas in buildings that have no other function than to present films to the public. Thus, after 1930, the first new Soviet cinemas appeared, built for a large number of spectators. Examples include the Udarnik cinema built in Moscow in 1933 and designed for 1,587 spectators, and the

Gigant cinema built in Leningrad in 1935 and designed for 1,400 spectators. The buildings were grand and spacious, often with two or more floors, also housing additional rooms that fulfilled various functions: billiard rooms, reading rooms, buffets, dance halls, corridors and generous foyers often adorned with columns and balconies etc. Most of these halls provided for two screenings for spectators who had to enter and leave without intersecting. This involved the construction of additional stairs and exits that unnecessarily complicated the cinema building[16]. Later on, the Soviet architects considered this type of construction uneconomical for central cinemas and chose to design and build multi-hall cinema buildings (initially with two, then with several halls). They were considered to be more adapted to the needs of the time – they brought minimalism in construction and savings in materials, efficiency of space distribution, an increase in film production, the emergence of sound cinema, and an increase in the number of spectators. The new cinemas also allowed for a restructuring of the cinema schedule, as the cinema could show several films simultaneously. The waiting time between film sessions was reduced (there was no need for foyers for the spectators waiting for the next feature), and the various additional rooms disappeared – the billiard rooms, the dance halls, the reading rooms – being transferred to other cultural institutions (clubs, libraries). The first Soviet cinema with two theatres of 300 spectators each was built in 1936 in the city of Chelyabinsk based on a project of the USSR Academy of Architecture. Later in 1938, the Rodina cinema was built in Moscow with two halls seating 600 spectators each. The Second World War marked a paradigm shift in the construction of cinemas. The era of experiments was replaced by an era of standardised solutions. The material difficulties of the Soviet state, the destruction of a

15 Денис Давыдов. Кинопередвижники. Как сельчан приобщали в 1920-е годы к 'важнейшему из искусств'. Source: <https://rg.ru/2016/01/20/rodina-kino.html>

16 Щербаков В.В., Быков В.Е., Белинин Г.К., Хазанов Д.Б. Архитектура кинотеатров. Серия: Архитектура советских общественных учреждений. Государственное издательство литературы по строительству и архитектуре. Москва. 1955. pp. 19–20.

The Biruinta ('Victory') cinema designed by Roman Bekesevich and built on the ruins of the Odeon cinema in 1945. Post card set, 'Planeta' publishing house, 1970

large part of the cinema network during the war (more than 500 cinemas were destroyed in the cities and more than 7,000 pieces of projection equipment were lost in the villages[17], amounting to half of the total number) required an austere investment regime in cinematography. Around 1950, the State Institute for the Design of Cinemas (Russian: Гипрокино) developed standard cinema blueprints for villages and towns, seating between 150 and 800 people. The composition of cinema buildings and their rooms began to be regulated by ГОСТ-2691-44[18]. The standardisation of the construction of cinemas boosted the construction of cinemas in the cities and towns of the USSR. In the Moldavian SSR, the first cinemas in the post-war period began to operate in existing buildings. The Biruinta ('Victory') cinema (architect: R. Bekesevich) opened in 1945 on the ruins of another cinema that in the interwar period was called Odeon[19] (the name it still bears today). A photograph of the cinema, taken in 1953[20], shows the sumptuous building of the cinema, with a façade decorated in an eclectic style: the entrance is marked by two columns, the walls contain decorative elements (stylised wreaths), and the ticket booths are located outside. Another picture of the Biruinta cinema

from the beginning of the 1960s presents a building in which the eclectic architecture has been replaced by a functional minimalism: the ticket booths have been moved inside; the columns have been completely removed, as have the decorative elements on the façade; and the construction lines are much straighter[21]. The cinema was rebuilt several times – in 1965 and 1982. In the 1970s, a special hall for children was built: Andries. The Patria cinema also opened at a former venue, this time in the building of the former club of the Assembly of the Bessarabian Aristocrats, built in the nineteenth century and rebuilt 'with architecture in the spirit of historical stylisations based on the Viennese Baroque (architect: H. von Lonschy)'.[22] In 1921 the building became the home of the National Theatre. In the post-war period, architects V. Voitsekhovski and M. Berber produced a new design for the building, adapted for the needs of a cinema. Patria underwent renovations at the end of the 1960s. The project aimed for the construction of a ventilation complex and the installation of a refrigeration machine and an air conditioning system. Patria became the most popular cinema in the city – visited by over 2.5 million people in 1982 alone[23]. Towards the middle of the 1950s the construction of new cinemas begins in buildings already built according to the standards of ГОСТ-2691-44 and according to the recommendations of Гипрокино. The first new cinemas were 'Chisinau' and 'The 40th anniversary of the Leninist Komsomol', both inaugurated in 1957. The Chisinau cinema (currently the former cinema of the Union of Filmmakers) was inaugurated on the occasion of the 40th anniversary of the October Revolution. As the first director of the cinema, Victor Andon, remembers the cinema was

[17] М. И. Косинова. Советская кинофикация и кинопрокат во второй половине 1940-х годов…'Трофейное кино' — спасение киноотрасли в период "малокартинья." Source: <https://cyberleninka.Ru/>

[18] Щербаков, р.33.

[19] Кишинев: энциклопедия, Кишинёв: Главная редакция Молдавской Советской Энциклопедии, 1984, р.141.

[20] <http://oldchisinau.com/forum/download/file.php?id=13297&t=1>

[21] Советская Молдавия. Кишинёв начала 1960-х. <https://apdance1.livejournal.com/23283.html>

[22] Nesterova, Tamara, Arhitectura din perioada postbelică a Moldovei sovietice, p. 99. See also Nesterov, T., Cinematograful 'Patria' din Chisinau, istoria edificării clădirii. Conference 'Patrimoniul cultural: cercetare, valorificare, promovare', proceedings, p. 115. Chisinau, Moldova, 29–31 October 2019.

[23] Кишинев: энциклопедия, р.396.

The 'The 40th anniversary of the Leninist Comsomol' cinema from the Telecentru district designed by Valentin Voitsehovski in 1957

built using a loan of 1.5 million roubles from the state bank. It was intended for 527 spectators. The 40th anniversary of the Leninist Comsomol cinema was built on a piece of land that was part of the Central Cemetery (some sources indicate that the tomb of the former mayor Karl Schmidt was located in the area where the cinema was later built). The one-storey cinema building was made according to a standard design (V. Voitsekhovski) and included an auditorium with a capacity of 668. In 1965, the cinema acquired an annex – a space for the lobby and several technical rooms[24]. A square was created in front of the cinema, in the centre of which stands a monument 'In memory of the fighters for Soviet Power' (erected in 1966 based on designs by sculptors A. Maiko, I. Ponyatovski, and L. Fitov)[25]. In 1959, the 'Tkacenko' cinema (Doina Street) opened in the Poşta Veche district, equipped with a single auditorium with 500 seats.

The other cinemas were built in the 1960s and 1970s. The 'Moscova' cinema was built in 1965 using a design made by the 'Mosgiproteatr' (architect: N. Kurennoy). The auditorium was intended for 940 spectators, making it one of the largest cinemas in the USSR at that time. According to reports, it was the only cinema in Chisinau that showed widescreen films (the projection was made on the screen using three projectors simultaneously). Some sources say that the name of the cinema was a return of courtesy by the Moldovan authorities – there was already a cinema called Chisinau in Moscow and it was 'logical' for the cinema in Chisinau to be named in honour of the union's capital. The cinema replaced the Cathedral of the Holy Archangels, 'demolished in order to eliminate its dominant position in the area and to replace it with a cultural site of a new type'[26]. The 'Shipka' cinema (Dimo Street, architect: G. Penbek) opened in 1967 and was built according to a standard design. The cinema had a single hall for 552 spectators. The 'Iskra' ('Spark') cinema on Trandafirilor Street was built in 1970 using a standard design (R. Bekesevich) for the celebrations to mark the 100th anniversary

---

[24] Кишинев: энциклопедия, p.464.

[25] Кишинев: энциклопедия, p.148.

[26] The Moscova cinema, Chisinau. Source: <https://romd.socialistmodernism.com/index.php/2018/08/21/cinematograful-moscova-chisinau/> Originally published in 'Cinematografele Chisinaului'. English version <http://bacu.ro/the-cinemas-of-chisinau-republic-of-moldova/>

The 'Moscova' cinema designed by N. Kurennoy in 1965 using a prototype design developed at 'Mosgiproteatr'

of the birth of V. I. Lenin[27]. The cinema's only hall was intended for 586 spectators. The 'Flacăra' ('Flame') cinema (Ion Creangă Street) was inaugurated in 1976 and built according to a standardised design (V. Zakharov). The audience hall, built in the shape of an amphitheatre, was intended for 500 spectators. In the Botanica district at the intersection of Teilor and Dacia Streets, construction of another cinema, 'Pacea' ('Peace', architects: F. Shostak, G. Zhinkin), was started but never commissioned. Apart from the cinemas themselves, the authorities started other forms of film screenings. Two of them are worth mentioning: summer cinemas and mobile cinemas. Both were viewed as provisional, temporary solutions to cover the huge demand for films from the public (and the requirements of political education through film mandated by the party) in the face of an obvious shortage of cinemas.

Several mobile cinemas operated in Chisinau in the early 1950s. The oldest is probably the 'May 1st Summer Cinema', inaugurated on 1 May 1952 in the lower part of the city (now Hîjdeu Street). The cinema building was actually a long wooden hall that could accommodate about 500 people. The film season would open in late

April and last until November[28]. Another open-air cinema was located on Lenin (Ştefan cel Mare) Boulevard opposite the 'Patria' cinema, and a third was at the entrance to Valea Morilor Park (the Central Leisure Park, entrance from Serghei Lazo Street[29]). We do not know the exact number of mobile cinemas (Russian: кинопередвижка) but we do know, from the direct testimonies of some participants and organisers of these screenings, that mobile cinemas played an important role in the spread of cinema in Soviet Chisinau. Viktor Andon says, for example, that mobile cinemas had a certain flexibility in choosing the repertoire of films (they could show award movies or foreign movies that were not part of the official cinema schedule[30]. Towards the end of the 1980s, with the construction of multiscreen cinemas, the importance of summer cinemas and mobile cinemas decreased. In 1983, the city had 10 cinemas, in addition to which there were six

27 'Вечерний Кишинев', 22 April 1970.

28 История одной фотографии: летний кинотеатр имени 1-го мая. Source: <https://locals.md/2017/istoriya-odnoy-fotografii-letniy-kinoteatr-imeni-1-go-maya/>

29 Ройтбурд, Елена. Где оно, 'Дневное кино'? // Кишиневские новости., 20 September, 2013, p.9. Source: <https://orasulmeuchisinau.wordpress.com/>

30 <http://oldchisinau.com/forum/viewtopic.php>

so-called film universities[31]. The Party's energetic efforts to promote the art of cinema and use cinematography in order to mobilise the masses in the construction of socialism were materialising in the growing number of spectators. Annually, in the urban localities of the MSSR, every inhabitant went to the cinema 22 times in 1960, and 24 times in 1970[32].

Instead of a Conclusion: The End of Public Cinemas – 1980s to 1990s

The history of cinema venues (cinemas and village/town clubs) with film screening capacities in the period 1980–2020 can be captured in a single figure: while there were 1,900 cinematographic installations in the Soviet Socialist Republic of Moldova in 1980, only 11 remained in 2018[33]. That is an over 100-fold decrease. The specific causes are multiple, but in general they must be interpreted as the concrete effects of a major transformation. The state, the monopolist and the sole agent of the active use of culture as a political tool, slowly relinquished this function, which it transferred to the market. The state left in the hands of the market both the production and consumption of cinema (as well as the cultural process in general). In a sense, the state abandoned its anthropological project by letting the New Man, the man adapted to the new market realities, be built by external and internal private agents. We also see a radical change in the way politics views cinema in particular and art in general: from one of the main political tools used to try social modelling (we can even speak of an anthropological experiment) to a sphere of activity without political significance and with primary connotations of prestige (art, especially 'high art' – painting, music, cinematography – becomes a sign of status) and entertainment. The depoliticisation of art means, in the context of the Moldovan capitalist society, not only the withdrawal of politics from art (as the main 'producer', censor, consumer) but also the withdrawal, for art, of any political function. In the new politico-economic reality, culture is no longer one of the main keys to political influence (it cannot even issue criticism or political messages) but instead just a consumer good. Cinemas, as well as libraries, theatres, music collectives, and other cultural institutions are merely victims of a process that has its origins elsewhere. The general history is that of Mikhail Gorbachev's attempt to reform the Soviet system and reenergise it by abandoning ideological adversity to capitalism and attempting to bring certain features of the capitalist system into the USSR. The particular history of cinemas in Chisinau in the post-USSR era is outlined as a result of processes taking place in the late 1980s. The general features of this history are as follows: the emergence of video theatres in the late 1980s and the liberalisation of economic initiative directly

31 Кишинев: энциклопедия, p.68
32 Народное хозяйство СССР за 70 лет: Юбилейный статистический ежегодник. Москва: Издательство "Финансы и статистика," 1987. Source: http://istmat.info/node/9311
33 The National Statistics Bureau, Chisinau, Anuar statistic 2019, p 196. https://statistica.gov.md/public/files/publicatii_electronice/Anuar_Statistic/2019/10_AS.pdf

Open-air cinema (demolished) from Valea Morilor Park (the Central Leisure Park), 1970s

Pacea ('Peace') cinema designed by architects F. Shostak and G. Zhinkin, refurbished after 2000 into 'Holy Trinity' Christian Centre

threw Soviet cinema products into a market in which they no longer had a privileged position and competed with films from around the world. Soviet films lost in the competition with foreign films, particularly with Western productions that were much more diverse and much more accommodating and adaptable to the needs of the masses than the Soviet films (which were cumbersome, pedagogical, etc.). And while in the beginning, for the first time in the late 1940s, foreign films (mostly 'Oscar movies') saved Soviet cinema[34] (by filling the gap created by a local industry that produced only a handful of films each year), the second wave of foreign films from the 1980s that arrived in an extremely flexible setting, in which the film could be consumed freely in any context, including at home, greatly undermined Soviet cinema (which had functioned throughout the period as a sole monopolist). As for the territorial and format flexibility of the video salons, we can judge it based on the curious case of a video salon that operated in the 1990s … in one of the carriages of the

Chisinau–Odessa train. To this we have to add the opening of private cinemas (so-called multiplexes) that offered viewers more varied choice and privacy in smaller screens. In 1989, the Goskino system was liquidated in the RSFSR and the other republics. The cinemas went under the full management of the local councils. De facto, this means that they depended on the whims of local public authorities but also on the entrepreneurial spirit of the leadership. In some cases, movie directors tried to be at the forefront – in addition to many cinemas, video salons were opened in order to meet the soaring demand for foreign films[35]. In other cases, the cinema directors rented out parts of the buildings to private agents (furniture and clothing factories, foreign exchange, etc.). In most cases the logic of commercial space gradually edged out the logic of culture. What do the results of these processes look like in Chisinau in 2020? Of the former cinemas, only two continue to screen films: Patria and Odeon. The

34 М.И Косинова. Советская кинофикация и кинопрокат во второй половине 1940-х годов. «Трофейное Кино» — спасение киноотрасли в период «малокартинья».

35 Олег Березин. Решения должны быть законными, но эффективными: кинотеатры в эпоху перестройки. Source: <https://kinoart.ru/texts/resheniya-dolzhny-byt-zakonnymi-no-effektivnyi-kinoteatry-v-epohu-perestroyki>

Former Shipka cinema, currently a house of worship for a Protestant religious group

former cinema was privatised in the early 1990s, while the latter is still municipal property. The Shipka cinema is currently a house of worship for a Protestant religious group. The Flacara cinema houses gyms and other commercial entities. The Columna (formerly Iskra) is a ruin under seizure, which has been pledged several times. Tkacenko is also a ruin and belongs to the Ministry of the Interior. The former Chisinau cinema has been inactive for about 15 years now. Gaudeamus (formerly the '40th anniversary of the Leninist Comsomol' cinema) is perhaps the most visible, but not for good reasons. A dubious scheme devised by the management of the cinema sacrificed the building to real estate interests. The complicity and complacency of the local authorities facilitated the scheme, and Gaudeamus is now a wreck after two attempted demolitions in 2018 and 2020.

The Shipka cinema designed by G. Penbek in 1967 according to a standard design from the Rascani district.

Socialist Realism

A

0   200 m

015

Grigore Vieru Ave.

Mitropolit
arlaam Str.

011   010

009

neneasca Str.   Ştefan cel Mare şi Sfânt Ave.

008

31 August, 1989 - Str.

Bulgara Str.

Strada Tighina

cureşti Str.

Ismail Str.

007

004

Negruzzi Ave.

Giuftea Str.

002   001

007   006   005   003   Yuriy Gagarin Ave.   002

Railway Station

1, Piata Garii Street
Leonid Chiuprin
1948

001 A

The space in front of the railway station was later planned to be used for a public square with a fountain and decorative elements, benches, decorative lighting, etc. In addressing the spatial composition of the building and further details, local architects were supposedly influenced by aspects of interwar architecture, namely the neo-Romanian school (for example, the sloping roof, the columns and arches at the entrance, the floral elements on the capitals and façade, and the use of glazed ceramics). In actuality, the building is a mixture of elements from the Slavic architectural tradition (with a roof inspired by vernacular and ecclesiastical architecture from the northern Russian Federation, *kokoshnik* elements used for the frames of the main entrance and windows, and red brick inserted in the window frames, among other details) with an added palette of symbols associated

In 1941, after the first phase of the Second World War, the railway station was among the first buildings in the city to be renovated. At that time, the old railway station, originally built in 1871 using a design by Henrik von Lonsky, was restored and could receive trains in normal operation. Following the destruction it suffered later in the war, in 1944, the old building could no longer be saved, and the authorities decided to rebuild it from the ground up. The reconstruction design was developed by architect L. Chuprin, partially using the foundations of the old architecture. The main consultant in this process was A. Shchusev, who exerted significant influence on the entire ensemble.

with socialist realism (including details such as the aurochs of the Moldovan coat of arms, floral elements, coats of arms with stars, grapes and cups and folios) in the frame of the main entrance. It is very probable that L. Chuprin introduced these elements at the suggestion of A. Shchusev, who had an affinity for ecclesiastical architecture. *Kokoshniks* have been used in Russian Orthodox architecture since the sixteenth century. Inserts made of ceramic and polychrome concrete elements persist in the decoration of the façade. The station's interior is indebted to the realistic-socialist style, while having abundant decorative details on the ceiling, a stairway, columns with capitals, suspended lusters, and other lighting elements in the upstairs waiting room. The last renovation of the building was completed in 2003. This was a complete refurbishment. The ticket booths were moved to the former location of the restaurant, and the offices in the hall were relocated. The station's platform was paved with stone. The major changes in the structure also required a new attached structure – the canopy along the main rails. The station's IT equipment was improved by installing a modern digital display panel.

A

The Railway Station Square Ensemble

Piata Garii Street
David Palatnik
1953–1957

002 A

At the time of the commissioning of the station, the building was surrounded by slums. It was here that the terminus station of the horse-drawn tram, or *konka* (the tram began operating in 1913), was located at the end of the nineteenth century. The Railway Station Square located between Aleea Garii Street and Gagarin Boulevard was planned according to D. Palatnik's project. During the incipient stage of Chisinau's development, it was the symbolic gateway to the city. The ensemble of the Station Square includes a plaza with a rectangular fountain and a series of three- and four-storey residential buildings arranged symmetrically on the perimeter of the square, three on each side, and extending to Gagarin Boulevard. Approximately one third of the territory of Station Square is occupied by a rectangular park equipped with a fountain, which is constructed from polished granite blocks. The fountain is flanked by several semi-circular benches built of sandstone and decorated with stylised vases placed on pedestals. Construction of the Railway Station Square ensemble extended over the period between 1953 and 1955. The break in style between the different buildings was due to the well-known decree issued by the USSR government 'On Architectural Excesses', which coincided with the construction. As a result, the south side of the square was built according to the original design, while the opposite side underwent substantial changes, namely completely forgoing decorative elements. On a symbolic level, the square as it exists today reflects changes in political discourse and is effectively a case study in this regard. The residential buildings on the sides of the square, designed with the same range of styles specific to the post-war period, were equipped with public spaces on

A

the ground floor (post office, pharmacy, bookstore, grocery store, etc.). The semi-circular elements of the window frames on the façades of the buildings, found both on the lower register where the commercial spaces were located as well as those on the upper floors, were designed to resonate with the elements of the vaulted entrance of the train station. The fountain is functional and the state of conservation of its components is satisfactory. The Railway Station Square ensemble, along with several other sites located on Gagarin Boulevard (the Cooperative Trade University, the Vibropribor plant building etc.), are some of the city's most coherent architectural constellations in terms of style and composition, and they are worthy of being historically listed and protected.

The Cooperative Trade University

8, Yuri Gagarin Boulevard
Robert Kurtz
1954

The building of the Cooperative Trade University, very peculiar from a stylistic point of view, is located on Yuri Gagarin Boulevard, and it is an example of well-tempered neoclassical style. Its architect, Robert Kurtz, who had a background in the school of European architecture, can be considered a master of eclectic style. This building combines elements of the neoclassical tradition that are arranged on a façade structured according to Renaissance canons: The surface is divided into registers, with the ground floor covered with *rusticated bossages*, with a prominent cornice with wide eaves, supported by modillions. The portal of the main entrance is an element inspired by the medieval architecture of Moldova, and the loggia with the arch above the entrance is indebted to Renaissance traditions. The term 'Stalinist Empire' architecture describes a style that is characterised by the use of architectural orders (Doric, Ionic, etc.) and has clear proportions and abundant decor. Marble and granite were often used in the decoration of façades. In the case of this building, constructed under austere circumstances, we find that the lower register is covered with a rendering that simulates granite, while the rest of the façade elements are made of limestone. Admittedly, this was part of a process of the archaisation of architecture – an imitation of historical style by which architectural elements (decorations, façade elements) were added to a reinforced concrete structure. The building of the Cooperative Trade University consists of the central study block, which was given particular attention by the architect, and that of the dormitory, which is much poorer in terms of detail. Both of these were aligned and set back from the boulevard, thus creating sufficient pedestrian space. The boulevard was part of Muncesti Street until 1961, but it was renamed Gagarin Boulevard after an event of global importance: the first manned flight in space. According to the city plan, the building completes the boulevard ensemble and is stylistically harmonious with the buildings of the railway station square ensemble aligned on the boulevard. At the other end of the boulevard is the square with the monument of G. Kotovsky, which, although set at a considerable distance, ties this area together in terms of style.

A

The square with the monument to G. Kotovsky

1, Constantin Negruzzi Boulevard
Fiodor Naumov, Lazar Dubinovsky
1954

004 A

The square with the monument of G. Kotovsky is located between C. Negruzzi and D. Cantemir Boulevards on the axis of Gagarin Boulevard. The five-metre-tall bronze equestrian statue is installed on a polished red granite pedestal and is surrounded by a carved crown. Together with the pedestal, the monument measures 12 metres in height, and the bronze sculpture weighs some 20 tonnes. Work on the monument took about four years, and the bronze was cast at the Mytishchi plant near Moscow. The elements of the square – the monument on its pedestal, two vertical supports with lighting fixtures, the group of stairs and the surrounding border with spheres set on pedestals – are solved in the manner of the 'Stalinist Empire' style. During the design and construction of the square, F. Naumov was the chief architect of the city, while the sculptor L. Dubinovsky worked as the head of the administration of the artistic commission of the MSSR until 1951. Between 1951 and 1953, he was part of the group of sculptors who worked on the monumental statue of Stalin for the Volga-Don Canal. Due to this experience, he was commissioned to build the monument to G. Kotovsky upon his return to Chisinau. For the construction of the monument, L. Dubinovsky invited the sculptors I. Pershudchev and A. Posyado and the painter K. Kitayka to function as collaborators. The team of artists who worked on modelling the equestrian statue arrived at a convincing implementation of detail without sacrificing proportion or a sense of monumentality. In the creation of the statue, the team took inspiration from equestrian sculptures from antiquity (for example, Marcus Aurelius, Rome), as well as from the Renaissance. Today the square seems somewhat isolated within the larger fabric of the city, but from a stylistic point of view, it is without a doubt the most successful architectural ensemble – a true oasis dating from the period of socialist realism. According to the original schematic plan, a building was to be built behind the square in keeping with the spirit of the time, but the plan did not materialise, and for a long time the square had a wall delimiting the area of the Gutsulevka slum with its low houses. The Cosmos Hotel was built behind the square much later in the 1970s.

A

Hotel CHISINAU

7, Constantin Negruzzi Boulevard
Robert Kurtz
1959

The building's architecture is an enigma in terms of style. Its central ascending volume dates from the Stalinist Empire era, but the façades seem to have been borrowed from another project. A number of elements appear to be somewhat isolated stylistically. The massive portal at the entrance made of polished granite and the glass tower form an ensemble with the hotel's marble-tiled interior and with the columns, heavy ceilings, and massive stairway complete with banister of its decor. This arsenal of burlesque ornament apparently survived the 'struggle against excess'. It is common knowledge that the construction of the hotel coincided with a turning point in policies, which dictated a radical reconfiguration of design and construction. At this time, budget austerity caused any extensive or costly decoration to be left out. The exterior walls of the building, lacking the ornament specific to the era, look like a person without a coat, and leave the building with an utter lack of personality. The building's silhouette and use of volume in its composition, especially its narrow core, resemble on a smaller scale the epitome of post-war architecture, namely the seven buildings nicknamed 'the seven sisters' that were erected in Moscow. The transparent tower placed on the central volume of the building represents a special feature; according to some sources, the tower is just a decoration, but others say that the tower was created in order to house a restaurant or café. In defence of the building, it has to be said that it presents a broad and well positioned landmark from the axis of Stefan cel Mare Boulevard and is therefore an elegant urban presence. The hotel used to have a post office and a hair salon as well as workshops for clothing and shoe repairs – a broad range of services that would not subsequently be offered in the hospitality industry. Apparently, Kurtz was the only architect who somehow managed to maintain a right to certain excesses in his projects, taking into account the elements that have survived (the glass tower, the granite portal, the hall decorated with columns, the hanging crystal lamps, the much-too-generous stairway in the atrium, etc.). As a whole, the interior of the hotel is indebted to the realist-socialist style, and a guest would feel teleported back into the 1950s in any of the rooms. Conforming to the decree and the austere funding, the hotel's walls, built with limestone, were left unfinished; it was only much later that it was decided to decorate them with ceramic tiles, which lends the building an unusual – to say the least – chromatic and aesthetic character. The trend of using ceramic tiles on buildings that had remained without final finishes swept the entire city during the austerity period of the 1950s and 1960s. However, this was met with criticism and disapproval due to poor workmanship; the adhesive deteriorated over time, and the tiles had to be replaced etc. The subsequent period was defined by the slogan 'the economy means being economic', offering no luxury options.

A

Academy of Science

1, Stefan cel Mare si Sfant
Boulevard
*Valentin Mednek, Aleksandr
Vedenkin*
1955

The Academy of Science building is located at the end of Stefan cel Mare Boulevard and aligned on one side with Ciuflea Street. It was originally designed to house the Offices of the People's Commissars and therefore its architecture promoted the tenets of dialectic materialism. Finished in 1955, it adhered strictly to the programme of socialist realism, in which the features of the French Empire style coexisted harmoniously with the canons of antiquity. Its profoundly eclectic character was rounded out by the addition of the Republic's coat of arms (later replaced by a bas-relief of the logo of the Science Academy) on the shield located on the parapet, and of the state symbols on the façade. The USSR subscribed to the Stalinist neo-classical tradition in architecture until the mid-1950s. In the case of Chisinau, this post-war style could be better described as a kind of Stalinist eclecticism. The building's layout follows the shape of the letter 'П' ('P' in the Cyrillic alphabet), with a longer main side and two short ones perpendicular to it. Like most of the buildings on the main boulevard, this too stands out due to its classical use of space and volume, which is through the classical orders and the accentuated use of local materials. The solemn character of the main façade is enhanced by the main entrance, which has three massive doors flanked by lean columns and octagonal windows placed at the level of the capitals, thus forming a symbolic archway. The façade is divided into three levels; the ground floor is decorated with *bossage*, but the other two levels differ in terms of colour and texture. The windows

A

of the first four floors are rectangular, but those of the top floor are arched, and this lends the building a good deal of refinement. Apart from its impeccable architectural forms, the building also stands out due to its unusual colour scheme: the ground floor and main entrance are finished in red granite, but the rest of the façade consists of white limestone, with a chromatic accent on the top floor. The building now houses the main block of the Moldovan Academy of Science.

The Republican Stadium

Bucuresti Street
I. Mnatzacanov
1951

The stadium is a unique piece of architecture situated in the centre of the city between Izmail and Tighina Streets and M. Kogalniceanu and Bucharest Streets. The construction was initiated by Leonid Brezhnev, the First Secretary of the Central Committee of the Communist Party of Moldova. Together with Valea Morilor Lake (formerly Comsomolist Lake), these are the two major projects realised by Brezhnev during the city's brief period of adjustment to the socialist system. Built in 1951, the stadium had a capacity for 22,000 spectators. Its football pitch was considered one of the best in the USSR. The two entrances stand out from the rest of the stadium due to the abundance of their decor. Texts and symbols carved in the stone make reference to the triumphal arches of antiquity, symbolically associating the stadium with an ancient sports arena or a mini coliseum. This 'triumphal' style reflects the general trend of Soviet architecture during the post-war decade, which was at first somewhat superficial and became ossified over time. The victory in the Second World War accentuated the stylistic pathos of the buildings and ensembles and gave predominance to the military and triumphal motifs in the decoration. Stylistically, the stadium complex fits the Stalinist Empire canon; it contains abundant decoration, including sculptural elements in ronde-bosse, columns with capitals, and bas-reliefs based on sports themes. The vegetal motifs borrowed from ancient architecture were generously employed throughout the sports complex, from the entrances to the surfaces of the stadium and the façades of the building on M. Kogalniceanu Street. After the war, the Soviet utopia turned into a frozen hierarchy – an ossified ideological system of symbols. This type of architecture and visual messages tailored for the masses took shape in the USSR in the 1930s. It arrived later to the MSSR, after 1944 and in recycled form. The ideological messages translated through the architecture and eclectic decor of the stadium embody a series of clichés and idioms of the official rhetoric of the Stalinist period. In 1974, the stadium was substantially modernised and upgraded to allow international competitions. It was equipped with rubber tracks, a billboard, lighting, and later with an inflatable pavilion. The athletic sections were

A

with training facilities and located opposite to the University Palace of Culture was used in winter. The winter basketball court was on the second floor of the main building. After independence, the stadium was the only place designated by UEFA for the home matches of the national football team. The stadium was no longer maintained in the 1990s and the sports facilities had visibly deteriorated. Rock concerts were organised in the stadium in the early 2000s to raise funds for the maintenance of the sports arena and the space was rented out for religious events on Sundays. Demolition of the stadium finally began in early 2007, and by summer the outer stone walls already surrounded an empty space. The two entrances and the main building are still standing.

organised in four rounded areas of the stadium ellipses. The space under the grandstands was used for smaller gymnasiums for winter, locker rooms, and sports equipment storage. Training was usually conducted on the pitches in summer (April–November); a building equipped

Ministry of the Food Industry 008 A

73, Stefan cel Mare si Sfant Boulevard

Valentin Voitehovski, Pavel Borisov
1954

The architecture of the building is characterised by a balanced spatial composition and a sober monumentality. Built in 1954, the edifice was designed to host the Ministry of the Food Industry. Later the building also hosted administrative offices such as the Economic Court, the Appeal and Registration Chambers, and today, the General Prosecutor's Office. The symmetry in the design of the building is typical of Voitehovski. This building, which extends between Armeana and Bulgara Streets along Stefan cel Mare Boulevard, has a plan based on an interior system of corridors for office spaces. The monumentality of the building is accentuated by an open loggia with a row of double columns situated in the central volume, which expressively highlights the main entrance. A similar Venetian-inspired loggia with arches can be found on the Mogosoaia Palace, a structure well known to the architect from his studies in Bucharest. The double columns on the perimeter of the loggia introduced by Voitehovski were also inspired by Byzantine ecclesiastical architecture and its echoes in medieval European buildings (for example, Saint Pons-de-Thomières Monastery in Occitanie and the Cathedral of Santa Maria Nuova, Monreale in Sicily). Lavishness can be considered one of the basic features of late Stalinist culture; its origins do not lie in the artistic field but rather in the political sphere. The political rhetoric of the post-war period was permeated by hyperbolisation and idiomisation ('the great leader and teacher Joseph Stalin'). Voitehovski managed to overcome phobic attitudes and tame the enthusiasm of the politruks, thus realising projects of an extremely refined artistic nature. The façade of the building is structured in several levels according to

a master of architectural ornament and stylistic combinations, Voitehovski did not hesitate to integrate the ideological symbol of the hammer and sickle into his decoration of the cornices, the window frames, and the column capitals. The technical solutions used in the construction of the Ministry of the Food Industry can be found in a series of later buildings designed by the architect.

the Renaissance tradition; a delicate base supports the core of the composition of the façade, consisting of a ground floor and two upper levels, all with smooth facing and compositionally topped with a discreet parapet. For the decoration of the façade, the traditional construction material of limestone was used and assembled without joints, and inlays with polychrome ceramic tiles were employed for the window frames. A tendency towards using the national architectural traditions is evident, such as stone carving and folk art motifs. Considered

A

Residential Building with 107 Apartments

126, Stefan cel Mare si Sfant Boulevard

Valentin Voitehovski, Svetlana Stalinskaia
1955–1959

The end of the Stalinist period in architecture is associated with Khrushchev's 1955 decree. By virtue of inertia, buildings of the Stalinist spirit continued to appear well into the 1950s. This is also the case with the residential building on Stefan cel Mare Boulevard between Vasile Alecsandri and Armeneasca Streets. In an effort to create an architecture with a solemn character and a demeanour appropriate for a building on the capital's main thoroughfare, the architects opted for a symmetrical composition. The main façade is divided into three volumes, slightly staggering the building's perimeter. The end corners are one storey higher than the main volume of the building. The central volume, jutting forward from the core, is enhanced by a gable on the balustrade level, while the side volumes form two lean towers at the corners. Their walls feature a number of bay windows on the upper levels, which are decorated with columns. Such decorations were rarely used in practice in Soviet architecture. The main façade is divided into three levels, similar to other buildings on the boulevard, with prominent *bossage* decorations on the ground floor. The top level, four storeys tall, has a cornice supported by modillions and culminates with a parapet running along the edge of the roof. The spaces between the loggia-styled bay windows on the main façade and on the side façades feature cantilevered balconies. In keeping with the festive nature of the façade, the building's ground floor was designed with tall and wide display windows, with broad portals for the entrances into retail spaces (sporting goods, traditional arts and crafts etc.). The apartments are on three floors, while the staircase is on the courtyards side and the entrances are on V. Alecsandri and Armeneasca Streets. Looking at this building reminds the viewer of the profoundly eclectic

façade ornamentation deserved special attention. Glazed ceramic was used in the intervals between the windows of the top floor, on the surfaces of the loggias, and on the modillions supporting the cornice. This enriched the decor of the façade and tied together the overall impression of the building. Extravagance as a central topic is represented symbolically through a range of floral motifs in stacked vases, decorated with five-pointed stars and ears of wheat. Over the course of the building's lifetime, some parts became damaged, and a gable was replaced with a galvanized steel structure. Elements of the building's façade are falling apart, but city authorities have not taken any interest in the state of the building. The apartment owners also contribute to the degradation of the façade due to the manner in which they understand and manage the issue of private property. The lack of strict regulations and building codes has allowed them to enclose the loggia spaces of the bay windows, thus concealing the building's outstanding decorations and creating a visual dissonance.

character of post-war architecture. At that time, the Stalinist slogan regarding architecture 'national in form, socialist in content' allowed the development of national motifs in the peripheral Soviet republics. While the architects generally did not understand the 'socialist content' component, they did take 'national form' as a call to action. In this context, the

A

The Moldovan State Philharmonic

78, Mitropolit Varlaam Street
Valentin Voitehovski
1962

As society was reconfigured according to new policies, musical creativity was encouraged, and the State Philharmonic Society of Moldova was founded in 1940. The late-nineteenth century building used to house the circus, and it was designed by Mikhail Chekerul-Kush. The building was considered the most appropriate location for housing the new society. During the reconfiguration process, the building – unpretentious but still solid – underwent substantial transformations. The metal columns supporting the cupola were removed, as they obstructed spectators' views, and the entrance was expanded and repositioned. However, the façade of the circus, which is still visible today, and part of the support structure were incorporated into the new building. Carried out based on designs by Voitehovski, the reconstructed State

Philharmonic building was equipped with a large, 1,000-seat concert hall and a smaller auditorium. The configuration and the comfort of the hall, with modernist highlights typical of the 'thaw' period, were obtained using a new architectural approach, contrasting in style with the building's façade and lobby. The main entrance boasts a neoclassical solution: a semi-circular portico supported by six columns. Due to this graceful structure, the exterior appearance of the building has taken on a demure but simultaneously solemn air, which is specific to postwar Stalinist architecture. In the 1950s and 1960s, the capital witnessed the reconstruction of several public buildings. Voitehovski was an architect who made an important contribution to this process and was engaged with the rehabilitation of the historical heritage. His concern for architecture monuments was the principle that guided a number of the architects of the era. In fact, there has been a trend towards rehabilitating the buildings constructed between the wars, as demonstrated by many examples: the train station, the M. Eminescu National Theatre, the former Moldova Hotel (currently housing Mobiasbanca – Groupe Société Générale), and the Patria cinema. Some of the buildings were fundamentally reconfigured, given that they did not fit the discourse advanced by the authorities after 1944. Other buildings, however, were reconfigured in order to correspond to the aesthetics and function of a socialist-type city.

A

Residential Building with 120 Apartments

132, Stefan cel Mare si Sfant Boulevard

Israel Shmurun, Serghey Vasiliev
1952

011 **A**

Located on the main boulevard of the capital not far from the Great National Assembly Square (formerly V. Lenin Square), the apartment building has an obviously festive character. Its inhabitants were the few who enjoyed the privilege of greeting marching crowds during demonstrations and parades after they had crossed the square. The building follows the tradition of the old city in terms of adhering to the street outlines,

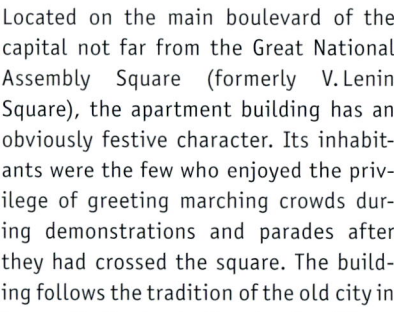

which resulted in the natural inclusion of new buildings into the historical texture of the capital. The inauguration of the building was a mark of progress in meeting the rigorous standards of the socialist city; thus, Chisinau joined the elite of Soviet capitals. Construction began in 1949 and it took four years to erect the building. No other post-war residential building can match the refinement of this block built for the Soviet elite of post-war Chisinau. The façade was decorated with granite, a material that is extremely costly and difficult to process, and the common spaces on the ground floor as well as the high ceilings of the apartments were on par with the most luxurious edifices in the USSR. At first, the occupants were the heads of ministries, academicians, and workers in the fields of culture and arts. The real estate market currently classifies the apartments in this building as 'stalinka'. For the imposing ground floor, the builders used granite; the plinth and cornice are palisaded; the walls are decorated with *rusticated bossages*; and the rest of the four-storey façade is finished using limestone without joints to create a smooth surface with the effect of 'white marble'. With its many sculpted details, balconies, and loggias, the façade of this

A

building creates the feeling that nothing is superfluous. Of special beauty is a carved cornice, supported by modillions resting on a smooth wall and perfecting the building's architectural volume. The specificity of this period was the use of classical orders on a large scale; at the same time, the elements of these orders were mingled with the symbols of Soviet propaganda. The capitals of columns included five-point stars, hammers and sickles as well as grapes and other elements from folk traditions – true to the slogan 'national in form, socialist in

content'. Also evident were shields and thematic cassettes featuring symbolic victory flags. Victory in the Second World War enhanced the dramatic quality of new buildings and developments, which prominently featured the military-triumphal motives in their decor. The nine 'cones' at the top of the building represent the culmination of a victorious society headed by a 'great leader'. Triumph is associated with abundance, represented by a number of elements not found on other buildings: perched on top of the capitals are horns of abundance, and higher still is a row of stacked vases decorated with stars and ambrosia symbolising the supremacy of Soviet ideology. Buildings of a similar type were built in other republic capitals, for instance, on Khreshchatyk in Kyiv and Independence Boulevard (formerly V.I. Lenin Boulevard) in Minsk. Without the benefit of preferential budgets from the 'centre' and with far less assets than these other cities, the authorities in Chisinau only managed to build a few buildings of this magnitude on the main boulevard. Besides, the authorities in Kyiv and Minsk had much more substantial resources and a longer period of time at their disposal (1935–1955) in order to design and build a city centre in a coherent style. During the time when the communist party was in power (2001–2009), this was one of the few buildings that was renovated using public funds. The façade was revamped, so that today it has an air of freshness about it, instead of languishing in grey neglect.

Posta Moldovei Central Post Office

134, Stefan cel Mare si Sfant Boulevard

Valentin Mednek

1961

The Post Office building located at the intersection of Stefan cel Mare Boulevard and Vlaicu Parcalab Street could be categorised in terms of style as neoclassical, with decorative elements specific to socialist realism. The building of the first post office in Chisinau was originally situated nearby at the intersection with Mitropolit Varlaam Street. The construction of buildings with public functions was generally approached according to stereotypes specific to the socialist era. One hypothesis states that V. Mednek's visual inspiration for this building had been the Central Telegraph Office (I. Rerberg, 1925–1927) in Moscow. In reality, the two buildings are different in terms of style and volume, with the one in Moscow falling into the category of rationalist modernism. In the case of the Chisinau building, the structural composition may have been inspired by art deco architecture, but it is largely indebted to the eclecticism of Stalinism. Because it is so controversial, Stalinist architecture is not easy to assess: some consider it unwieldy and grandiose, while others see it as the work of talented architects. One of the advantages of this building is its successful integration into the texture of the city. It fits well with the scale of the surrounding buildings. The construction process was troubled, with the design undergoing adjustments due to the regulations introduced after 1955. The resulting building has a sober appearance, even an austere one compared to other buildings on the boulevard. The Posta Moldovei Central Post Office has an angular layout consisting of two blocks aligned with the street perimeter and connected by a tower. Access to the building is through the massive doors of the tower cylinder. The façades of the two blocks are divided into levels, with windows on all floors and arched windows on the top level. The tower block has an additional level, which is decorated with windows separated by columns apparently girded by a horizontal band bearing leafy motifs placed too high for the street-level viewer to notice. The façade and the plant-like motifs are made of limestone. As archive pictures indicate, the roof of the tower block used to support a radio antenna, which was later removed. For a brief period, a neon globe advertising the Soviet Postal Service was perched on the tower. The globe disappeared after 1990 and has only been preserved in memory by the 1962 movie *Man Follows the Sun*.

A

Gemenii Department Store
136, Stefan cel Mare si Sfant
Boulevard
Valentin Voitehovski
1961

013 A

Construction of the Gemenii Department Store (formerly Magazin Universal and Lumea Copiilor, or Children's World) not only resulted in a well-positioned building but also produced an important highlight in the ensemble of the central square (currently Piata Marii Adunari Nationale, or Great National Assembly Square). At some point, the store had a reputable fabric and sewing section, which took up almost an entire floor on the main boulevard. The shoe department also used to be well-stocked. The store developed in several stages. The department store was built in 1954 – a building with a façade organised according to the Doric classical order, with clear proportions and abundant decor. Practically speaking, the building was a plain and functional structure, to which a Stalinist Empire façade had been added. Later on, the store was expanded to face the main square of Chisinau (and named

Lumea Copiilor, later Centrul Comercial Gemenii, or the Gemenii Shopping Centre). The building received an addition in 1961 – a tower block placed at the corner connecting it to another block aligned with Pushkin Street. The construction process used the typical modern spatial solutions and local building materials. In terms of style, the building's architecture was not very different from the architecture of the transition period from Stalinist eclecticism to Soviet modernism. Owing to the new trends in construction, the building remained unadorned; from the original design only the portal at the entrance – made of polished granite (similar to that at the Hotel Chisinau) – survived. In order to add a dose of eclecticism, the store was decorated with elements stylistically associated with international modernism: wide windows on the lateral façade, flooding the interior with light, and providing a fine view of the square and the park of the cathedral. In terms of use of space, the building closed off the ensemble of the square. The tower block on the corner, together with the building of the Trade Union Council (R. Kurtz) across the

![Photograph of the Gemenii Department Store, a multi-storey light-coloured building at a street corner with a traffic light in the foreground and pedestrians crossing the street.]

A

street, form a symbolic gateway, a pro-pylaea, as it was called in classical architecture, through which the marching columns of parades would pass. This element was present in other capitals of the USSR as well and constituted a ritual signifying an entrance into the 'bright future'. The latter was one of the fundamental myths of Soviet society, a moment that was constantly postponed or replaced with other major objectives, such as the conquest of space and later the accession to developed socialism – a perspective eventually cancelled out by *perestroika* and *glasnost*. In order to meet the needs of the city, the general store was moved to a new postmodern building in the 1980s, which was called UNIC (M. Orlov, V. Lepskii, and A. Varshaver) and located at number 8, Stefan cel Mare Boulevard.

The Trade Union Council

24–26, Alexander Pushkin Street

Robert Kurtz

1953

014 **A**

One of the buildings of the National Federation of Trade Unions (of agriculture and the food industries, known as Agroindsind) is located at 26, Pushkin Street, on the corner of Stefan cel Mare Boulevard close to the governmental building and Gemenii Shopping Centre. In order to facilitate officers' access to the government building, the entry was arranged directly from Pushkin Street instead of from the courtyard, which would have been the natural path of entry. Kurtz, the architect and designer of the Trade Union Council building, was also responsible for the project of reconstructing City Hall (A. Bernardazzi), which was severely damaged during the Second World War. The façade of the National Federation of Trade Unions (originally the Trade Union Council) adheres to the orders of classical architecture, having clear proportions and being decorated with pilasters and capitals. The tower on the corner is two storeys taller than the rest of the building and is accentuated by an additional row of columns and arched windows, which are flanked by round windows. The lower level is covered by bossages, but the facing is made of local limestone on the rest of the façade's levels. The cornice is supported by modillions and the composition is topped by a parapet. The tower on the corner was consciously designed at a height that would create a

hand, they diminished the importance of the triumphal arch built during the Russian Empire, while on the other hand, they marked the symbolic path to a new era. Later on, both buildings were decorated with neon lights forming the image of red flags, which were visible at night. The image of Chisinau as a 'city of white stone' and the 'Chisinau by Night' attraction were promoted intensely. The city's architectural heritage was well managed and protected by the city's former authorities. The buildings were catalogued, and they were equipped with informational plaques. This building was one of the first to exceed the permitted height in the city's historical area. The building is currently in a precarious state. It has not been properly maintained and was recently put up for sale.

landmark visible from the boulevard. After the Gemenii store was completed, these two buildings formed the symbolic gates of the main square. On the one

Residential Building
19, Grigore Vieru Boulevard
Pavel Ragulin
1951

015 A

One of the first buildings on Grigore Vieru Boulevard (formerly Tineretului or 'Youth' Boulevard) was based on a design by Pavel Ragulin and was intended for elite members of the Moldovan Communist Party as well as officials from MSSR ministries and departments. The building used to have a small garden with a fountain, and the apartments – each with three and four rooms and three-metre-high ceilings – were furnished with beech floors. A grocery store was installed on the ground floor and is still operational today. The block was supposed to be a prototype for Tineretului Boulevard, which was later replicated in other areas of the city. Austerity was the watchword in construction in 1955, and the structures built around it no longer had any personality; later on, the boulevard filled up with mass-produced compact buildings. Although the decor of the building is pretentious by comparison, it is not in the same league as the buildings on the central boulevard. The façade is structured with horizontal levels, whereby the ground floor and the three upper floors are finished in white limestone. The building is capped by a cornice supported by modillions. On the main façade, pairs of pilasters flank open loggias on three levels. The top floors feature cantilevered balconies between the loggias. The side façades are decorated in a similar manner but lack balconies. The

flower vases, while the loggias are festooned with laurel garlands and wreaths. Tineretului Boulevard, which used to be called 'the main radius', ran for 1.7 kilometres, starting at the Cathedral Park and ending at the Bic River. The boulevard was part of the three-radius system (the so-called 'trident') foreseen by the master plan adopted in 1951. Tineretului has meanwhile become the main urban thoroughfare, as it connects the city centre and the district of Rascani. Drawing this main radius was part of the complex process of reorganising the lower part of the city, which was coordinated by Robert Kurtz and Pavel Ragulin. As a result of these changes, the old core of the city, with two markets and two churches, disappeared, and only a few isolated elements remain (on Pushkin Hill).

abundant decor of the façade includes elaborate capitals and panels decorated with wheat sheaves and overflowing

A

The National Library of the Republic of Moldova

78A, 31 August 1989 Street
Agasi Ambartsumyan, Serghey Vasiliev
1957

016 **A**

The Library of the Republic was founded in Chisinau in August 1940 in the newly created Moldavian Soviet Socialist Republic. It was housed in the former building of the Romanian Central Library, which had recently been evacuated across the Prut River. Starting in 1944, it operated as the state library of the republic, and in the summer of 1961, the library moved into the current central block of the National Library. During that particular stage of the city's development, the inauguration of the building was an important public event. The central structure of the National Library was built according to a standard design (L. Rudnev), which was adapted by Agasi Ambartsumyan in cooperation with Serghey Vasiliev. Vasiliev was in charge of the design for the building's façades and interiors. He was also one of the architects who contributed substantially to the development of post-war socialist realist architecture in Chisinau. The two architects had worked together previously on the building of the Institute of Arts (originally the dormitories of the Party School of the republic). The library building, profoundly indebted to Stalinist design, was started in 1953 and finished a few years after the 1955 decrees regarding excess in construction. Nevertheless, it preserved all of its style and corresponding decorations. One of the design versions shows a façade with much more refined decor, with a Renaissance-type organisation, highlighted by sculptures in niches. In the end, the chosen solution was an austere one, excluding any decoration of the side façades, and the library's logo was cast from concrete. The result was a graceless façade, with a row of half-columns and several massive doors at the entrance – a structure readily resembling a government building in an anonymous periphery town. The library

was designed using a stylised classical order, but the poor workmanship of those who made the limestone façade diminished the architect's original vision. The interiors and the furniture preserved to this day have the air of a public institution of the 1950s. The library was named after N. Krupskaya. In term of representation, it was supposed to be a temple of knowledge. The shield sitting on the building's frontispiece – a book bathed in sunrays – underscored the ideological programme on which the library was founded. Located on 31 August Street close to the government building (S. Fridlin) and the National Concert Hall (formerly the October Hall, S. Fridlin), the library visibly clashes in terms of style with the other buildings in the administrative area of the city, which was developed in the spirit of Soviet modernism. Currently, the National Library is one of the main sites that houses the written and printed cultural heritage of Moldova.

A

Patria-Loteanu Cinema

103, Stefan cel Mare si Sfant
Boulevard
Valentin Voitehovski
1952

017 **A**

The cinema is located on the central boulevard a short distance from the main entrance to Stefan cel Mare public park. The park used to be the location of a café called Guguta (the former Noroc restaurant) close to the cinema, which was a major social gathering point in the 1970s and 1980s. The Opera and Ballet Theatre (N. Kurennoy, A. Gorshkov), which was built in 1980, is across the street. Together with the public garden and the cinema, the opera solidified the area as a culture and leisure destination in the city centre. The Patria-Loteanu cinema (originally Patria) was erected on the foundations of the Aristocrats' Club, built in the 1870. Beginning in 1921, the club building hosted the National Theatre of Chisinau. In 1935, a decision was made to refurbish the building, but the repairs were delayed until 1937. Shortly afterwards, work stopped altogether and the site remained at a standstill through the war up until 1944. Bearing in mind the role of cinema in ideologically shaping the new Soviet man during the post-war period, the decision was made to reconstruct the old building and transform it into a cinema. Despite the configuration of the existing foundations, Voitehovski managed to change the appearance of the building. In fact, a new building was erected on that spot and its compositional centre became a hall for film screenings and concerts. Apart from the cinema hall, which features the balconies on the first floor, the building also had a smaller auditorium for special screenings. The resulting cinema complex also included a buffet restaurant, administrative spaces, and offices. The new project preserved the volumes and the height of

the old building, and the details of the façades reflected a neoclassicist style, while including elements specific to socialist realism. The interior and the ceiling of the cinema gave off an air of solemnity and luxury due to the abundant decorations. Both the exterior and the interior were embellished with ornamentation and decorative elements made of stucco. In the early 1970s, the Patria cinema underwent a modernisation process according to a project developed by the Moldgiprostroy Institute (A. Vaysbein, F. Shostak, and M. Berber). Substantial changes were made; the main auditorium was expanded; a modern air conditioning system was installed; and the projection equipment was upgraded. The cinema currently has three auditoriums, with a capacity of 436 seats. It continues to be a favourite destination among the residents of Chisinau.

A

![lower photograph of the building with bare trees in front]

Residential Building with Tower

142, Mitropolit Dosoftei Street

Anatoly Kolotovkin

1954

018 **A**

The building is placed on a corner with its adjacent sides aligned with Mihai Viteazul and Mitropolit Dosoftei Streets. There are other similar buildings in Chisinau designed in the same period by S. Vasiliev. There is also one in Tiraspol designed by V. Smirnov, but none of them can compare to this design by Kolotovkin in terms of proportions and use of volumes. Between 1964 and 1970, Anatoly Kolotovkin held the position of chief architect of the city. He was subsequently appointed director of the Moldgiprostroy construction engineering institute, and in this capacity he contributed substantially to the development of the city. The building's architecture uses a classical order, and in terms of composition, the façade divides the surface into levels decorated with pilasters. The ground floor and the cornice are well detailed, and the middle level is built with masonry made from limestone. The building was finished before the austerity period, but nevertheless the façade is sparsely decorated. Only the top two floors have cantilevered balconies, and the column capitals are made of stucco. Two gables stand on the cornice on each side of the building at the corner, which is dominated by a squat tower with arched windows and columns. After 1945, architecture was intended to inspire optimism, glorious ideas, and confidence in the future, and monumental buildings therefore became part of the arsenal of visual propaganda. The structuring of façades

![Photograph of the residential building with tower at a street corner, with cars parked along the road and a street lamp in the foreground.]

in levels and the use of towers on tall buildings, based on the classical architectural orders, represented a continuation of the neoclassicist architecture favoured in Leningrad (now St. Petersburg), the so-called 'Palmyra of the North'. The building's stern countenance and the fact that it was set outside the limits of the old city demonstrate that the buildings of the socialist realism period would completely change the topology of Chisinau. The ground floor, with its arched windows, was reserved for services and retail spaces – a useful and necessary feature for an apartment building. This format was supposed to be replicated all along Mihai Viteazul, but very shortly afterwards the area became intensely industrialised, and residential buildings changed radically. Soon afterwards, 'series 143', a seismic-resistant, nine-floor prefabricated panel residential building would dominate construction; in 1980 Kolotovkin was awarded the State Prize of the MSSR precisely for the development of the 'series 143' design.

A

The Waterfall Stairway

113/1, Alexei Mateevici Street
Robert Kurtz, Svetlana Stalinskaya
1954

`019 A`

One of the entrances to Valea Morilor Park leads to a walkway heading towards a circular colonnaded pavilion, known as the Rotonda, and a waterfall stairway. The stairway, split in two by a series of pools arranged in a cascade formation, is flanked by pillars with lamps that light

the way during night-time walks. A fountain consisting of stacked basins decorated with plant motifs is situated on one of the steps of the waterfall. The stairways leading to the lake are interrupted by belvedere terraces with parapets, which face the lake. One of the terraces hosts another round fountain, larger than the first, in the shape of a bowl supported by rococo elements. The circular pavilion has a cylindrical base, and two access stairways lead to an open terrace with columns set in a circle and supporting a dome. The prominent cornice of the dome is supported by modillions, and its perimeter is decorated with laurel garlands. Fitting the larger picture of the 'garden city', the waterfall stairway is a landscape architecture concept inspired by a type of garden and park very popular in the 1930s. The *proletkult* ideology did not influence the vision of Moldovan architects until after 1944. The park entrance leading to the waterfall stairway, along with the circular pavilion (Rotonda), are a celebration

the USSR in the 1930s, is associated with a general 'warming' (Vladimir Paperny, Culture Two). It also serves as a nod to the Orient in Stalinist landscape architecture (hence the interest in tropical vegetation, for the 'Crimean and Caucasian spa resorts' etc.). The complex was neglected by the authorities in the interval between 1990 and 2015. Some of the components of the waterfalls fell apart, and park visitors were met with a desolated landscape. At the initiative of urban activists and NGOs, the complex was revived. It was cleaned of mud and debris, and events were held that facilitated its restoration. In February 2015, repair work started on the waterfall stairway and the Rotunda in Valea Morilor Park. The works were carried out according to a restoration project designed by Chisinauproiect and approved by the National Council of Historical Monuments. The complex opened to visitors in October 2016, but the fountains did not start working until later, after several deficiencies were remedied.

of opulence and triumph in pure form, as found in other sites around the city (e.g., the façades of the residential buildings on Stefan cel Mare or the Railway Station Square). The multi-coloured lighting of the waterfalls, designed by Robert Kurtz, helped enhance the park's image as an area of leisure and exoticism and recall the atmosphere of spa resorts on the Black Sea, which were very popular after the Second World War. The 'cult' of water, which was invoked here and was generally expanded through the abundance of fountains in the public spaces of

A

The Central Entrance to Valea Morilor Park

77, Alexei Mateevici Street
Robert Kurtz, David Palatnik
1954

Valea Morilor Park, designed by Robert Kurtz, was originally called the 'Central Culture and Leisure Park of the Leninist Komsomol'. According to the date engraved on a granite stele (which was removed in the 1990s), the park was built in 1950 at the initiative of Leonid Brezhnev, First Secretary of the Central Committee of the Moldovan Communist Party. The park stretches over 114 hectares, of which the lake occupies 34. A 2.5-kilometre walkway runs around its edges. The basin for the lake was dug with much enthusiasm by members of the young Komsomol, a Soviet youth organisation, between 1951 and 1952. The park has two entrances, both of which are on Alexei Mateevici Street (formerly Livezilor Street) and were created between 1956 and 1958. The design of the main entrance, located at 77, Al. Mateevici Street with its stairway descending towards the lake, was developed by D. Palatnik. The main entrance to the park recalls a propylaea of the Doric order and it references the style of ancient temples. The top register of the colonnaded gallery walls used to be adorned with mosaics showing athletic scenes. There was a visible dissonance between the socialist realist aesthetic of the entrance and the modernist one of the red granite steps. The descent to the lake took the shape of a stairway with red granite steps, in a minimalist solution. The monumentality of the stairway as a

whole was well thought-out. The length of the steps is comfortable for the walker and there are intermediary landings for resting during the climb. According to Marxist-Leninist theory, a culture and leisure park must be a combination of visual propaganda, culture, entertainment, and sports activities aimed to maintain citizens' fitness, and the park adheres to this formula for a socialist proletarian park. The entire arsenal of artistic devices used to influence the human psyche

was subordinated to this formula: The park was equipped with a number of facilities with various functions, including an open-air theatre with a seating capacity of 5,000 and a matinee cinema (now demolished). The MoldExpo Centre, formerly the Moldavian SSR Exhibition of Achievements in National Economy (VDNKh MSSR), stands next to the park. Over the years, the lake in the park has served as a training facility for various water sports. At one point there were three rowing schools active in the park. Athletic areas and fishing spots for leisure fishers were also created. In wintertime, the frozen lake became a municipal skating rink. There used to be a parachute tower in the park, accessible to the public, as well as a parachuting sports club with trained instructors.

A

Soviet Modernism

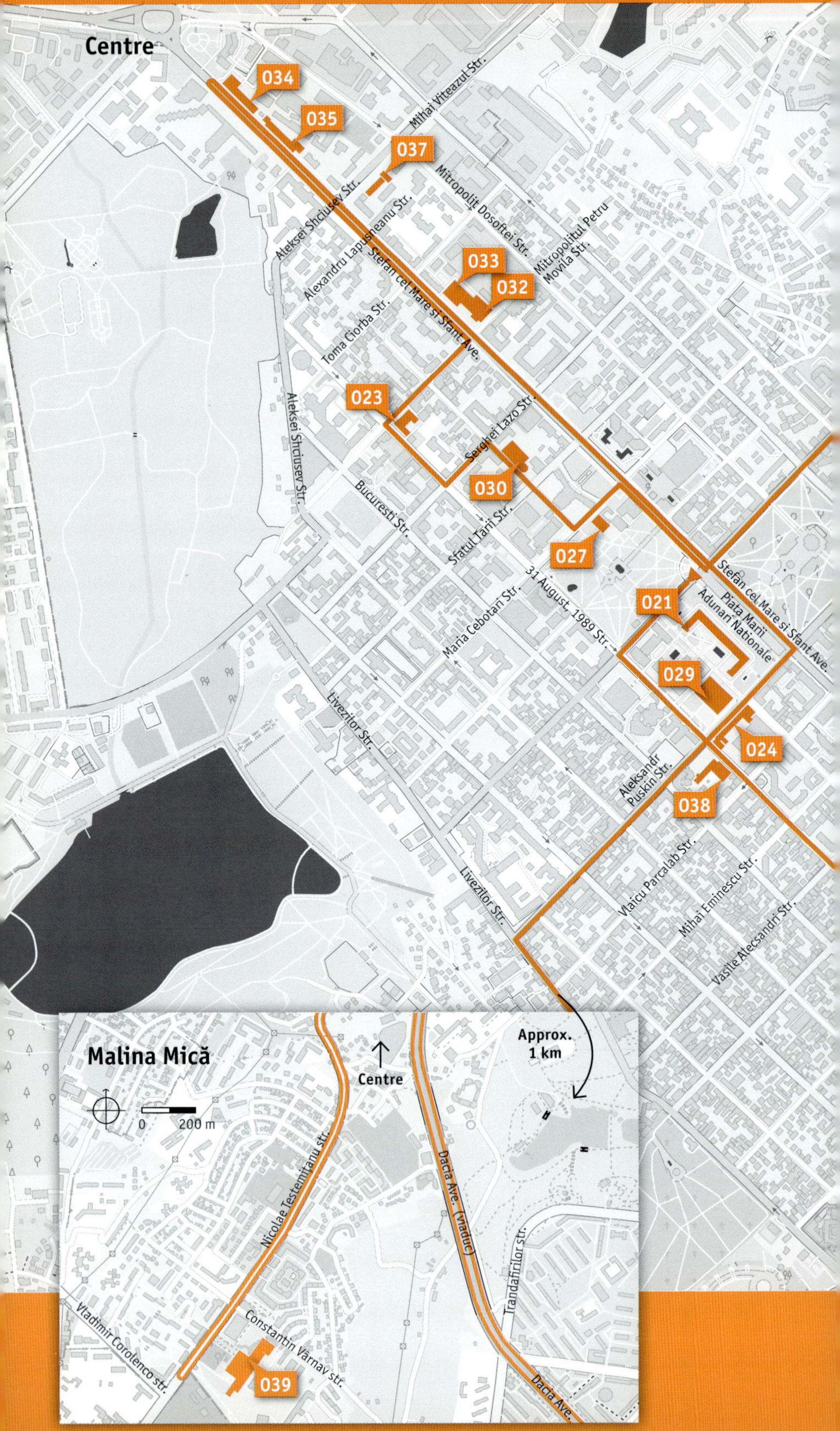

Centre

034

035

037

Mihai Viteazul Str.

Mitropolit Dosoftei Str.

Aleksei Shciusev Str.

Alexandru Lapushneanu Str.

Mitropolitul Petru Movila Str.

033

032

Toma Ciorba Str.

Ștefan cel Mare și Sfânt Ave.

Aleksei Shciusev Str.

023

Sergihei Lazo Str.

Bucuresti Str.

030

Sfatul Țării Str.

027

31 August 1989 Str.

Maria Cebotari Str.

Ștefan cel Mare și Sfânt Ave.

Plața Marii Adunări Naționale

021

029

Liveziilor Str.

Aleksandr Pușkin Str.

024

038

Liveziilor Str.

Vlaicu Pârcalab Str.

Mihai Eminescu Str.

Vasile Alecsandri Str.

Malina Mică

0   200 m

↑ Centre

Approx. 1 km

Nicolae Testemițanu str.

Dacia Ave. (Viaduc)

Trandafirilor str.

Vladimir Corolenco str.

Constantin Varnav str.

039

Dacia Ave.

031

022

028

026

025

036

040

Airport

Approx.
12 km

0   200 m

0   500 m

Renașterii Naționale Ave.

Andrei Doga Str.

Andrei Doga Str.

Calea Moșilor Str.

Albișoara Str.

Grigore Ureche Ave.

Calea Moșilor Str.

Mitropolit Varlaam str.

Ștefan cel Mare și Sfânt Ave.

Bulgara Str.

Strada Tighina

Ismail Str.

Negruzzi Ave.

Muncești str.

Dacia Ave.

The Government Hall

Grand National Assembly Square

Semyon Fridlin

1964

021 B

In terms of style, Government Hall is an undisputed testament to the reform period initiated by Nikita Khrushchev. Gagarin flew into space. Stalin's personality cult was abolished. Socialism 'with a human face' dawned on the horizon. The Soviet modernism associated with the thaw period embodied confidence in the idea that everything would be fine. Reforms in architecture took the form of an openness, transparency, and airiness characterising the new buildings constructed throughout the USSR. Government Hall (initially the offices of the Council of Ministers of the Moldavian SSR) is a clearly shaped volume. The layout is shaped like the

Russian letter 'П' with the front extending along the plaza and two short wings. The structure fits modernist canons to the letter. The rhythm of the pillars that alternate with inset vertical strips of windows gives the building a cool dynamic. Overall, we are reminded of the structure of an ancient temple, but one whose elements are pared down and abstracted. The streamlined presence of the six-storey building, placed on a high stylobate, is conveyed by the balanced proportions of the wide windows and the elegant detailing of the casings of the aluminium frame windows (a technology imported from the West). The entrances have black granite facing that contrasts with the white limestone facing of the pillars and with the tessellated effect of the windows. The design process developed out of a long series of abandoned projects. A design made in 1946 by architect Alexei Shchusev adhered to the traditions of Russian classicism; as a result, the building was stylistically linked to the ensemble of the Cathedral, the Bell Tower, and the Triumphal Arch – three nineteenth-century architecture monuments located across the street in Cathedral Park. Shchusev's design was kept 'in the drawer' by the state government, as it was very expensive. Another design followed,

B

developed by a team of architects from Kyiv led by S. Tutuchenko. This was visibly influenced by the triumphal architecture of Moscow buildings and largely responded to the presence of the monument to Lenin, which had been erected previously, and to the enlarged space of the square, which was already a designated place for mass events. The third design for Government Hall emerged from different political and ideological circumstances (after the 1955 decree) and was created by a team led by architect S. Fridlin, who was invited from Kyiv. Construction work ended in 1964. In terms of style, the façade of Government Hall has parallels with the iconic building of the Palace of Soviets (Mikhail Posokhin) in the Kremlin, which had a strange fate but possessed a special symbolism. The project began in 1937 (designed by Boris Iofan) and was abandoned in 1957; a new building was erected instead, but not at the site picked by Stalin, but rather inside the Kremlin. The project was kept under wraps and inaugurated in 1961. It was at the Palace of Congresses, designed in the style of Soviet modernism, that Khrushchev criticised the cult of Stalin and triggered the 'thaw'.

The TURIST Hotel
9, Grigore Vieru Boulevard
Roman Bekesevich
1971

022 B

The Turist Hotel was conceived for tourism within the USSR. As the Republic of Moldova became increasingly attractive in terms of its industry, agriculture, and cultural offering, it became a preferred destination for travellers from other Soviet republics. The hotel, which appeared on the city's map in 1971, was designed by R. Bekesevich, originally from Ukraine and a graduate of the Lviv School of Architecture. He taught for a while at the Construction Engineering College in Chisinau. One of his projects in Moldova was the reconstruction of the Biruinta ('Victory') cinema (formerly Odeon). The six-storey building is located on Grigore Vieru Boulevard near the former Moscova cinema (currently the E. Ionesco Theatre). The Turist Hotel also has a restaurant with a spacious terrace sheltered by a pergola. The hotel and restaurant buildings are situated on a corner at the intersection between Grigore Vieru Boulevard and Ierusalem Street. The hotel's façade faces a monument to the young heroes of the Komsomol (sculptor: L. Dubinovsky, architect: F. Naumov) and a small square. In terms of its spatial composition, the hotel building is not dissimilar to an apartment block, since it was assembled from prefabricated elements, and all the balconies were placed on the side facing the boulevard. The volume housing the restaurant protrudes slightly from the block-like volume of the hotel and is complemented by the ground-floor lobby. At the top of

depriving the building of an element that lent it elegance and lightness. The rooftop terrace and the ground floor volume are accented with a row of vertical cylinders that add dynamism to the façade. The restaurant and the nearby monument made the hotel an attraction, not just for tourists, but also for local residents. Its favourable location on Grigore Vieru Boulevard, with access to the pedestrian walkway extending down the middle of the entire boulevard, created a leisure area that attracted crowds throughout the summer, despite intense traffic. The boulevard is one of the few areas of Chisinau that was designed and finalised according to a rigorous urban development concept. The result is compact and well organised, and everything – the buildings, the monuments, the cinema, the green spaces – makes sense.

the hotel there is a sundeck, which used to operate as a leisure facility. This sundeck was later reconfigured, and the gap in the terrace roof was covered over, thus

Writers' Hall

98, 31 August 1989 Street
David Palatnic, Victor Yavorsky
1974

023 **B**

Construction of the building dedicated to the Republic of Moldova Writers' Union took place between 1969 and 1974. The main block parallels 31 August Street and has a lobby, four floors of offices, and a bookshop, Luceafarul, which is located on the ground floor with an entrance from the street. This is one of the few artists' union buildings to be equipped with a conference hall, an inner yard, a canteen, and a summer terrace in addition to the main structure. The building also houses the 'Mihail Kogalniceanu' National Literature Museum, with access from the lobby. The design stems from David Palatnic, who studied at the architecture faculty of the Civil and Municipal Construction Institute of Odessa between 1934 and 1939. In 1955, Palatnic was employed by the Moldgiprostroy Institute, where he worked for over 40 years. The architect's creative skills came to the fore after 1957, when the developments in housing construction made standardised technology a focus for architects' unions and engineering organisations throughout the country. The main block is built on a grid-like prefabricated reinforced concrete structure, which supports prefabricated panels. The walls are made from blocks of limestone and brick. The windows on the façade are arranged in a grid running vertically and horizontally. The façades themselves are finished in limestone with characteristic nuance. One distinctive element of the building is the sundeck on the roof, a reference to constructivist practice and specifically to the rooftop terrace of Le Corbusier's Unité d'Habitation. This modernist element can also be found in the Lumea Copiilor building (A. Kolotovkin) and in the prefabricated panel apartment block on A. Shchusev Street at the corner of Sfatul Taii Street. The terrace occupies the entire area of the building and is virtually an open yard, where the visiting writers could have coffee or take walks

undisturbed by the street traffic. The windows on the main façade are flanked by a grid formed by vertical and horizontal profiles – a brise-soleil offering protection against the sun's rays during the day. The building's entrance is shaded by a stylish overhang resting on two columns. In keeping with the spirit of Soviet modernism, the side façades of the building were decorated with a mosaic; its motif is not proletcultist in tone, as might be expected, but instead the mosaic forms an idyllic image of white waves floating on a green background, bathed in the rays of the sun. Currently, parts of the building are in need of renovation, particularly the basement, which houses the collections of the Literature Museum.

B

The House of the Press

22, Alexander Pushkin Street
Semyon Shoikhet, Abram Vaysbein
1967

024 B

The House of the Press ('Casa Presei') is located on Pushkin Street, occupying a plot delimited by 31 August Street and Veronica Micle Street. The building is functionally divided into spaces for various services on the ground floor, with access from the street, and publisher's offices for newspapers and magazines on the four upper floors. Access to these offices is through the entrance at the intersection of Pushkin and 31 August Streets. The printing press used by all the publications is located immediately behind the building. The House of the Press is part of a set of utilitarian buildings inserted into the city's texture in order to house a wide range of services. Similar in typology, they were all built in the same period and include, for example, the National Bank (A. Vaysbein, S. Shoikhet) and the Telephone Exchange (V. Dubok).

The architect Semyon Shoikhet studied for seven years at the Architecture Faculty of the Tashkent Polytechnic Institute; he graduated in 1956 with the degree of 'engineer-architect'. As a young specialist, he managed to obtain the approval to move to Chisinau. The first project to which he was assigned was developing master plans for seven cities, among them Leova, Comrat, and Cahul. These projects were a springboard for the young professional, whose career soon took off. The House of the Press design – the first collaboration between S. Shoikhet and A. Vaysbein – was integrated organically into the administrative district of the city, which was stylistically dominated by the National Palace and Government Hall (S. Fridlin). The square with a fountain in front of the palace is an open space, from which the House of the Press is visible in its entirety. In terms of its use of volume, the industrial appearance of the building's elongated block is indebted to the constructivist tradition. The windows are aligned in stripe-like

B

horizontal bands running across the entire façade; the brise-soleil situated above the main entrance is another distinctive mark of Soviet modernism. A signature of the Khrushchev era, the original design of the roof included access to a sundeck, but this element was later scrapped. The drawings made by the architects, which bear witness to the atmosphere of the 'thaw', show a clock above the entrance on the brise-soleil; it also did not make it into the final design. Currently, the House of the Press and other buildings in the neighbourhood are the object of major real estate transactions, which may potentially result in irreversible changes to the entire ensemble.

Inter-city Telephone Exchange 025 B

12, Stefan cel Mare si Sfant
Boulevard
Victor Dubok
1967

Housing the central offices of Moldtelecom since 1993, the building was designed by the Ukrainian architect Victor Dubok. It became a prominent structure in the city landscape not only due to its function and positioning, but also due to the fact that it heralded a new trend in the architectural typology. Having just abandoned the Stalinist practice of recycling classical heritage, post-war Soviet architecture required a new architectonic and ideological mindset as well as professional justification for new architectural paradigms. Apart from its main tenet of condemning the 'excesses' of Stalinist style and requiring economy in construction, the 1955 decree 'On Architectural Excesses' invited Soviet architects to 'more boldly master the advanced construction technologies used in the USSR and abroad'. Victor Dubok was the chief architect of Giprosvyaz (the Union-wide communications enterprise). In addition to the Chisinau telephone exchange, he also designed exchange buildings in Kyiv, Kharkov, Aktobe, and Vilnius. The central positions of the telephone exchanges in these cities represented a distinctive mark of progress, underlining the prominent place telephone communication had taken in everyday life. The first automated exchange in Chisinau was commissioned in 1938 (architect: Constantin Nanescu); it was situated behind the Post Office on a street closed off by a café (later

B

demolished and replaced by a McDonald's located between the Gemenii shopping centre and the central Post Office. The interwar exchange could no longer cope with the increasing number of clients and telephone connections. The new automated telephone exchange built in 1967 became an extremely busy place. The exchange not only offered calls to foreign countries and other USSR republics, but also bill payment and technical assistance desks. The architecture of the building is one of the first examples of the use of brise-soleil structures for sun protection across the entire façade as a modernist functional element. A similar feature was later used for other buildings, such as the House of the Press and the National Bank. The grid in itself is not very sophisticated. It is constructed from prefabricated elements, and the entire structure is slightly set off from the building. The exchange is built from prefabricated reinforced concrete elements, and the surfaces of the exterior blocks are rendered in a coarse material in order to contrast with the windows. The seams between the blocks remain visible to this day. Other distinctive marks of Soviet modernist style include the strip of windows on the side façade, the asymmetrical interlacing of the building's volumes, the generous spaces on the ground floor, and the use of monumental art on the side façade. Another distinctive element is the lobby, which provided access to the hall for inter-city calls and to the hall dedicated to customer service. Access to these halls was via two flights of stairs set above the ground floor, which allowed people to look out into the street traffic through the windows while waiting for their call to be put through. The two halls, running along the main boulevard and Tighina Street, are accented by an overhang, which shields them from the sun in summer and visually sets the public part of the building apart from the technical, back-office section. In addition to these stylistic and functional transformations, Soviet modernist architecture also created a synthesis with monumental art, as exemplified by the mosaic panel on the façade facing Tighina Street, which portrays telephony as a symbol of global communication.

The A. P. Chekhov Russian Drama Theatre

026 B

75, Vlaicu Parcalab Street
Roman Bekesevich
1966

The building of the Russian Drama Theatre is considered a reconstruction based on the designs of architect R. Bekesevich. The theatre project is unusual in that it used the foundations and some of the walls of the Choral Synagogue. Built in 1913, it was the main house of worship of the city's Jewish community and has a total area of 1,350 square metres. The theatre operated on the premises of the former synagogue beginning in 1945, though the building was not adapted to function as a theatre until 1966. The renovation was actually an entirely new project resulting in the construction of a different type of building. Political directives and construction regulations were followed to the letter by the engineers and architects of this era, who had little interest in ethical considerations and instead focused on rigorously adhering to technological and engineering requirements. The theatre designed by Bekesevich is modest in terms of volume and bears clear references to the tradition of modernist architecture – the spirit of the era in which it was created. In his organisation of space, the architect used a full and diverse range of masterful devices. The main façade is divided into two levels. The top one is a high terrace with a roof that extends over both levels and is supported by columns. The terrace, open towards the square, recalls an *aywan* (an open summer terrace with a canopy) – an element borrowed from Eastern and Central Asian architecture, which was adapted here in order to shade and ventilate the building during the summer. The ground floor was designed as a block with floor-to-ceiling windows inspired by constructivism. This transparency forms a rhythm with the opening by the terrace. From the ticket booths on the ground floor, the visitor proceeds into a narrow hallway leading to the auditorium. The audience hall is spacious; it has a balcony and is equipped with comfortable seats. The theatre used to have an extension into the public space – a square

B

with trees, streetlamps, and a fountain that offered a refreshing space during summer, an oasis of coolness and calm. The square has recently been refurbished, but unfortunately the stylistic integrity and the coherence with the building's architecture were lost in the process. The original lampposts were inexplicably removed, and the pavement and the street furniture were modified. The appearance of the theatre building now no longer reflects the original; it would take a diligent effort and close study of archive photographs and original designs in order to restore it to its initial form. Today the lobby is covered with double-glazing, unsightly frames, and opaque glass; it no longer reflects the spirit of transparency promoted during the era of Khrushchev's 'thaw'. Another important aspect is the façade and its colour scheme – also far removed from the original. The building is now topped by a kitschy element that has replaced the theatre's logo. Bearing in mind the need of the Jewish community to reclaim its former heritage, today we are faced with the dilemma of choosing between preserving the theatre and rebuilding the synagogue, the walls of which are still visible today.

Guguta Café (formerly Noroc Restaurant)

027 B

Stefan cel Mare Public Garden
Vladislav Kudinov, Victor Zakharov
1967

The building, currently a derelict café, is a reconstructed version of the Noroc ('Cheers!') restaurant, located in the Stefan cel Mare Public Garden in a protected area of the city. In terms of its spatial composition, the building was originally designed as a raised structure supported by columns. The space on the ground floor was used as an open-air terrace and daytime serving area. Access to the hall used in the evening was through an elegant stairway attached to the main façade. The image of the restaurant was highlighted by a stylish neon logo. The duo of architects thus successfully came up with a simple yet attractive spatial-volumetric solution in keeping with the trend of Soviet modernism and the open spirit that dominated society at the time. It was designed as a transparent block, assembled from glass panes with delicate metal frames, recalling a gigantic aquarium, radiating light and cheering up partygoers in the evening. Located in the centre of the city behind the Patria cinema, the restaurant became a destination of choice for city inhabitants. It would fill up in the evenings, attracting customers with its cuisine, which brought it European-wide fame. Noroc restaurant was also the site of a memorable anniversary. It was chosen as the venue for the festive banquet celebrating the first 50 years of the MSSR Communist Party. The event was attended by members of the Central Bureau of the USSR, led by Leonid Brezhnev, as well as a few hundred guests from other republics and from abroad, who were treated to a select menu of traditional Moldovan dishes. The restaurant is also considered an iconic location due to the glorious spirit of the 1960s, defined by the pop bands (or VIAs, 'vocal-instrumental ensembles', as they were called) which used to perform here. After the building of the Central Committee (A. Cherdantsev) was

erected in 1976, the restaurant fell out of favour with the authorities due to its extreme popularity and the image it cultivated in a neighbourhood that was virtually hallowed ground for the government. Therefore, the space was redesigned (S. Lebedev, N. Zaporojan, 1976) into a mundane cafeteria for children, under the name Skazka ('Fairytale'). The hasty reconstruction disfigured the building, covering it in papier-mâché-like decorations that jarred with the building's modernist aesthetic. However, the structure and the original features remained intact. Currently abandoned, the building of the Guguta Café used to be one of the iconic buildings of the city, and it occupied a prominent place in citizens' lives and memories in the 1970s and 1980s. The Public Garden brings together the collective memories of various ethnic and age-related communities in peaceful co-existence. In recent years, the garden has not only become a place where the cultural memory of Moldovan society is preserved (due to its historically significant monuments), but also a living place, where the struggle to preserve this memory and to redefine the identity of the city centre is being constructed and organised. As a result of a number of real estate transactions, the building was privatised and is currently owned by a company that is planning to demolish it and instead build an eight-storey business centre (80 rooms and 68 parking spaces), an inappropriate project for this strictly protected area of the city – a business endeavour masquerading as a cultural centre. Architect V. Kudinov also designed the Codru Hotel, which was demolished in 2018, and it would be a pity for the city to be deprived of his one remaining remarkable building.

B

The National Bank

1, Grigore Vieru Boulevard
Grigore Vieru Boulevard
Abram Vaysbein et al.
1973

028 B

Starting in the 1970s, tall buildings began appearing on Grigore Vieru Boulevard (formerly Tineretului), and the flagship of this new trend was the nine-storey edifice of the National Bank (originally the State Bank). The building was designed by A. Veysbein in collaboration with S. Shoikhet and G. Kalyuzhner, and construction work lasted from 1972 to 1973. During Khrushchev's time, this new architecture was just finding its way, exploring new construction methods and a new aesthetic; Soviet modernism reached its maturity around 1967. After 1968, when Soviet tanks entered Prague,

the attitude of society shifted – the former optimism and belief in a bright future faded considerably. The bank is placed on a corner at the intersection of Grigore Vieru Boulevard and Constantin Tanase Street. The building stands out due to its pared-down use of volume. It is formed by two elements: a tall, slender office block and a flatter second element extending beyond the footprint of the tower where the entry hall is located. The two elements are connected through a gallery, with a different volume, which has a hallway and adjoining spaces, protected by an elegant brise-soleil for sun protection. The ground floor gallery, slightly set off from the rest of the building, continues on C. Tanase Street and is accented by an elegant overhang. The constructive and functional element of the brise-soleil was intensely explored

B

instance, brise-soleil with similar elements are found in the House of the Press (S. Shoikhet, A. Vaysbein) and on the House of Technology (V. Zakharov). Starting in the early 1970s, the illusion of a better future faded away, and creative élan diminished. This was very palpable in architecture journals, such as *USSR Architecture*, which became increasingly dull. With its straightforward spatial composition, the design of the bank fits perfectly in this paradigm. The verticality of the taller block, enhanced by the stacked narrow windows, is accented by the thin metal profiles running from the ground floor to the roof on all the sides of the building. Despite its plainness, the building still meets today's aesthetic and functional demands; fortunately, the recent renovation has not robbed it of its characteristic features.

in modernist architecture. It is important to remember that Moldova is a country with high temperatures in the summer, and therefore this element, inspired by other cultural contexts (Central Asia), was widely applied in combination with microclimate control inside buildings. A very diverse range of materials were used for this construction. For

'Nicolae Sulac' National Palace
21, Alexander Pushkin Street
Semyon Fridlin
1974

The National Palace (initially the 'October Hall') was inaugurated in 1974 to celebrate the 50-year anniversary of the establishment of the MSSR and the creation of the Moldovan Communist Party. The main guest at the event was Leonid Brezhnev, whose political career had started in Chisinau. The palace was designed as a multifunctional building, meant to host the congresses of the Communist Party of the MSSR, ceremonial assemblies, extended political and international congresses, conferences, concerts, and shows. The building is located across the street from the House of the Press and faces Pushkin Street; it is thus harmoniously enmeshed in the city's texture. As with Government Hall, architect S. Fridlin was invited from Ukraine and he designed the palace under the influence of the reforms started by Khrushchev. Shunning Stalinist neoclassicism, Khrushchev insisted that new buildings clearly fulfil the functions they had been designed for, and he had little interest in aesthetic considerations. However, he was vague in his statements and pointed out that architecture should nevertheless have an attractive appearance, citing the modern buildings of the West as examples. From his position as First Secretary of the USSR Communist Party, he insisted on simplicity, laconism, balanced proportions, and a clear relationship between form and function. Despite the fact that Khrushchev was removed in 1964, this working agenda remained unchanged, and architects continued to design and erect buildings according to the programme he had initiated. The National Palace was not finalised until 1974. It had been designed in the spirit of Soviet modernism, but the 10-year time and style gap between the Government Hall and the palace is virtually non-existent. The three-story building has a clear and functional layout divided into a lobby area, a visitor area, technical and management area, and a space for performances and events. The main façade facing Pushkin Street showcases the floor-to-ceiling windows that

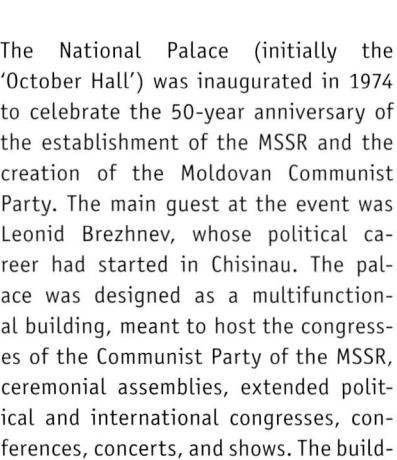

B

run the length of the building and are punctuated by the vertical rhythm of narrow pillars. The wide stairway and escalators take visitors from the spacious lobby to the second floor. The auditorium (with approximately 2,000 seats) consists of a ground floor with an amphitheatre and a balcony. At the edges of the auditorium and placed on various levels, there are lighting and sound booths, a projection box, radio and television control rooms, and interpreting booths. The restrained architecture and the balance of volumes lend the building an imposing air, conveying a sense of grandeur both in the interior and on the exterior. Located at the intersection of two streets and elevated by a recessed base of a glass and metal construction on the ground floor along the lateral façades, the building has a stately and elegant appearance. In the spirit of openness and transparency, the building also opens onto a generous square surrounded by spruce trees and featuring a fountain that gives it an even more festive appearance.

The Parliament Automotive Fleet Garage

10, Anatol Corobceanu Street
Anatoly Dubrovsky
1978

The building of the Parliament's Automotive Fleet Garage was designed by A. Dubrovsky, originally as the Council of Ministers' Garage, in order to house the official Volga and ZIM cars used to transport the political elites of the MSSR. It is an enigmatic building that has been hidden from the eyes of the world for a long time, as it was strategically placed in an obscured position in the vicinity of the parliament building (A. Cherdantsev). In the USSR, architects not only paid attention to the organisation of the traffic or the internal structure of such buildings, but also to their appearance. The garage building is part of a Soviet architectural tradition regarding such buildings; some of the more remarkable automotive structures include the Intourist Garage (1934) designed by K. Melnikov and the Bakhmatyev Garage (1927), both built in Moscow. The building faces A. Corobceanu Street, but its most beautiful façade can be seen from the yard of Herta House or from the windows of the Ministry of Agriculture. The windows on both façades are covered with a grid of cut-out elements recalling the portholes of a ship. This feature lends the building a unique appearance. Because the building was not in a highly visible location, it was neglected for many years. However, it is now considered a landmark of utilitarian architecture in Chisinau. In terms of

functionality, the design makes reference to the multi-storey car parks used in the West. The city did already have a multistorey car park at the time – much more modest in design – used by the taxi service on Calea Iesilor Street. In the case of the Parliament Garage, the innovative and compact solution resulted in a five-storey building that saved space in the city centre. The side façade facing the parliament building has an unusual profile; it has a curved, semi-cylindrical shape that is crossed by bands of windows running at a horizontal angle following the spiralling ramps that took the vehicles to the upper floors. Given the extent to which the city is now overcrowded with vehicles during the day, mainly in the centre, the lack of car parks has become a pressing problem. A viable solution suggested by the Municipality of Chisinau would be to transform part of the Parliament Garage into a paid parking area.

Tennis Arena

59, Eugen Coca Street
Semyon Shoikhet, Alla Kirichenko
1968

031 B

The Tennis Arena belonging to the Sports School of the Republic, Tennis Specialisation, was developed by the Moldgiprostroy Institute and designed by S. Shoikhet and A. Kirichenko as part of a sports and leisure area including Alunelul Park. After graduating from the Architecture Institute in Moscow in 1961, Alla Kirichenko was assigned a position in Chisinau. She dedicated her entire career to systematic urban planning for housing developments and to designing buildings. Together with S. Shoikhet, she produced several remarkable projects. The Tennis School has an arena that includes a building made of curved structures, housing two indoor courts, several adjacent spaces for rest and recovery, and several outdoor clay courts. In the early 1970s, this complex managed to produce a solid team of world-class athletes and champions. During the harsh winters of the 1970s, the clay courts were turned into hockey and skating rinks used by children and youths. Undeniably, the Tennis Arena can be categorised as an embodiment of the most advanced trends in Soviet modernism. Its arched roof is a tensile structure secured in the ground at the extremities of the building. A series of vertical ribs dominate the appearance of the front façade. The sides of the arena consist of floor-to-ceiling windows, allowing light to penetrate the entire building and creating a feeling of airiness. The construction developed by the team of architects was realised by Moldovan construction engineers with what at the time was cutting-edge technology. The result was a novelty, not just for the Republic of Moldova. When it was built, the sports complex was on par with the most competitive tennis schools in the USSR. The entrance to the arched space is a rectangular volume attached to the left side of the building, which comprises a lobby and a small cafeteria, in addition to the locker rooms and showers. At the entrance, a monumental sculpture representing a tennis player preparing to serve the ball complements the ensemble in concept and style. Alunelul Park was designed by the urban planning department of the Moldgiprostroy Institute in order to create a relaxing leisure area for the inhabitants of the Buiucani

district. A rectangular fountain is situated in the centre of the park and connected to neighbouring streets through a network of walkways and paths. At the top end of the park, a broad stairway with several flights of steps leads upwards to the Tennis Arena complex. The area now encompassed by the arena and Alunelul Park overlaps with part of the old Jewish cemetery; before structural changes introduced during the interwar period, the latter extended as far as Calea Iesilor Street. This Jewish cemetery is one of the oldest in Chisinau. It is a national historical monument, currently occupying an area southwest of the arena along Milano Street. S. Shoikhet designed a memorial to the victims of the 1903 pogrom (completed by sculptor N. Epelbaum); it was installed in the park in 1993 – a silent witness to the demolition of the old cemetery.

The Fashion Centre

182, Stefan cel Mare si Sfant Boulevard

Victor Zakharov, Liudmila Gofman, Gennady Zhinkin

1970

The Fashion Centre (the 'Casa Modei' or 'Fashion House') is part of an ensemble developed in the late 1960s that includes the building of the Publishers' House – belonging to the Chisinau City Executive Committee. The Fashion Centre is a counterpoint to this building in terms of spatial composition. The ensemble, located on the central boulevard, is one of the few large-scale projects that reflected the influence of modernity. In terms of its function, it combined the spheres of graphic design (an intrinsic instrument of the publishing industry and political sphere) with clothes design (a luxury for the everyday citizen). It is important to note that certain trends, especially architectural styles, tended to reach the peripheries of the USSR with some delay. In view of the city's architecture in the 1970s, this explains why these buildings seem to have been teleported there from another dimension – an impression enhanced by the techniques and materials used for the façades. The design was developed at the Moldgiprostroy Institute (later called Urbanproiect) by a team of architects led by V. Zakharov. Construction work was coordinated by the Union of Architects, the USSR Gosstroi (the State Committee for Construction), according to the decisions of the USSR Gosplan (the State Planning Committee). It was completed in 1970. The total surface of the building measures 9,307 square metres, with an adjacent plot of 0.658 hectares. The Fashion Centre consists of two volumes: the largest, main volume is set back from the boulevard line, and a much smaller volume extends forwards, resting on pillars. Its sides are covered with a relief cast in concrete with plant motifs. This is a classic feature of Soviet modernism, which intensively made use of monumental art. During that particular period, society was fascinated not only by the exploration of cosmic space, but also by the charting of the ocean's depths, especially by the French oceanography expeditions led

B

by Jacques-Yves Cousteau from his ship, Calypso. Cousteau was interested in studying submerged built habitats and human ability to live under water. The minimalist façades dominated by a modular metal structure and motifs recalling aquatic contexts reflect the influence of these exploration campaigns. They create a feeling of transparency when combined with the texture of the concrete. In terms of function, the building was divided into several areas: a section for presenting clothing designs, the workshops, and the administration offices. In recent years, the Fashion Centre has been the object of various lawsuits. It has been foreclosed and transferred to different mediators and assignees. The ground floor spaces, home to a number of businesses over the years (the Exchange Boutique, La Placinte restaurant, the Felicia chemist shop), indicate the extent to which the role and function of the building have been degraded over the years; excessive advertising displays and strident logos used by the businesses have denigrated its appearance.

The Publishers' House

180, Stefan cel Mare si Sfant
Boulevard
Victor Zakharov, Liudmila Gofman,
Gennady Zhinkin
1980

033 B

After inauguration, the building of the Publishers' House became a landmark in terms of its architectural composition and no other building in the city centre corresponded with it. Despite having been scheduled for construction in 1969 and conceived to form an ensemble with the Fashion Centre built in 1970, the Publishers' House was not realised until a decade later. The building is set back from the boulevard line and aligned with Mitropolit Petru Movila Street. Spatially it consists of two slightly staggered block-like volumes that lend the design a discreet dynamism. The block closest to the boulevard houses the staircase and is accented by the jagged pattern of its windows. The lateral façades of the building are covered with aluminium siding that protrudes from under every window, thus creating a uniform grid suggesting both volume and movement. The building is set on a slightly raised platform. A hallway connects the building with the Fashion Centre. The façade is clad with limestone, which offers a contrast to the coloured elements in the metal grid-like structure used for the balconies, which create the impression of a series of open book covers. The construction of the Publishers' House was planned by Chisinau's City Executive Committee in order to celebrate the 50th anniversary of the establishment of the MSSR. The building was meant to house the State Press Committee (the MSSR Department for Publishing, Printing, and Book Trade), state publishing houses, the State Book Chamber, its archive, and a bookshop, among other organisations. The design was developed by a team of architects at the Moldgiprostroy Institute. Due to a lack of funding, the construction process was delayed, and the building process lasted from 1975 to 1979. The construction was also completed due to the fact that 1980 was the year of the Moscow Olympics, and the torch was supposed to pass through the city. The building has 14 floors above ground and two underground and is accessed through two entrances, one on Stefan cel Mare Boulevard and another on Petru Movila Street. The third floor includes a conference hall. Another conference hall, meant for the top tier of the MSSR State Committee, was designed for the eighth floor. The fourth and 10th floors used to house the employees' canteens. Current occupants of the building include the offices of the Republic of Moldova National Book Chamber, the Special Schoolbook Collection, the 'Lumina State' Publishing House, the 'Bogdan Petriceicu-Hasdeu' Institute of Romanian Philology, and various departments of the Ministry of Education, Culture, and Research. A monument honouring the Metropolitan Petru Movila (architect: I. Halupneac, sculptors: B. Dubrovin and G. Dubrovin) was erected in front of the building in 1996.

'C. Stere' University of European Political and Economic Studies (USPEE)

200, Stefan cel Mare si Sfant Boulevard
Victor Zakharov
1970

034 B

In the 1960s, new forms of expression were introduced by architects, who were inspired by documentation they brought back from trips abroad as well as the values of the free world. Both contributed to an optimism surrounding the potential for architecture to bring social change and inspired utopian visions for a better world. However, there was never any public mention of the new ideology promoted in that era. It was maintained that the primary role of architecture was to solve social problems, and aesthetic issues had to take a back seat to utilitarian considerations. In the case of USPEE (initially Technology Hall), a strictly functional design was chosen, as this was a building intended for clerks, engineers, researchers, and lecturers. It consisted of a main block-like building and a secondary edifice, both of which face the central boulevard. The new principles of Soviet architecture were also manifested in the use of new construction technologies, such as the use of a prefabricated grid-like framework. Technological advances enabled the replacement of massive brick walls with prefabricated panels and much lighter structures, which were not

B

overloaded with any additional decorations. Moreover, the approach to the architecture of administrative buildings changed. These designs became fertile ground for experimentation and served as laboratories for cultivating a completely new image. The construction process for the USPEE structures employed a typical method for the time: prefabricated panels were set onto a structure of concrete pillars, and the façade consisted of textured prefabricated elements. The aluminium profiles covering the entire surface of the façade not only had the effect of providing shade, but they were also aesthetic, creating an organised structure of repetitive elements. The smaller rectangular structure, designed for conferences and other public events, is very dynamic in shape; it is supported by a row of industrial-looking elements, recalling the teeth of a wrench and giving the building its unique identity. This block is connected to the main building through a gallery, where the central entrance is located. Part of the gallery is transparent, with glass windows and doors, and part of it is covered with concrete brise-soleil elements, much like those used for the House of the Press (S. Shoikhet, A. Vaysbein).

Urbanproiect Institute (currently the National Anticorruption Centre)

035 B

196, Stefan cel Mare si Sfant Boulevard
Robert Kurtz, Roman Bekesevich
1967

In the 1960s, government institutes were established for carrying out large-scale construction and engineering projects, their main mission being to accelerate building processes and reduce the cost of construction through the use of standardised designs and prefabricated materials. The process of creating such designs involved teams of architects working in different departments and sharing responsibilities based on their specialisations. Architecture was driven by the standardised building industry, and only edifices of special importance were designed as individualised, customised projects. Soviet modernism gave rise both to exceptional buildings, which were lauded by the press, as well as hundreds of unexciting microraions scattered across the republics. Opening up to an international context and gaining an awareness of other countries' building practices did

not cause the architectural profession to become any freer in the USSR. Once L. Brezhnev became the leader of the USSR, experimental élan and creativity were dampened, and buildings became increasingly simplistic and devoid of expression. The Urbanproiect Institute was founded as a construction engineering establishment, part of the republic's Moldavstroyproyect trust in accordance with decision no. 168 of 13 August 1944 of the MSSR Council of People's Commissars. In 1954, Moldavstroyproyect changed its name, becoming Moldgiprogorselistroy, and it became the state institute for construction engineering known as the Moldgiprostroy Institute in 1957. This institute used to have a city planning department with an 80-person team and regional divisions – Central Moldova, South Moldova, North Moldova – with over 300 employees. The institute also had teams working on industrial construction projects, although the separate Promstroy Institute was in charge of developing industrial sites. Today there is no longer any administrative body dedicated to industrial projects. In 1998, the institute was designated the National Institute of Research and Engineering and named

Urbanproiect. The building's façade is typical for the modernist period; the windows are arranged in bands that follow the perimeter of the building; these are punctuated by slender concrete profiles. The construction technology – concrete panels installed on a structure of reinforced concrete columns and a façade made of prefabricated elements – is also characteristic of the era. However, a throwback to 1950s architectural typologies includes the two basement storeys, which are clad on the exterior with Cosauti sandstone. The entrance features an awning, which enlivens a little the industrial appearance of the building. An impressive number of buildings were developed over time by the institute's specialists, and it is hard to understate the symbolic importance of this particular site in defining the city's architectural landscape. At various stages, the institute had in its service V. Voitekhovski, D. Palatnic, R. Kurtz, A. Kolotovkin, A. Ambartsumyan, S. Shoikhet, V. Kudinov, G. Solominov, and R. Bekesevich, among others.

B

The National Hotel

4, Stefan cel Mare si Sfant
Boulevard
*Vladimir Shalaginov, Adolf
Gorbuntsov*
1978

036 B

The National Hotel (formerly the Intourist Hotel) designed by architects V. Shalaginov and A. Gorbuntsov is undoubtedly a landmark building and an epitome of modernity not just in the context of the architecture of Chisinau, but also that of the entire republic. The slender and airy structure was built with prefabricated reinforced concrete elements. From the very moment it was erected, it took on a symbolic status. The construction of the 17-storey building took four years and was finished in 1978. In the late 1980s, the international Intourist network operated some 458 hotels, eight of which were located outside the borders of the USSR. Elegant in its proportions and typifying modernist architecture, the ensemble of the National Hotel includes a restaurant and a square with a fountain placed between the hotel and the boulevard. The first two storeys of the building were dedicated to management, services, and utilities; the rest of the floors were occupied by guest rooms. The restaurant's volume has a dynamic shape with two banquet halls placed on separate levels. The architects found an ingenious solution – a walkway – for connecting the hotel's 17-storey block with the somewhat detached body of the restaurant. The hotel complex is well positioned, being visible along the Ciuflea Street axis. The volumes of the restaurant and the hotel fit well into

the intersection of Stefan cel Mare and Negruzzi Boulevards. In its heyday, the Intourist Hotel in Chisinau was the destination of choice for foreign guests taking part in various international events, congresses, and competitions. In addition, the hotel ran the Berezka shop – the only shop in the city that accepted foreign currency and offered a wide range of local and imported quality goods. The hotel had two bars and two buffets, a hair salon, a post office, a newsstand, a consignment room for luggage, and other facilities. During the transition period, the hotel lost most of its business and it was privatised in 2006. Nowadays, the fate of the building is uncertain, but there are signs that the current owner plans to demolish it and build a new hotel complex. In an ironic twist of fate, the hotel gained its name of the National Hotel during the period of change brought about by the national movement that dominated Moldova in the 1990s, but it then fell into private hands. The political spectrum has meanwhile become more diverse, and the hotel has now transitioned to owners who are exclusively profit-driven. In the absence of a functional state and city mechanisms for regulating and protecting architectural heritage, the latter has remained vulnerable and subject to decay.

The County Government building (Buiucani district)

2, Mihai Viteazul Street
Boris Shpak
1969

The building of the County Government offices (originally the Frunze Raion Committee) on Mihai Viteazu Street stands out through its massive, top-heavy volume, which is showcased by the building's location on an upward slope. In the early years of the USSR, the architecture of its cities was dominated by ideological concerns, which aligned with the demands made by the party's apparatus and the ideal typology of the socialist city; these constituted a series of unwritten rules that continued to define the mentality of state architects throughout the era. In the late 1960s, several buildings meant to house the raion party committees, composed of the residents of the various city districts, were designed and built in Chisinau: for example, on Kiev Street for the Rascani district (Octombrie raion), on Bulgara Street for the Central district (Lenin raion), and on Mihai Viteazul Street for the Buiucani district (Frunze raion). Identical standardised designs were used for each of these buildings. Only minor adaptations were made respective to each construction site. The building of the County Government offices for the Botanica district is an exception, as it was built according to a different design. New technological developments were accompanied by the practice of holding competitions for standard projects: residential buildings, administrative buildings, hospitals, clinics, schools,

cinemas, and shops. In order to save time and boost efficiency in construction, these were generally designed and erected in a modular manner, assembled from an array of standardised components. Young architects began winning such competitions, while veterans wondered about this approach to assembling buildings like LEGO. A wave of emulation followed, and some of the architects turned out to be extremely economical in terms of design: some of the newly designed buildings – both residential and administrative – could be built using just two dozen elements. The building for the County Government of the Buiucani district consists of two elements: the main block with five storeys and an adjacent one, smaller in size, meant for executive conferences and meetings. The two are connected through a ground floor gallery. Stretching out before the building is a terraced lawn, which is followed by an ascending slope and then a stairway leading to the main entrance. In contrast with the rest of the building, the elevated and cantilevered volume of the conference hall, equipped on one side with a modest but graceful concrete fire escape, is the building's defining feature.

Gh. Asachi High School

038 B

113, 31 August 1989 Street
Semyon Shoikhet, Alla Kirichenko
1969

The building of Gh. Asachi High School (originally Scoala No1) is located in the historical centre of the city. Facing Pushkin Street, it occupies part of the block between 31 August and Bucuresti Streets and is situated next to the nineteenth century chapel of the Girls' Secondary School (A. Bernardazzi). The high school has a prominent reputation and long-standing history, as it is the oldest education establishment in the republic, with its teaching and educational traditions extending back some 155 years. Its educational approach is still considered innovative and interactive today. The high school was founded in 1864 by Janette Dubois, and it was originally located in the founder's personal home at 64 Podoliei Street (now Bucuresti Street). The school's new building is based on a design developed at the Moldgiprostroy Institute (currently Urbanproiect) by S. Shoikhet and A. Kirichenko. At the time, S. Shoikhet had acquired some prominence as an architect and was quite influential due to the projects he had already completed. Together the pair was extremely productive, realising important projects in the period during which Shoikhet was the institute's chief architect. The building was to be erected in record time in order to commission it before the start of the school year. The architects and builders chose to assemble it using prefabricated concrete elements, while employing a limited range of construction options. A look at the original drawings shows that certain initial spatial solutions were discarded due to the constraints imposed by a limited budget and existing regulations. The high school building consists of a main four-storey block with classrooms and a smaller

two-storey block that faces 31 August Street and houses a gymnasium. In terms of its overall composition and use of volume, the building stands out due to the intersection of its long horizontal volume with the vertical body housing the stairwell, which juts out from the façade in an expressive manner. The vertical volume of the staircase is accented by narrow strips of windows that alternate with concrete profiles creating a wavy geometric pattern. These individual shapes appear on every façade, in a manner underscoring the 'modular' nature of the building. An additional notable detail is the use of square concrete cast panels with a geometric pattern. Alternating horizontally with the glass panes of the windows, these white panels create a pattern that lends the ensemble a visual dynamic. The gymnasium is decorated with a continuous frieze made from the same cast concrete elements, which run along the top of building as a kind of cornice. The gymnasium's volume is enhanced by two concrete wing-like elements projecting from the lateral sides of the building and apparently supporting a balcony running the width of the first floor. On the main building, several horizontal bands run across the top of the building, increasing the height of the building without adding another storey and lending the structure a sense of monumentality. The fact that horizontal elements were added to the top floor of the building creates an effect of monumentality; these also visually connect the main structure with the intersecting volume of the stairwell. The high school's building coexists with the neighbouring chapel designed by Bernardazzi, which used to house the Museum of Atheism – a function that saved the church from demolition. Due to the particular positioning of the buildings, the area of the school and Pushkin Street has remained unbuilt, providing an open space and good visibility.

The Republic's Clinical Hospital

29, Nicolae Testemitanu Street
V. Baklanov et al.
1977

039 B

At the time it was built in 1977, the tall block of the Republic's Clinical Hospital was not just an impressive landmark situated on Malina Mica Hill; the structure also signified the new level of healthcare services being provided to the public. It was designed by the KievZNIIEP (V. Baklanov, P. Bezrodnyi, S. Yahnenko, T. Mosneaga), a state research and design institute for civil engineering in Ukraine. At the time, it was one of the largest institutes specialised in the design of buildings and structures in seismic areas. The organisation still carries out sophisticated static and dynamic field tests today. Prior to the new structure, the Republic's Clinical Hospital used to operate from a building on Spitalului ('Hospital') Street and was very similar to a provincial hospital. With this new building and the accompanying up-to-date equipment, the hospital managed to greatly improve the quality of healthcare services that it provided, perfecting and diversifying diagnostic methods, laboratory operations,

and the work of various departments. Over 181 new diagnosis and treatment methods were implemented here. The improvement in treatment quality was significant, and the wide and bright wards showed the medical system in a new light. The elongated volume of the building, underlined by the horizontal pattern of the balconies, recalls a luminous ship coming to the rescue of those adrift. Radiating a sense of purity and safety, the hospital has 15 floors, of which two with higher ceilings are used for surgical procedures. Most floors contain wards for inpatients and offer access to large and comfortable loggias. The 14th floor is entirely occupied by rooms used for various procedures and by the intensive care units. The 15th floor contains an operating theatre with a cupola on top, allowing medical students to watch operations. The hospital design included a large garden, with spaces and pathways where those convalescing could walk. The hospital's surroundings were therefore also an important consideration, with a need to provide light and air for the welfare of the patients. The Republic's Clinical Hospital currently has 795 beds in 20 specialised departments. It also serves as the clinical base for 12 university chairs, and it

B

serves as a teaching hospital for Nicolae Testemitanu State University of Medicine and Pharmacy (USMF). This function and the input of the teaching staff enable the hospital to provide modern, cutting-edge medical services. The hospital complex also includes a cardiology institute and the recently-built surgery unit. The cardiology institute is housed in a rectangular building located next to the main hospital block; together the two form a stylistically coherent ensemble.

The Chisinau International Airport
80/3, Dacia Boulevard
A. Eksner et al.
1974

The first Chisinau airport was built in 1960 and was based on a standard design that reflected a simplified socialist realist style. The design had already been implemented in Donetsk (Stalin/Stalino) in 1957. It was later replicated in Kazan and Karaganda. The first flights operating from Chisinau Airport went to Moscow, Leningrad (now St. Petersburg), Kyiv, Minsk, and cities in the Caucasus and Crimea. The design for the new airport was developed by the team at the Lenaeroproekt Institute in Leningrad led by A. Eksner. The new airport building, constructed next to the old one, increased processing capacity and fundamentally changed the image of the capital. As a symbolic gateway to Chisinau, the airport architecture suggested a new type of spatiality, different in style and functionality from the previous facility. In 1987, processing capacity reached one million passengers per year, and the Moldovan capital was connected by air to 20 destinations domestically and over 80 cities in the Soviet Union. The airport was equipped with a 3,590-metre runway – one of the longest in Eastern Europe – and operated 24 hours a day. The airport building has balanced proportions. It sits on an elevation, and the wing-like shape of its roof is visible from a distance. In terms of functionality, the building is divided into several areas. The passenger processing area is connected to the check-in desks through an elongated hallway. The top floor contains a café and a passenger lounge. A number of upgrades were made to both the interior and the exterior of the building after the airport acquired international status in 1995. Airports generally tend to be buildings that can cause an elevated level of emotional discomfort caused by the large number of passengers and the

intensity of the processes taking place. This is the reason architectural solutions for terminals aim to create a pleasant and comforting emotional environment for passengers, while using design solutions as effectively as possible in order to convey a coherent artistic image. The arrival area, once quite basic, was expanded substantially in order to accommodate an intensified level of traffic after the year 2000. The departure area was also modified in 2000 and later in 2010. The series of reconstruction projects and the extension designed by M. Eremciuc et al. (Arhiconi Grup SRL) in collaboration with HALCROW Co, UK (2000) and 'Hochtief AirPort GmbH' (2010) significantly changed the appearance of the airport. One of the walls of an extended hallway was decorated with an indoor mosaic; a stairway running along this wall led to the waiting area, from where the passengers had access to a terrace. After the reconfiguration of the spaces, the wall with the mosaic was included in the departure zone. There used to be another mosaic on a wall of the public terrace that opened towards the runway. After the airport was refurbished, access to this particular terrace was closed to the public and the mosaic disappeared, its destination unknown.

Postmodernism

The Centre for Culture and Art – Ginta Latina

18, Sfatul Tarii Street
Abram Vaysbein
1975

The building of the Centre for Culture and Art – Ginta Latina, originally designed as the House of Political Education, is located in an administrative area, set back from the central avenue in an oasis of peace and shade. The area was designed for a number of buildings that ensured the functionality of the central apparatus of the Communist Party (CP), such as the building of the Central Committee of the CP (A. Cherdantsev, G. Bosenco), the headquarters of the Central Municipal Committee (G. Solominov), and the CP Archive from the MSSR (A. Cherdantsev). This district constituted the new 'sacred area' of the city, and it was well guarded and well maintained. Several apartment blocks were built nearby specifically for party officials. The apartments were much larger (approximately 100 square metres) than standard units; they were very comfortable and had different configurations than the norm. First-class architects were selected to design the infrastructure of the general headquarters of the state leadership, and the budget was much more generous compared to other sites in the city. At the same time, the architects had no creative constraints and were encouraged to freely use their imaginations. Considerable efforts were made to finish the buildings using a wide range of materials, some of which were imported. Abram Vaysbein was one of the guiding lights of Moldovan architecture during this period. In collaboration with other colleagues, he designed a number of buildings characteristic of this phase of

Soviet modernism. He was also the designer of the apartment block type known as the 143 series, which was constructed from prefabricated panels and introduced improved apartment layouts. For this achievement, he was awarded the USSR State Prize in architecture. The building of the Centre for Culture and Arts has a prominent rectangular volume with multiple floors. Stylistically, the design of the façade places the building within the transition phase from Soviet modernism to Soviet brutalism. The block of the upper level is defined by a series of prominent triangular concrete lesenes, or pilaster strips, running around the building and jutting out over the lower level. Placed between the windows, they cause the windows of the upper two levels to appear as one vertical unit. The two upper levels are set on the glazed gallery of the ground floor, whose windows run around the perimeter of the building, giving the upper section a levitating effect. The pattern of the lesenes on the façade is altered above the entrance, where five of them are grouped more tightly together, a device that is repeated on the side façades and highlights the transparency of the ground floor. The building sits on a low base, whose delicate concrete steps lend the structure a floating effect. Functionally, the building is no different from a house of culture. A rectangular volume, with a smaller footprint than that of the rest of the building, goes beyond the level of the roof, being a natural extension of the concert hall. The ground floor contains a spacious lobby, a café, and changing rooms, and both levels have administrative and technical offices. The building is under the aegis of the Ministry of Culture, and it houses the Fara Nume Theatre ('the theatre with no name'), among other institutions.

The Republican Council of Trade Unions

129, 31 August 1989 Street
Vladislav Kudinov
1977

042 C

The unions were considered to be at the forefront of Soviet society and embodied the labour movement. Thus, the head office of the Republican Council of Trade Unions was placed in the headquarters area directly across from the Party Committee of Chisinau alongside the Central Committee of the MSSR. The Council of Trade Unions previously operated from its old headquarters, built in the 1950s (R. Kurtz) and located in the

city centre at the intersection of Stefan cel Mare Boulevard and A. Pushkin Street. During the reconfiguration of the city centre and the development of the administrative area, a new building was erected. From a distance, its façade can be associated with a succession of vertical banners resembling an agitprop display. The intermittent rhythm of the curved vertical elements aligned on the façades creates the impression of a perfect building for the work of party officials. The elongated nine-storey volume protrudes over the base of the ground floor, which has a transparent front covered with large windows. Setting the upper volume of the building apart from

the foot was a stylistic technique often used in the modernist period. Behind the building, an extension on the ground floor houses a cafeteria for employees, which is still functional after so many years. Naturally, the design of a site like this would only be assigned to an architect with very good standing in the union of architects and one possessing flawless professional qualities. Kudinov studied at the Faculty of Architecture of the Institute of Civil Engineering in Leningrad and then transferred to the Institute of Civil Engineering, Kyiv, in 1960. After graduating in 1963, he was employed at the Moldgiprostroy Institute in Chisinau, where he advanced from his position as a staff designer to become the chief project architect. His projects were well-known, although many have suffered sad fates: the Codru Hotel, built on the same street, was recently demolished, and the former Noroc Restaurant (Guguta Cafe) is currently slated for demolition as well. The Trade Union building is still standing, but when the first-floor offices were taken over by an influential businessman, the building suddenly underwent radical repairs, which altered the façade and the original characteristics of the building. These renovations were not the first. The elevators had been previously changed and turnstiles had been installed at the entrance. The building is now practically indistinguishable from an ordinary office building dating from the 2000s.

The National Opera and Ballet Theatre

043 C

152, Stefan cel Mare si Sfant Boulevard
N. Kurennoy, A. Gorshkov
1980

Due to its imposing stature, the National Opera and Ballet Theatre could easily be mistaken for the Palace of Culture, a building housing the executive city government, or even the Parliament (which actually operated here for a short while in the 1980s). The structure references the layout of a classical temple with its sober, slightly schematic formula. Although clad with marble slabs, the building still has a somewhat brutalist appearance. The design made by the Muscovite architects was based on a standard blueprint developed by the Central Institute for Scientific Research for Experimental Engineering in Moscow. The same design had also been used for the opera and ballet theatre in Vilnius. In the case of the Chisinau version, the standard design was adapted in order to find a balance between the volume of the building and the generous space allotted to the theatre by the authorities. In addition, the theatre in Vilnius is very different in terms of the aesthetic and layout of the standard blueprint. It is obvious that the Lithuanian architects produced a somewhat more sophisticated structure. The solution for the building in Chisinau was to employ simple volumes. In terms of function, it consists of a concert hall with 1,200 seats, a large lobby, as well as technical and administrative spaces on the ground floor. The elevated core structure is surrounded by a portico with delicate rectangular pillars. A broad, imposing stairway leads from the ground up to the main entrance on Stefan cel Mare Boulevard. The main façade features two white marble bas-reliefs that mirror the vertical rhythm of the columns and flank the main entrance. The reliefs portray two groups of muses (B. Dubrovin, G. Dubrovina). The white slender pillars of the portico support a massive frieze – a meander with a traditional folk motif designed by V. Novikov and produced in copper sheet. It depicts a succession of musical instruments and geometric elements in a modulated rhythm. The construction incorporated materials imported from all over the USSR – marble from the Ural mountains, granite from Karelia, light fixtures, wood and even bathroom furniture brought from countries such as Czechoslovakia and Hungary as well as regional resources, such as limestone and sandstone. A wide range of decorative

artworks were placed liberally throughout the interior, including plaster ornaments, paintings, tapestries, and ceramic works. The auditorium's walls were finished in wood. The downstairs lobby features sculpture groups representing the muses, made by Nely Sajina. As in many other architectural contexts, the 'national in shape, socialist in contents' formula was carefully emphasised by the creators here. This is also affirmed in various interior and exterior elements: not only a massive frieze with folk art elements, but also the muses of the façade and the interior, who are dressed in traditional Moldovan costumes, as found in the prints of the fine artists I. Bogdesco and F. Hamuraru. Two rectangular fountains placed in symmetry with the main entrance enlivened the extended square in front of the theatre. The downstairs spaces of the building are currently being used by private businesses (Andy's Pizza, Mojito Terassa, etc.). This situation is testimony to the precarious nature of the theatre's maintenance and financial arrangements: it has been forced to compromise its image as a high-quality cultural institution in order to survive. The empty space in front of the building is used mainly as a car park. It turns into an open-air cinema-cum-beer garden during European and global football championships and is filled with crowds.

C

Ministry of Foreign Affairs

80, 31 August 1989 Street

Gennady Solominov

1977

044 **C**

The building originally intended for the City Committee of the MSSR Communist Party is an outstanding piece of work in all respects. The offices of the City Committee were located behind the MSSR CP Central Committee next to a hotel in a removed, quiet area. Nowadays, 31 August is an avenue with heavy traffic, and the building, which is currently used by the Ministry of Foreign Affairs, is very visible and popular. It stands out due to a robust and dynamic reinforced concrete structure, which is slightly flared at the top, suggesting the shape of traditional

C

houses without their slanting roofs. The concrete structure was clad in white lime-stone. Recessed and supported by this structure is red brick-clad volume, which

seems to be suspended above the ground. The different volumes of the building suggest the symbolism of a Chinese puzzle, which contains hidden or well-guarded knowledge. As an architect, Solominov began his career in Dushanbe, Tajikistan, and was later invited to Chisinau (1967), where he worked on a number of notable projects. The monumental quality of the building was attainted through the almost sculptural use of volume, in which the architect broke with design principles of the past. Solominov brought a fresh wave and sense of liberation to the architectural scene in the MSSR through robust shapes and an aesthetic influenced by brutalist and contemporary Japanese architecture, especially the Metabolist movement (Kenzo Tange, Kisho Kurokawa, etc.). The building's exostructure forms a colonnade behind which is a glassed-in ground-floor area, which is set back from the building's perimeter. The fact that the architects opted not to use a visible concrete surface and instead chose stone cladding reflects a trend typical of the era: pairing red brick walls with large surfaces of white stone. The interior of the building features a balanced rapport between the individual rooms and light-flooded hallways, where, as on the exterior of the building, the architect aimed to create a carefully considered balance of volumes and an equilibrium between light and shadow. Today the building houses the Ministry of Foreign Affairs and it has maintained its status as an elite site. Maintenance work on the building has brought only minimal changes to the façade and the building's components.

Ministry of Agriculture, Regional Development, and Environment

045 C

162, Stefan cel Mare si Sfant Boulevard

Abram Vaysbein, Semyon Shoikhet, Alexei Chmykhov

1980

The building is located in the administrative area of the city in the neighbourhood of the Offices of the President and the Parliament, set back from the boulevard. It was specifically designed for the Ministry, formerly the Council of Kolkhozes and of the Food Processing Industry, since the latter's old building, erected in the 1950s, was no longer appropriate in terms of style and function. The new building

was, quite literally, a leap forward in time and space. In comparison to the unassuming, three-to-four-storey constructions in the city centre, the tall building of the Ministry of Agriculture stands out due to its imposing size, which rivals that of skyscrapers in various world capitals. As this is a functional structure, the designers opted for a formula that would provide enough space for all the agencies and institutions under the umbrella of the ministry. In order to keep costs down and save time, the load-bearing structure of the building was made through the continuous pouring of concrete (slip forming) – an effective and already proven method. The building has a sophisticated use of volumes: it consists of two rectangular, slightly staggered blocks connected

through a taller, also rectangular volume. The façades have a common feature: sharp 90-degree corners alternating with rounded ones, and the surfaces cross from one volume to the next. Thus, the blocks have an overall streamlined shape. The façades are clad entirely in white limestone, and the windows, placed in a stacked vertical pattern, alternate with blue plastic panel elements, on top of which are anodised aluminium profile elements. The rectangular shapes formed by the profiles enhance the verticality effect. Another interesting construction element is the base that includes the ground and first floors and connects the vertical volumes, extending beyond the footprint of the towers. The top part of this volume is accentuated by prefabricated reinforced concrete elements placed at regular intervals along the upper floor and balcony. This upper level extends out beyond the perimeter of the ground floor with its glazed façade and is supported by narrow columns. The ground level is entirely covered with windows and appears slightly withdrawn into the depths of the building. The main entrance is marked by an elaborate gateway-like configuration. The lawn between the boulevard and the building is unusually large for the staff of a public institution. However, with minimal effort it was possible to reorganise the area and make it accessible to the general public and inhabitants of the city.

Parliament of the Republic of Moldova

046 C

105, Stefan cel Mare si Sfant Boulevard

Alexander Cherdantsev, Grigorii Bosenko

1976

When the detailed master plan for the central area of the city was approved in 1971, it signalled the beginning of a new phase for the architecture of the city. This initiative attempted to overcome the 'monotony and uniformity' of the 1960s. In order to support this ambitious

programme, significant funds were allocated to finance a number of buildings. That very same year, the Moldgiprostroy Institute announced a competition for the design of the administrative building of the Central Committee (CC) of the Communist Party of Moldova (MCP). Aleksandr Cherdantsev, who at that time headed the institute's urban planning department, also took part in the competition. As the winner, Cherdantsev started designing the structure in 1972, and the project lasted several years. Although the construction was supervised by the First Secretary of the CC of the MCP, Ivan Bodiul, the building was not inaugurated until 1976, and the final budget amounted to some six million roubles – twice the amount originally allocated. For the Communist Party of the MSSR, the building represented a most important goal, and its construction used the most modern methods available at that time. In the 1970s, Moldova was also the USSR's testing ground for monolithic construction technology. In the case of the CC building, it was decided that the construction of the pillars of the central part of the building would be carried out through a continuous pouring of concrete using slip forms, so that the side blocks could be erected using the advanced method of jump forms and the rear structure would be assembled using prefabricated elements. Thus, the building process used three different construction methods. The building consists of a central section with four pillars, which extend from the ground to the roof, and two elongated wings, which each meet the central block at an angle. The overall shape of the building is that of an open book standing upright and thereby referencing the fundamental work of Marxism – Karl Marx's *Capital*. The entrance canopy and the roof are tilted upwards towards the front, creating a sense of lift-off. The façade of the building was clad with several types of stone in various shades: pink limestone with a porous texture on the walls, white limestone on the columns, and red granite on the walls of the first two levels and on the central stairway. The narrow rectangular windows of the top two levels are interspersed with thin, half-rounded pillars that extend into the roof structure, enhancing the feeling of lift and weightlessness. The interior of the building, designed by Grigorii Bosenko, was decorated in an extremely luxurious fashion. A great deal of attention was paid to the shades of wood used for the floor, for frames and doors, and for the furniture in the First Secretary's office. Multiple exterior and interior elements of the construction as well as its use of space and volume stylistically place the building in the postmodernist realm. While in the modernist period, architecture coexisted with monumental art in an organic symbiosis, sculpted elements had a different role in Soviet postmodernism, serving instead a complementary function and being volumetrically and stylistically detached from the architecture of the building itself. This is true for this building, where the figure of Karl Marx was placed next to that of Friedrich Engels (sculpted by L. Dubinovsky) on a bench located on an alley paved with red granite slabs in front of the building. However, the monument did not survive the tumultuous times of *perestroika*. It was shattered in the clashes that took place between law enforcement and the demonstrators demanding the democratisation of society. The tree-filled grounds of the building and the location far back from the boulevard line were designed to shield the structure from the noise of traffic and preserve the peace for the officials.

Ministry of Justice
82, 31 August 1989 Street
Alexander Cherdantsev
1978

The building was originally designed to house the Institute for the History of the Communist Party, affiliated with the Central Committee of the Communist Party of the MSSR. The building of the History Institute is striking due to its sophisticated use of volumes. At the time of its inauguration, it evinced an unusual combination of textures: stone finishes on the façades and polished wood on the exterior – an unexpected combination in modern architecture, where the interplay between concrete, glass, and metal tends to predominate. The volumetric solution derived by architect Cherdantsev stands out among the designs of the period. It was influenced by Scandinavian architectural practices emphasising a symbiosis between tradition and modernity. The phrase 'organic architecture' promoted by Alvar Aalto and other Finnish architects was not unfamiliar to the architects in the USSR. Cherdantsev was familiar with the designs of Finnish colleagues. Such work was known in the USSR since the 1970s, especially as a result of the 'Finland is Being Built' exhibition presented at Lenexpo (Leningrad), where Aalto's work was exhibited and where the design of Vyborg Library was upheld as exemplary. At the same time, the composition of the ministry entails clear references to the work of Le Corbusier, whose

formal processes have become part of a vocabulary embraced by architects from all continents. The façades of the building are resolved organically, so that no one is more important than another. The building is perceived as a whole, with no side predominant. The curved profile of the roof, which somehow emerges from the inside of the building, creates a unified body with the façades and changes the classic perception of the wall-roof relationship. The building was recently renovated and, unfortunately, some original characteristics were irreversibly altered. The wooden eaves were replaced with an 'alucobond' metal profile, which caused the roof to lose its continuous surface and the organic flow of its form, which was originally composed of wooden strips. A series of elements on the exterior were modified without taking their original condition into consideration. The building is also known as the Party Archive and now houses the Ministry of Justice. As a public institution, the ministry does not have the necessary budget to maintain it properly or potentially invest in preserving the structure as architectural heritage.

C

The Palace of the Republic

16, Maria Cebotari Street
Ivan Zagoretsky, Alexander Shevtsov, Mikhail Orlov, Stanislav Makarchuk
1984

The building is located in the city's administrative district. It was initially designed as Friendship Hall and stands out due to the exuberance and eclecticism of its exterior, which is complemented by the abundant decor on its inside. The entrance portal is modelled on an ancient gateway, having a festive air. At the same time, it makes a reference to the façade of a traditional Moldovan house, specifically to the *casa mare* ('the good room') as the centre of hospitality in the private home. The main entrance is highlighted by a glazed gallery on two floors, restrained by the imposing structure of the portal. The rest of the building has vertical niches decorated with glass and other ornamental elements. The fact that the Palace of the Republic consists of several volumes with façades and elements of the most diverse shapes and textures makes the viewer wonder whether its designers deliberately used every means of expression available at the time. The availability of imported materials does not seem to have been an issue: from dark glass and anodised aluminium to granite and marble in a wide range of hues. All these elements were the result of the work done by the team led by Ivan Zagoretsky. This team was not only responsible for the design of the building and its luxurious halls, but also decorative art and monumental artworks that made the building into a veritable art museum collection. Ivan Zagoretsky began his career in Tselinograd (Astana/Nur-Sultan),

Kazakhstan, and in 1964 he moved to Chisinau, where he worked for the Moldgiprostroy Institute – first as an architect, then as a team leader, and later as the head of the number one design department from 1986. The design and construction of a new venue for events was intended to coincide with the celebration of the MSSR's 60th anniversary. As to be expected, this was a project for extremely demanding customers. The result is a luxurious complex with a suite of audience halls (seating 550, 80, 40, and 30), a hotel, a cafeteria, and rooms for technical facilities. The complex has an inner courtyard with a fountain accessible to hotel guests. The building has two entrances: the main entrance on Maria Cebotari and the hotel entry on Nicolae Iorga. For a while, the building hosted the Eugen Ionesco theatre, and this is currently where the Onisifor Ghibu library operates. The lobbies of the main audience hall and hotel were adorned with artificially lighted stained-glass panels, while other rooms were decorated with works produced by visual artists. The staircases have works of decorative art – compositions in ceramic and glass – and the main hall features a monumental ceramic mural designed by L. Iantsen and produced in collaboration with E. Saakov. While the Parliament building was being renovated (2009–2014) following the devastation caused by the events of 7 April 2009, Moldova's so-called Twitter Revolution, the assemblies were held in the top floor auditorium of the Palace. The venue is used today for large-scale events, from international conferences to weddings and private parties.

The State Circus

049 C

38, Grigore Vieru Boulevard
Alla Kirichenko, Semyon Shoikhet
1984

The building on Visterniceni Hill, surrounded by a suburb, is a singular public edifice with a sophisticated silhouette assembled from elements with a futuristic, sci-fi air. Visterniceni Hill, a suburb of Chisinau in the nineteenth century, is now involved in an unevenly matched competition with real estate developers who have gained a foothold there through the construction of a gigantic housing complex. The circus originated from funds allotted by the USSR's top leadership for the development of a number of buildings on the occasion of the city's 530th anniversary.

Around the same time, the Union's State Circuses Association (Soyuzgostsirk) proposed building a structure with a standard design that had also been realised in other cities (such as Ryazan, Kursk, Kemerovo, etc.). The engineering work for the final design was carried out by the Moldgyprostroy Institute after the institute's team persuaded the leadership of the USSR's Ministry of Culture to agree to an alternative design made from scratch. The building was originally supposed to be built using the continuous pouring of concrete (slip forming) method, but the allotted funds were insufficient. The next option was to assemble it from prefabricated concrete structures and install a façade made of metal structures. The design process took a long time, and after a host of revisions and recalculations, it finally came to an end in 1979. Construction work did not start for another year. Eventually, the building was inaugurated in 1984, on another anniversary – 60 years since the establishment of the USSR. The contours of the building's layout, reminiscent of a Star

Trek star ship, consisted of two components: the performance area and the administrative segment. The entire building is partially inserted into the slope of the hill. Part of the administrative area and most of the auxiliary and technical rooms are located in the basement. The administrative block has two levels and two closed-off inner courtyards. The main section, hosting the performances, is the most expressive in terms of its use of space and volume. It has a lobby, dressing rooms, ticket booths, administration offices, restrooms, and utility rooms. The main audience door is in the basement; from there, spectators have access to the theatre and the arena. The next floor (at ground level) contains an entrance to the audience hall, a buffet, restrooms, a circular lobby, and an exit to a circular terrace offering views of the city. The circus' auditorium features an arena measuring 13 metres in diameter, amphitheatre seats, a stage, an orchestra pit, and a cupola. The zigzag of the pillars running around the perimeter creates a dynamic pattern, a geometrical motif influenced by the ornamentation of the local traditional costumes. The trapezoidal panels on the balcony line and at the top of the façade appear to be stylised borrowings from the local traditional architecture. The roof is capped with a structure plated with zinc, recalling a radio transmitter. This underscores the building's futuristic quality, while still complementing the geometric texturing of the cupola. The façade elements, clad in local natural materials, add weight to the architecture, while also highlighting various constructive elements. Highlighting the purpose of the building, the sculpture of a circus clown above the main entrance was installed as late as 1988. Inside, the walls are covered with murals (encaustic paintings) and ceramic panels. A significant dose of circus-themed monumental art complemented the architecture. The circus closed for renovations in 2004, but work was suspended due to insufficient funding and the building fell into disrepair. The training arena was repaired in 2014, and the small arena opened later that year and the circus relaunched.

The Central Bus Station

58, Mitropolit Varlaam Street
Ivan Zagoretski
1974

050 C

The ensemble of the Central Bus Station is a work of modernist architecture that has survived despite the unfavourable circumstances leading many others to disappear without a trace. The complex includes a building and the adjacent open area with platforms arranged around the building's perimeter. The terminal is one of the three major stations in Chisinau, with a capacity for 800 passengers. It is located in the central district of the city, directly behind the Central Market. For a long time, the station served domestic passenger transit within the Republic of Moldova (mainly providing access to the towns surrounding Chisinau) and international traffic (Ukraine, Romania etc.). It has been expanded, altered, and adapted countless times in order to accommodate increasing demand and passenger numbers. The elongated rectangular volume of the station is divided into a waiting hall and administrative offices. A vertical volume intersects the horizontal block. Framing the stairwell to the upper floors and roof, its side walls terminate in a sloping angle that accentuates an upward movement. From the original plans, one can infer that the roof was originally conceived to feature an open terrace with a panoramic view on the city, but this never materialised past the design stage. In terms of structure, the frame of the building was assembled from prefabricated reinforced concrete elements. The façade was clad according to

C

the same principle, leaving the joints visible. The station building includes a waiting room, ticket booths, storage rooms, various shops, an information desk, a barbershop, and administrative offices. Access to the top floor cafeteria – currently used as office space – was originally via an elegant stairway cast in reinforced concrete. In keeping with the trends of the time, the wall of the waiting hall is covered with a monumental mosaic presenting the city under construction, with some of the buildings already finished – an emblematic memento of a certain stage in the city's development. The idealised representation of the city blossoming with the new buildings is countered today by the current development boom and chaotic urban planning. In terms of style, the original concrete brise-soleil structure that used to cover the waiting hall has been removed. The epic mosaic, the profile of the indoor stairway, and the zigzag placement of the platforms are all characteristic of the modernist period, whereby the building adheres to the formula for utilitarian constructions of this era. The station recently underwent major renovation works. As a result, its style and colour scheme have been altered. The façade has been clad entirely in alucobond-type sheeting, and the platforms have been covered with a peculiar-looking, armour-like metal sheeting.

The State University of Moldova

60, Alexei Mateevici Street
Bronislav Morgun, Alexandr
Cherdantsev, Leonid Voronin
1987

The newer five-storey building of the State University of Moldova is located in the city quarter outlined by A. Mateevici, M. Kogalniceanu, Banulescu Bodoni, and A. Pushkin Streets. Set below street level, the building is accessed through a footbridge from A. Mateevici Street. There is also a ground floor entrance accessible from Banulescu Bodoni Street, which leads past the auditoriums to the entry doors under the footbridge. In terms of composition, the building is characterised by an elongated, S-shaped block interrupted by a vertical volume. Placed in front of this are three detached rectangular volumes that house the auditoriums. These are set in staggered positions on a diagonal to the main building and are connected on the ground floor. There is a large lobby with a café inside

the main building, and the top floors contain the classrooms and the offices of the teaching staff. While the exterior of the building is plain, the interior is downright austere. The circumstances of the design and construction process at the time cannot be compared with those of the present. There were restrictions on the use of construction and finishing materials; often materials were in short supply. In order to obtain quality results, designers were forced to engage in a certain degree of subterfuge. For instance, they would initially get minimal budgets for finishes approved, and then later on when the construction was drawing to a close, they would plead before the USSR State Committee for Construction and Architecture (Gosgrazhdanstroy) to have additional resources allotted for more interesting, better-quality materials. A fine aluminium grid covers the façade, recalling the brise-soleils used in the modernist era. Here the metal structure has a more prosaic role, merely serving as a visual accent for a utilitarian building. The grid consists of

overlapping rectangular elements made of gold-coloured anodised aluminium, providing a protective shield for the high loggia created by the set-back windows of the upper three storeys. The main entrance to the top floor was altered and covered in alucobond panels; it currently looks as if it were affixed to the building as an afterthought, since it is completely different from the rest of the edifice. According to an official city development plan created during the Soviet era, the entire area between the university and the Republican Stadium was supposed to be demolished in order to make room for the expansion of the university complex. However, economic stagnation meant that the plans had to be minimised, and the remaining funds were redirected towards less ambitious projects and buildings. Thus, the university complex remained within its original quarter, its only extension being this particular brutalist building, which is connected to the modernist university building designed by I. Shmurun and A. Sobolev in 1967.

C

The Railway Workers' Palace of Culture

052 C

2, Decebal Boulevard
Semyon Shoikhet, Abram Veysbein, Tatiana Lomova
1980

The Railway Workers' Palace of Culture is one of a kind. Housing one of the city's most complex cultural infrastructures, the building is located on an elevated terrace at the intersection of Decebal and Gagarin Boulevards. It was built according to a design by Semyon Shoikhet resulting from a competition organised by the Moldgiprostroy Institute. Built in 1973, the ensemble is stylistically poised at the juncture between Soviet modernism and postmodernism. In 1983, some 40 amateur dance troupes and numerous clubs and initiatives operated in the Palace of Culture. In terms of appearance, the building's spatial concept is influenced by constructivist architecture, although the general image of the building is dominated by the limestone and brick facing of the façades. It is regrettable that the rough and expressive concrete surfaces typical of the modernist era were abandoned in favour of this trend towards surface decoration. The ensemble of the Palace of Culture consists of a

main block used for concerts and events and a secondary structure designated for sports and workshops. The two volumes are connected on the second floor through a flat curved footbridge set on

columns, whose shape recalls the gears of an engine. Other elements of the main building, such as the grids on the ventilation shafts and the gear-like outline of the double bands of brickwork encircling the upper levels of the façade, enhance the industrial aesthetic of the building. This jagged pattern is carried over into the footbridge, which rests on a row of columns with shapes and detailing suggesting the form of a wrench. The vertical element of the main building, which houses the staircase, adds to the unusual appearance of the building. Leading from the front plaza, three separate flights of steps provide access to the main building, the terrace beneath the footbridge, and the secondary building. The complex is currently managed by the Moldovan Railway Company, and it is still used by various sports and dance ensembles. It has a concert hall/cinema with a capacity for 380 people, where public conferences and events are held. The main building also contains a winter garden with tall palm trees and other tropical plants. The secondary structure has a dozen rooms for workshops and clubs, two libraries, and two gyms. The wide plaza in front of the complex is planted with trees and shrubs and has a network of footpaths. At its centre is a circular fountain featuring an abstract sculpture in the shape of a stylised flower (sculptor: Valeriu Rotari).

The Cosmos Hotel

2, Constantin Negruzzi Boulevard
B. Banykin, I. Kolbayeva
1983

Prominently visible along the axis of Y. Gagarin Boulevard, the Cosmos Hotel is a visual landmark in the city centre. It stands at the juncture where Negruzzi and Cantemir Boulevards diverge. Designed by a team of architects from Leningrad, the hotel soon became a recognisable building for anyone entering the city from the railway station or travelling by bus from the airport. At the time, the space programme became part of the agenda driving the sweeping political reforms launched by Nikita Khrushchev – an impetus that powered most of the USSR's great achievements. Under Khrushchev, the fist man-made satellite, Sputnik, was launched and the first cosmonaut, Yuri Gagarin, was sent into space. The exploration of space simultaneously became a recurring motif in design and architecture. Soon residential buildings and public edifices began resembling interplanetary spaceships, satellites, and flying saucers. Yuri Gagarin Boulevard was given its name precisely during this trend, and when the Cosmos Hotel was built, the exploration of the universe was still a major subject of speculation. However, the cosmic theme did not materialise in the building's structure or in any monumental artworks associated with it, as one might expect. Instead, it was merely reflected in the hotel's name and logo, which included neon stars. The 18-storey hotel was commissioned in 1983. The design process had lasted a long time, and construction had stretched over the period of a decade. Today, striking elements of the building include its façade, with the grid of its balconies creating a chessboard pattern. The unusual effect is obtained by the alternation of sets of windows with and without balconies. The building is topped by a volume with broad windows, which was designed as a café with a panoramic view of the city. An upward tilting canopy roof covers the café space. Set slightly to one side, it lends the hotel an iconic accent. Extending beyond the footprint of the high-rise structure, the ground floor and the first floor form an elongated volume, which houses the lobby, the restaurant, and technical and administrative spaces. One side formerly contained a very popular bar, which could be entered from Negruzzi Boulevard. The rectangular block of the restaurant space dynamically overhangs the ground floor. Its façade is a continuous glazed surface, and the framing is accented by four highlighted incisions, which lend it a brutalist air. The side opposite the base was extended in 2002 with a shopping centre

C

annex, known as the Grand Hall, which was expanded considerably in 2011 and thereby visually competes with and distorts the hotel's complex. It is now no longer possible to admire the hotel without associating it with the shopping centre. This is hopefully a somewhat temporary (reversible) arrangement. In 2007 the complex suffered economic difficulties, which had unforeseeable consequences. The hotel was first privatised and then sold to a new owner in 2011. This precarious situation may result in the disappearance of an exceptional architectural feature of Chisinau's urban landscape.

City Hospital for Children Nr. 1 054 C

7, Serghei Lazo Street
Gennady Solominov
1972

Designed between 1968 and 1969 and erected in 1972, the hospital demonstrates a form of spatial organisation that places it firmly within the avant-garde of architectural practice in the MSSR. The building is a rare example of a jagged blueprint that recalls the teeth of a saw and emphasises the diagonal axes. The architect opted for an architectonic solution in which the building almost seems to have unfurled itself, staggering its balconies to face the sun. Contrary to the modernist practice of protecting the façade exposed to the most sunlight with a dynamic grid (a brise-soleil), solar protection was achieved here by repositioning the rooms. In terms of typology, the building introduces to the city a type of structure usually found at the seashore: the windows and the balconies all face the same direction. This ensures better cooling for the rooms during the summer due to the shade provided by the balconies and the heat being absorbed by the side walls. In terms of construction, the building does not entail any innovations, as the load-bearing structure is a carcass built from prefabricated components. Panels were added to this skeleton in a manner that left certain walls open – gaps that were then filled with limestone and brick. The constructive solution chosen for the balconies has a rather expressive quality: the reinforced concrete elements that support the base and front panels of the balconies are interlocked in a manner reminiscent of wooden joints. This element originates from traditional architecture, but it was also an aesthetic used in the modern Japanese architecture of the 1960s. This effect is enhanced by rain gutter elements above the windows and the balconies. The almost ephemeral welded metal structure placed on the sides of the balconies was also part of the modernist aesthetic. Vines were supposed to climb on them and bring a green accent to a façade dominated by the white of the limestone. Enhancing the intended greenery of the building's surroundings, the landscaped area between Bucuresti Street and the building was equipped with a fountain whose style matched that of the building, and the ensemble was complemented by abstract concrete shapes filled with earth and decorative plants. The building contains many innovative details and solutions introduced by the architect, such as the tall, narrow windows at the joints between the walls, which bring light into the corridor spaces deeper within the building. The interiors

of the building follow the structure of the façade, having a configuration that is slightly puzzling without being uncomfortable. The load-bearing structure is highlighted and is an integral part of the volumes of the corridors. The main street entrance, unlike the auxiliary entry from the courtyard, is very striking in terms of its shape and expressive form. It is showcased by a massive protruding frame – an extension of the building's architecture into sculpture. The hospital was recently renovated. It is the first medical institution in the country to be completely weatherproofed, and the roof, basement, façade, and boiler rooms are now covered with an exterior cladding, which has unfortunately transformed and distorted the appearance of the building.

The House of Nationalities

109/1, Alexei Mateevici Street
Yuri Tumanyan, Victor Yavorsky
1982

055 C

Conceived to serve multifunctional purposes, the building designed for the House of Friendship with Foreign Countries was ambitious in scope and expression. With its sharp angles and ascending and descending lines, the building seems to reference the sacred architecture of a hermetic culture. The futuristic silhouette of the building originated from a period in which architects were obsessed with experimenting with the potential shapes and properties of reinforced concrete. In 1975, Yuri Tumanyan was invited to Chisinau

as the head architect of the municipal Chisinauproiect Institute, which used to be one of the leading ventures of the USSR State Committee for Construction and Architecture (Gosgrazhdanstroy) for the design of reinforced concrete buildings. The House of Nationalities was planned in 1985 at around the same time as when Tumanyan headed the reorganisation of the Cosmonauților ('Cosmonauts') Boulevard. A consummate professional, he was obsessed with perfecting every detail, and the projects he managed to realise in that particular period earned him high acclaim. The façades of the building are clad in limestone, and the curved cantilevers supporting the sharply slanting roof are made from reinforced concrete. Had the designers relied even more on exploiting visible concrete surfaces, the building might have had a better chance of being considered an exceptional work of Soviet brutalism. The interior of the building is decorated with marble, with other kinds of stone providing other nuanced tones, but white remains the dominant colour. The main entrance is the most dynamic and expressive. Jutting out from the main corpus of the building, its dominant form is complemented by other volumes and angled surfaces. This

C

pyramid-like volume houses one of the auditoriums in the building. Designed in order to enhance the policy that dominated the USSR in Brezhnev's era – in which culture and diversity were fully implemented as political instruments – the House of Friendship was aimed to serve as a ziggurat of cultures and nations. The building has several halls for conferences, cultural events, and receptions, as well as offices and rooms for educational activities.

The large space between the edifice and Mateevici Street is now used as a car park. The back façade faces one end of Valea Morilor Park and from here spectacular vistas of the lake are available from the top floor terrace. The relationship between the building and its surrounding greenery has not been sufficiently explored, despite the fact that two flights of stairs connect the ground floor to a square that corresponds with the park.

The Republican Centre for Children and Youth (ARTICO)

056 C

169, Stefan cel Mare si Sfant Boulevard
Kiev ZNIIEP Institute for Research and Design
1986

This complex facing Stefan cel Mare Boulevard was designed by the Kiev ZNIIEP Institute for Research and Design in order to house the Pioneers' Palace and was built between 1983 and 1986. The construction process was interrupted by the political stagnation and the economic breakdown of the 1980s. In the 1990s, another period of stagnation and economic troubles, the building fell into the hands of private investors, who took advantage of legal loopholes and a power gap in the local government, at a time when government authorities lost control over public buildings. For more than a decade, the building housed a business centre, where space was leased to various companies and merchants. The building was designed as a lightweight and semi-transparent structure elevated on columns and set on the slope of a hill. Two remarkable characteristics of the structure include its orientation towards the Dendrariu ('Arboretum')

Park and the step-like organisation of the building's volumes. In fact, the orientation of the ensemble towards the park was one of the advantages posed by the site that the architects exploited most successfully, even if their approach to volume was not as well conceived. One example is the section of the complex containing the observatory, which consists of three blocks with two storeys each. An open platform connects it with the main body of the Pioneers' Palace, thus integrating the structure into the surrounding park. The other, lower end of the building, which follows the same layout, consists of a sequence of rectangular blocks organised on a diagonal, which were intended as gathering places for clubs and workshops. The structure was built using prefabricated reinforced concrete elements, and the walls are made of brick and limestone. The façade, clad in polychrome anodised aluminium panels, also has large glazed segments – a solution that aptly plays with the contrast of voids and solids. After political reconfigurations and a reassessment of public spaces and facilities, a decision was made to terminate the contract with the new owners and renationalise the complex. In 2007, the Republican Centre for Children and Youth

(the ARTICO Centre) was established, and it was lavishly inaugurated in 2008. The centre was the consolidation of the National Creative Palace for Children and Teenagers, the Young Tourists' Centre, the Republican Centre of Young Naturalists, and the Pupils' Centre for Technical and Scientific Creation, which today operate as departments of the ARTICO. Following reconstruction works in 2007, the building's appearance was redesigned and completely altered. The main façade of ARTICO faces the boulevard and an open terrace area leads to the entrance here.

One of several new elements added during the renovations includes the pyramid-like structure enclosing the entrance and the gaudy plastic cladding of the façade with the staircase made of metal piping. Meanwhile, the observatory has fallen into decay and is veritably dilapidated, in stark contrast to the centre. In terms of function, the ARTICO promotes good practices and programmes in terms of extra-curricular offerings, aiming at strengthening and bringing together communities of children, youth, and educators, just as the original centre intended.

Kentford Business Centre

202, Stefan cel Mare si Sfant Boulevard
Architects not identified
1984

Visible from the central axis of Calea Iesilor Street, the building is a dominant landmark on Cantemir Plaza. The main tower is a three-part volume: a central volume is flanked by two volumes that connect to it at an angle in a manner recalling an open book. An open terrace consisting of a structure of thin frames, which is an extension of the vertical ribs of the façade, occupies the entire area of the roof. The delicate framework of the terrace outlines the volume of the building. On the ground floor, the building features a horizontal structure extending out from the footprint of the tower. This transparent semi-circular gallery with a glazed front contains the lobby. The side facing Stefan cel Mare Boulevard has a rectangular, two-storey annex that connects to the low gallery. The building carcass is a reinforced concrete structure, whose lateral exterior walls were made of prefabricated panels. On the original façade, the rows of windows are alternated with bands of coloured plastic panelling, a pattern replicated across the entire surface. The aluminium frame windows form a giant grid across the façade, while metal vertical ribs add accent and structure. The building is an example of how a rigid concrete structure can be made to seem less massive through the addition of affordable lightweight materials. When the city redrew its urban plans, approving a new master plan in 1969, Cantemir Boulevard (then Frunze Boulevard) was meant to extend across

the old city and reach Cantemir Plaza. In order to symbolically mark the site, the roundabout in front of the centre was supposed to hold a monument to M. Frunze (which was never produced). After 2000, a proposal circulated to feature a monument to Dimitrie Cantemir there. The plan first foresaw that the monument be installed in the square in front of the building, but later on it was decided that the roundabout was more appropriate and more visible from all of the converging roads. In order to ensure access to the planned monument, the roundabout had already been connected to the surrounding footpaths through a network of underground pedestrian passageways (architect: M. Rusu), which were decorated with mosaics (artist: F. Hamuraru). The passageways currently lead to an empty surface. The square in front of the building has been the subject of a heated debate related to the construction of an Orthodox church with a necropolis for the capital's wealthy elite. After urban activists sounded the alarm about this misappropriation of public property, the building permit was withdrawn and the square remained intact. Today the annex facing Stefan cel Mare Boulevard contains a restaurant (Andy's Pizza), while the tower houses various companies and media agencies.

C

Casa Radio ('Teleradio-Moldova' Public Company)

1, Miorita Street
Architects not identified
1974

The Teleradio-Moldova Company was established in 1940–1941 at a time when radio services were coordinated by the Committee for Radio Networks and Radio Broadcasting within the MSSR Soviet of People's Commissars. The first television broadcast in Moldova took place in 1958 from a studio built in the 1950s. That particular TV complex, located on Hancesti Road at the intersection of Lech Kaczyński Street, housed the administrative offices, television studios, editing rooms, and the actual broadcasting antenna. Between 1957 and 1989, television and radio broadcasting was coordinated by the various MSSR Committees. The National Radio and Television Broadcasting Service was created in 1990. The building on Miorita Street, nicknamed Casa Radio ('Radio House') was built in the 1970s. It consists of a nine-storey vertical block connected to a rectangular block on two levels, with recording studios, editing rooms, offices, an archive, and administrative spaces. The load-bearing structures of each volume are assembled from prefabricated reinforced-concrete elements, and the façades are made of concrete panels with vertical ribs. Horizontal rows of windows alternate with bands of white concrete panels on the façade of the high-rise structure. The top floor is much taller than the others, and it houses the technical equipment. The window casings are accentuated by thin concrete lesenes running the height of the building and visually accentuating its verticality. The

ground floor is covered in black marble slabs, and the platform of the complex is made of red granite. As a building with a utilitarian function, the architecture forgoes any sophisticated use of volumes. However, its sober, even ascetic character as well as the monumental art on the façades give it character and situate it within the modernist style. The entrance on the first floor previously featured a bas-relief made of stainless steel – one of the few works of abstract sculpture in the city's architecture programme with such a high quality of expression and execution. It consisted of convex elements representing the shape of radio waves. The annex on Miorita Street used to house the employee canteen, which is currently rented by a private operator. The main façade of the annex is covered in limestone, and the side façades repeat the pattern of the main block. The annex also features another exceptional artwork: a mosaic mural with three-dimensional stainless-steel elements, repeating the motif of the waves found at the entrance. The building was renovated in the 2000s without any major alterations. However, the stainless-steel piece at the entrance suffered a less fortunate fate and was replaced by a new logo made of alucobond-type sheeting.

C

The Romanita Tower Block
29, Arheolog Ion Casian-
Suruceanu Street
Oleg Vronski, Octavian Blogu,
Serghei Krani
1986

 059 C

The high-rise, with its one-of-a-kind silhouette, stands on a hill in Valea Trandafirilor ('Rose Valley') Park; note that the Cardiology Institute and the Republican Clinical Hospital are on the north-western side of the park. This type of building was not a novelty in the former USSR. Comparable towers were built in Minsk and Kyiv; also noteworthy is the Yerevan Youth Palace (S. Khachikyan, H. Poghosyan et al.) in Armenia, which was very similar in structure to the Romanita Tower and called *Krtsats-Kukuruz* (Armenian for 'gnawed corn cob'). Built a decade prior to the Romanita Tower, it was demolished in 2006. The original technical brochure issued by the Chisinauproiect Institute states that the Moldovan building was meant to be a dormitory with separate rooms and shared infrastructure. The building operated as such until 1997. According to the authors, the building was supposed to be part of an ambitious project of the Soviet Union's Ministry of Construction. Apart from the spectacular 22-floor tower block, the complex was intended to include a banquet hall, a cinema, a gymnasium, and a library. The comprehensive project was only realised in part, and construction of the block faced many difficulties and delays. Although it was designed in 1978, actual construction work did not start until 1984. Later on, after many of the apartments had been sold to private owners in the 1990s, the tower's status was changed to that of residential building. In terms of its use of space and volume, the building consists of a cylindrical block featuring 16 floors with apartments and four lower floors with auxiliary spaces (planned as laundry, drying, and cleaning rooms, as well as utility rooms). The layout of the apartments is based on the principle of a unit

with two rooms connected through a hallway, and a bathroom, with six such units on each floor. Each floor was supposed to be equipped with a shared kitchen and dining room. In the 1990s, the shared-space concept was abandoned, and the apartments were reconfigured as autonomous units. The load-bearing structure is a monolith that entails a sequence of rings, each 40 cm thick, which connected through a network of radial walls 20 cm thick – the same thickness as the plates between the floors. The structure was built through the continuous pouring of reinforced concrete (slip forming). In order to obtain the stability adequate for the seismic features of the area, the block was placed on a base and a foundation consisting of a solid plate of reinforced concrete (engineer: A. Marian). The silhouette of the Romanita block is eye-catching due to the wavy profile of the loggias, a movement which flows from one unit to the next, creating a continuous pattern. The repetitive elements of the loggias – prefabricated cast concrete components – form a brutalist-style armour, the architectural feature that has captured the attention of architects and fans of Soviet modernism in recent years and has brought the building online fame. The top two floors of the building form a circular structure that could be mistaken for a spaceship that is just resting for a moment on the cylindrical block. The wavy pattern of the loggias appears to be a symbiosis of these two elements, crystallised in concrete. The top two levels of the block provide a panoramic view of the city, but otherwise form an impractical structure that is not readily accessible. Although it had been placed on the axis of Independent Street (Botanica district), the visibility of the building is now compromised by a church placed at the corner of the street and a crowded housing complex, both built after the year 2000. Due to developers wishing to achieve as much profit as possible, a host of apartment blocks have crowded out the Romanita Tower, gradually concealing its iconic architecture.

C

The 'Yuri Gagarin' Republican Youth Centre

1, Melestiu Street
Nikolay Klyushnikov
1972

This complex, consisting of several interlocking block-like volumes, was originally meant to house activities of a political, cultural, and educational nature. Construction began in 1970, and the building was made possible by funds raised by Komsomol members and other young citizens during so-called *subbotniks* (groups who worked on public projects on the weekends and volunteered their pay). Located in Valea Trandafirilor Park (originally V. Lenin Park), the Youth Centre, together with the Railway Workers' Palace of Culture, formed a complex infrastructure designed for workers' families and young people in the Central and Botanica districts. After Muncesti Boulevard was renamed Yuri Gagarin Boulevard to mark the first manned flight into outer space, the Youth Centre followed the same trend a decade later. In the 1970s, space exploration was on the rise, and it inspired the names of multiple sites in the city – including the Cosmos Hotel (B. Banykin, I. Kolbayeva) built in 1983. In the case of the Youth Centre, this inspiration was not only in name; the main façade features a monumental mosaic, *Cosmic Ploughman* by Aurel David, an artist who developed a special mosaic technique using shards of industrially manufactured polychrome glass. A bust of Gagarin was installed in the generous lobby; together with the architecture of the ceiling, it created a celestial ensemble. The centre has a spacious lobby featuring a gallery on the upper floor and fountains on the ground

floor, an audience hall for large events (800 seats), a concert hall (400 seats), ballet studios and gymnasiums, as well

as facilities for various clubs and thematic activities. The complex also used to include the Trandafir Hotel, the Valea Trandafirilor Restaurant, and a library. The Trandafir Hotel belonged to the Sputnik Bureau of International Travel for Youth run by the Komsomol's Central Committee and mostly used to host foreign travellers. Designed at the Moldgiprograjdanselistroy Institute, the complex consists of a five-storey tower set perpendicularly on an elongated lateral block with a glazed front. The tower volume includes the foyer and juts out from the lateral volume with the wall covered by the mosaic, which constitutes the central element, around which the restaurant and the hotel are aligned. The restaurant is set back and runs perpendicular to the hotel block. The elongated space of the lobby has strips of windows, while the restaurant's façades feature strips of windows framed by aluminium profiles. The load-bearing structure consists of a framework of reinforced concrete elements. The walls are made of brick and limestone extracted from the local vicinity. After 1991, the building of the Youth Centre was privatised. Concerts and fashion shows were organised here, and the MALS disco later opened in the centre and remained active until the year 2000. Around that time, a new owner terminated all activities, and the building began to decay.

Soviet Brutalism

073

065

0   1 km

Bogdan Voievod Str.

Moscovei Ave.

Alecu Russo Str.

Kiev Str.

Renasterii Nationale Ave.

Calea Iesilor Str.

080

Ion Creanga Str.

Stefan cel Mare si Sfant Ave.

Aleksei Shciusev Str.

Alexandru Lapusneanu Str.

Aleksei Shciusev Str.

Stefan cel Mare si Sfant Ave.

Approx.
3 km

Toma Ciorba Str.

Mitropolitul Petru Movila Str.

Serghei Lazo Str.

Sfatul Tarii Str.

062

Bucuresti Str.

Maria Cebotari Str.

31 August, 1989 Str.

Stefan cel Mare si Sfant Ave.

Aleksei Shciusev Str.

Livezilor Str.

074

Nicolae Iorga Str.

Mitropolit Gavriil Banulescu-Bodoni Str.

Aleksandr Puskin Str.

Piata Marii

Adunari Nationale

061

Vlaicu Parcalab Str.

Mihai
Eminescu

Aleksandr Puskin Str.

Aleksei Shciusev Str.

079

Onisifor Ghibu Str.

Alba-Iulia Str.

0   200 m

Sucevita Str.

Parts Str.

Alba-Iulia Str.

Ion Pelivan Str.

The Chisinau Directorate for Culture and the Licurici Theatre

061 D

68, Bucuresti Street
Yuri Tumanyan, Oleg Vronsky
1986

According to original project documents, this building, with its unattractive façade but an expressive use of volume, was designed to host the Victoria, a horticultural production and research institute. In terms of function, one section of the building was designated for production and laboratories. It was connected to a specialised sales area and a hall for exhibiting samples. However, the building's purpose was abruptly changed during the construction process just before the building was inaugurated. In 1985, the country's leadership was concerned about the problems facing young people. It decided to have the building reconfigured and turned into the Palace of Youth, repurposing the extension on 31 August Street for the Licurici Puppet Theatre. Thus, the planners and builders from the Grazhdanstroy Institute were forced to remodel the already completed facilities to accommodate the newly assigned purpose. This included building a stage and an auditorium in an extension that was inappropriate for a theatre. According to the master plan, the cultural district of the city comprised three museums and a number of public buildings: the Opera Theatre, the Cathedral (the Artists' Union Exhibition Hall prior to 1989), the Chekhov Theatre, the Philharmonic Society, the Eminescu Theatre, and the Organ Hall. The Palace of Youth and the Licurici Theatre were meant to round out the cultural offerings of this area. In the 1990s, the Palace of Youth came under the jurisdiction of the city's Directorate for Culture, which installed its offices in the building. The remaining spaces were rented out to cultural enterprises (jazz bands, folk music collectives, publishers, etc.). Around the same time, the facilities situated between the theatre and the directorate's offices, as well as rooms on the ground floor, were rented out to businesses – a casino, bars, and

nightclubs. This created a maze of parasitic spaces, distorting the appearance of both the building and the adjacent structures. The building consists of three interconnected volumes. The main structure, a slender, six-storey block, has an unusual configuration, in which its two side wings are angled so as to partially embrace the theatre complex behind it. At the front of the building, the first two floors accent the main entrance; the upper floor forms a massive windowless projection over the entry and transitions into a series of staggered window modules creating a zigzag form across the front of each side wing.

The second block is shorter, with a rectangular footprint. It serves as a connector between the section housing the directorate and the Licurici Theatre. The theatre wing consists of four symmetrically arranged octagonal elements with a space in the middle. The theatre walls are clad in a combination of white and pink limestone. In terms of layout, the three volumes form a pictogram resembling a flower with two leaves at the base. The façade of the volume facing Bucuresti Street looks like the head of an enormous robot. The rows of windows on its façade are outlined by aluminium profiles, which are then also used as cladding to create bands of aluminium alternating with the windows. Enclosing the building along the roof and sides is a giant frame-like overhang lacking windows and covered in a combination of white and pink limestone. At the front of the building, the presence of an underground space is indicated by several vents emerging from the ground, whose volumes complement the shape of the building. At some point, the square in front of the directorate was turned into a car park, which prevented pedestrians from being able to walk past the building and employees from using the area during breaks. As of 2008, however, the artistic community reclaimed the area and turned it into a venue for various public events, which gave the square back its function as a genuinely public space. Part of an ongoing effort to reoccupy public spaces in the city included in the artistic work of Flat Space/Apartmentul Deschis (designed by Stefan Rusu), which was installed on the square by the Oberliht Association as part of the Chiosc Project and supported by the Architecture Department and the Directorate for Culture.

The Moldovan Presidential Office Building

062 D

154, Stefan cel Mare si Sfant Boulevard

Yuri Tumanyan, Arkady Zaltsman, Viktor Yavorsky

1987

The Presidential Office Building for the Republic of Moldova (originally the Presidium of the MSSR Supreme Soviet) is located in the administrative district on the central boulevard – ironically, across the road from the Parliament building (the former Central Committee of the MSSR CP). The building, with its cubist volumes, was built during *perestroika* in the interval between 1984 and 1987, a period marked by political transformations. Tumanyan assembled the project team while working as the chief architect of the newly established Kishinevgorproiekt Engineering Institute (Chisinauproiect), which he had been invited to join in 1975. Tumanyan had previously studied at the Faculty of Architecture of the Polytechnic Institute in Tashkent and had then been active in Kazakhstan at the Kazgorstroyproiect and Almaatagiprogor engineering institutes. During that period, he developed the master plans of several cities, such as Kustanay, Djambul, and Tselinograd, and he also produced designs for residential districts and

individual buildings. However, the project that made him a household name was the ensemble of the Republic Square (formerly L. I. Brezhnev) in Almaty, which was built between 1971 and 1978 and for which he was awarded the state prize in 1982. This sizeable achievement was his ticket to a management position at the Institute in Chisinau. The Presidential Office is situated on a plinth with stairs leading up to the monumental volume, which is connected with two symmetrical lower wings on the ground floor. The building's entrance is a portal resembling an abstract rendition of a triumphal arch. This brutalist canopy structure is visibly set off from the rest of the building and dwarfed by the tower structure. The latter is inspired by a floral motif, which was exploited by an entire generation of architects, with this building among the most successful interpretations of this kind. At the central core of the building, an elongated geometric shape covered in zinc juts up like a pistil of a flower – serving as the flagpole for the national flag. The façade is covered in white limestone, while the ground-level stairway leading to the main entrance is clad in dark red and black marble. The load-bearing structure consists of a carcass made of reinforced concrete elements; the vertical elements, covered in stone, alternate with glazed façades of narrow windows, the glass of which corresponds chromatically to the anodised aluminium profiles. The overall resulting effect is one of opaqueness and refinement. Designed to withstand earthquakes up to a magnitude of nine (although no earthquakes in the area have registered a magnitude greater than eight), the Presidential Office could not withstand the violent protests of 2009 and was severely damaged. The glazed surfaces were most impacted by the damage, but the interior was also significantly destroyed. It took a decade to complete the repair works, which were funded through a grant from the Turkish Government and finished in 2018.

D

The Oncology Institute

30, Nicolae Testemitanu Street
Oleg Vronsky et al.
1992

The Oncology Institute occupies a vast territory in an area assigned to hospitals and diagnostic centres in the vicinity of Nicolae Testimiteanu Street. The Republican Hospital, Medical Laboratories, the National Medicine and Pharmacology Institute, and the National Centre for Nursing are situated here, among others. In the 1980s, Moldova's Oncology Research Institute was one of the five top institutes of the Soviet Union. It was included in the international programme run by the Council for Mutual Economic Assistance member states, which was dedicated to creating a unified cytological classification of tumours (in concert with the GDR, the Hungarian People's Republic, the USSR, and Czechoslovakia). In 1980, a polyclinic opened here, featuring cutting-edge equipment and a daily turnover of 750 patients. In 1992, a nine-storey building was erected, featuring patient wards with a total of 500 beds and 20 operating rooms. An important development for patients was the inauguration of a four-storey hotel-style accommodation facility, making it possible for people from remote areas to stay overnight in order to undergo extensive examinations and have time to discuss treatment plans. If the layout of the State Circus building (S. Shoikhet, A. Kirichenko) can be described as a Star Trek spaceship, then the institute building appears to have been modelled after a newer generation of star ship, with a much more elaborate use of volume and a more sophisticated interior. The skeleton structure was built as a framework of precast concrete elements, and the façades consist of prefabricated plates and modules, each configured with an individual design. The building has a massive central rectangular block with an entrance consisting of two semi-circular elements. Slightly detached from the building's

cylindrical structure with windows on the ground floor, which is intersected by another much smaller cylindrical block with an auxiliary entrance from the courtyard. These cylindrical elements correspond to the structures at the building's front entrance as well as the thin oval openings in the lattice-like curtain element crowning the building on its upper levels. These forms are typical of the sci-fi aesthetic employed by many architects of this era. The open area in front of the institute features many elements that correspond with the entrance: several cylindrical vents and two circular fountains, currently not in operation. After the republic gained its independence, considerable efforts were made to improve the institute's facilities and technical equipment. A major overhaul of the radiology department was carried out in 2009 in order to accommodate a linear accelerator. A gamma room was installed and a laboratory for radionuclide diagnosis was created in 2010 with the support of the International Atomic Energy Agency.

main corpus, they symmetrically flank the entry portal, which has a curved lintel. The entrance and the ground floor sit on a plinth with a semi-circular flight of steps. The complex includes another volume perpendicular to the main building and connected to the oncology polyclinic facing Grenoble Street and also to the canteen at the back. Near the corner is an additional two-storey extension – a

D

UNIC – Central Department Store

064 D

8, Stefan cel Mare si Sfant Boulevard

M. Orlov, V. Lepskyi, A. Varshaver
1983

When it was inaugurated, the Central Department Store was the largest retail centre in the city, with a surface area of over 10,000 square metres. More than a thousand sales assistants and cashiers served an average of 100,000 customers each day. Standing on a massive plinth, the four-storey building faces the central boulevard to the front and runs along Ismail Street on one side. A car park behind the store exits onto Mitropolit Varlaam Street, which leads to the central market. The plinth itself contains retail spaces that are one level lower than the plaza of the main entrance; access to these shops is via the building's interior and stairways at the back of the building. The ground floor facing Ismail Streets includes the halls and technical spaces used for merchandise deliveries. The composition of the building reflects the classical typology of modernist architecture, in which smooth stone-clad surfaces alternate with narrow strips of windows. The building consists of a core rectangular volume, with several narrower volumes of the same height staggered around this corpus, forming a compact but dynamic monolithic block. The façades are covered with white limestone, alternating with narrow strips of windows, which are accented with lesenes made of aluminium profiles. The front façade has a protruding volume that houses the staircase and visually frames the fountain on the plaza. The space in front of the store is a wide plaza featuring a rectangular fountain that is perpendicularly aligned with the boulevard. The fountain consists of overlapping rectangular surfaces and several devices that spout water, the central one consisting of four cylindrical stainless-steel elements positioned vertically in an unusual design. Each side of the plaza has four semi-circular niches with seating surfaces, which are part of the walls that enclose a planting bed on each side. These seating areas offer weary shoppers a place to rest, and they are popular gathering places for young people. After closing hours, the plaza serves as a public park and has an animated holiday-like atmosphere. In 2018 substantial renovations were undertaken on the building, to which many changes were made, although the main volumes of the building remained unchanged. The interior spaces were reconfigured, and the staircases on the main façade were equipped with elevators that were housed in additions clad with alucobond panels, which have a different appearance from the rest of the building. The space in front of the store has become more multifunctional. For instance, the fountain has been turned into a stage for open-air performances – a venue for concerts and public events. These events have taken on an increasingly commercial and promotional character in recent years.

D

The ACVAPROIECT Institute

1, Alecu Russo Street
*Anatoly Kolotovkin, Tatiana
Lomova*
1980

The complex of the Water Management Systems Engineering Institute (ACVAPROIECT, formerly Molgiprovodkhoz) consists of a 1960s structure facing Alecu Russo Street and a more recent tower block facing Moscow Boulevard. The institute's new building was designed by A. Kolotovkin at the time when he was director of the Moldgiprostroy Institute (beginning in 1977). Under his supervision, the building of the Ministry of Construction and Industrial Materials was designed in collaboration with T. Lomova (1975), as was the entire town of Alonka (1980–1982) in the Russian Federation, which was situated along the Baikal-Amur Railway (BAM). The collaborating architect for ACVAPROIECT, T. Lomova, had already worked on a number of public buildings with S. Vasilyev and later S. Shoikhet. The 16-storey tower block soon became a visual landmark on the boulevard, in an area with heavy traffic. It consists of two interlacing towers, each rectangular in shape but staggered in height. The tallest has radio antennae on its roof. A third lower volume follows the corner outlined by a street intersection. The three volumes are perched on a base formed by the two lower floors. The upper of the two is highlighted by a succession of semi-cylindrical elements with windows placed in unusual repeating geometric configurations. The load-bearing structure of the building is monolithic, constructed using the slip forming method – a technology successfully applied in the construction of other tall towers. The tower block can easily be mistaken for a residential building adapted for public use. The façades have broad windows, with rhomboidal side casings. This detailing, in combination with the semi-cylindrical elements at the base, are suggestive of an aquatic theme. Possible sources of inspiration range from a submarine to an underwater colony. A wavy pattern appears is the cast concrete elements that alternate with the windows of the two tower elements, which give the façade an undulating effect. At the top of the building, the utilities level has vent-like openings. The same motif is repeated on the side of the corner volume. The visible surfaces of the tower's façade are plastered in some areas, and the base volume is clad with limestone. The building took on a different function in the wake of the social changes that occurred in the 1990s. The complex now houses several shops and commercial dealers. Instead of a public building, it is now a commercial hub called Casa de Comert SOIUZ (Union Commercial Facility). This block used to house a cinema, which began operating in an era dominated by the screening of movies pirated from VHS tapes.

Moldtelecom

10, Stefan cel Mare si Sfant
Boulevard
*Alexandr Kireev, Nicolai Dorofeev,
S. Mukhin, Vladimir Shalaginov*
1983

066 D

Close to the UNIC shopping centre on Stefan cel Mare Boulevard, there is a tall building originally designed as part of an ensemble belonging to the MSSR Communications Ministry. At a time when technological innovations in telephony and communication were rapidly advancing, more space was required, and the complex belonging to the Communications Ministry (currently Moldtelecom) was expanded. A slender tower block was thus built next to the Inter-City Telephone Exchange (Victor Dubok), which was constructed in the 1960s. Between them is a shorter building with an expressive architecture. All three form an integral architectural ensemble. The 16-storey building, consisting of two volumes juxtaposed back-to-back, bears resemblance to other edifices on the boulevard in the heart of the old city, such as the Publishers' House (V. Zakharov, L. Gofman, G. Zhinkin) and the Ministry of Agriculture (A. Vaysbein, S. Shoikhet, A. Chmykhov), which were built according to the detailed city plan adopted in 1971. According to this plan, high-rises were intended for construction in the upper part of the city as well, but after First Secretary Brezhnev passed away in 1983, modernisation efforts began to slow down, and the massive vertical development of the city centre was postponed. The building's architecture is striking due to the almost primitive expression of its monolithic structure, which was constructed using slip forming. Such tall buildings accorded Chisinau, located in an area of significant seismic activity, the status of a modern city. Counterintuitively, the lateral façades, with their rounded corners, have been plastered in order to hide the rough concrete, and the narrow spaces between the vertical strips of windows were covered with grey-white limestone. The façades, which are dominated by vertical strips of windows, are given a chromatic contrast by the plastic panels that punctuate the windows. The overhanging technical floors on opposite sides of the building, which are supported by curved cantilevers, give the structure a somewhat top-heavy appearance. These contain air vents, whose openings are expressively outlined by rhomboidal casings. Due to poor maintenance, the rounded corners of the façades have lost some of their surfacing, revealing the rough texture of the concrete below, which is much more resistant to the natural elements. A metal structure on the roof simulates the form of an emitter antenna. Consisting of cylindrical elements, it is in keeping with the style of other details on the top of the building, which give the entire structure a certain futuristic aesthetic. A unique element among the city's utility buildings is the stainless-steel entry canopy, which is an advanced design solution for an everyday entrance – a metal wing with a dynamic profile.

Residential Complex – Four Tower Blocks with a Social Infrastructure

067 D

27–37, Dacia Boulevard
Gennady Solominov, Oleg Vronski
1974

This series of towers with similar silhouettes that line the main axis road of the Botanica district are the most impressive of all the residential complexes built in the city. A construction boom took place in the MSSR in the 1970s and 1980s. Large investments were made in this sector at this time, which coincided with a period of spectacular economic growth due to the oil exports of the USSR. Starting in 1972 and in anticipation of the 50th anniversary of the establishment of the republic and the MSSR Communist Party, the USSR leadership allotted colossal budgets to the revamping of the Moldovan capital. Due to the infusion of resources, design and construction advanced in spectacular fashion in the city. Small, single-building projects were soon replaced by the development of entire microraions and residential districts. It was during this phase that the Rascani, Ciocana, and Sculeni districts and Dacia (formerly Pacii) Boulevard in the Botanica district were created. One of the flagship projects of this period of maximum potential was the group of monolithic towers on Dacia Boulevard. In essence, this complex could be described as the materialisation of a utopian projection of the future, not only in terms of the use of space and volume, but also in terms of politics and economics. This massive scale, previously unimaginable, was made possible by new construction technologies, namely the slip forming of reinforced concrete structures, in alternation

with the jump forming method. The complex was built between 1973 and 1974 and designed by a team led by G. Solominov at the Moldgiprostroy Institute. It heroically withstood the strong earthquakes of 1977 and 1986. For G. Solominov, the complex became the *pièce de résistance* of his career, for which he was awarded the MSSR State Prize in 1978. The complex consists of four tower blocks resting on a platform that is set slightly below the level of the boulevard and thus forms a kind of souterrain level. Between the towers and connecting them are three volumes in the shape of stepped pyramids, rhomboidal in section, which sit on the platform, which thus forms a continuous structure stretching from Traian Street to Cuza Voda Street. The essential aim was to connect the housing blocks using a more complex formula than in the 1960s, with specialised furniture stores, grocery

D

shops, and even fashion salons at the feet of the towers. The retail spaces on the souterrain level and the restaurants and the fashion centres on the upper level between the blocks formed a complex and almost self-sufficient circuit together with the residential buildings. A similar model is the Neminga housing complex implemented in Minsk. Another example, but in a different political context would be the Barbican Centre in London. Both of these sites are emblematic of the brutalist style, and both have become obsolete, having been criticised for a range of faults. They are at risk of demolition today. The blocks are 19 storeys in height. Each has a technical floor, and the souterrain level is accessed from broad walkways. Three of the blocks have a fountain at the front. Another important aspect is how this ground level also serves as an elevated walkway, providing a panoramic view of the district and the boulevard. Access from the boulevard was possible via the stairways in front of the commercial centres or via four spiral staircases that enhanced the futuristic appearance of the building.

Apa-Canal Chisinau Joint Stock Company/MoldovaGaz Company

38, Albisoara Street
Leonid Voronin
1986

As the development of the city advanced, the buildings became more diversified in terms of their use of volume than they had been during the modernist period when the emphasis was on simple volumes and balanced proportions. Were it not for the neon company names and logos on the roof, one might easily assume that this futuristic looking building was a research station or an astrophysics institute. The sole shareholder of one of these companies, Apa-Canal Chisinau, is the Chisinau City Council. Occupying half of the building, the company is the city's water and sewage provider. It also supplies central heating in the Codru, Aeroport, and Costiujeni housing districts. The company has been in existence since 1892. The other half of the building houses the MoldovaGaz company. The motif of the stepped pyramid, inverted and raised up on pillars, was a recurrent theme in brutalist architecture, with one of the most prominent examples being Boston City Hall in Massachusetts. Such ideas were inspired by new construction technologies, especially the still untapped potential of the novel construction material of reinforced concrete. The building runs along Albisoara Street and consists of an elongated seven-floor volume, which is intersected towards the centre by two prominent vertical elements giving the impression of pillars lifting the building off the ground. The building's volume decreases from top to bottom, following the principle of a reversed pyramid. The suspended effect is enhanced not only by this step-like shape, but also the transparent ground floor with its glazed front. This sense of lift is also fostered by the façade colour scheme. The first floor is clad in rosy porous limestone, while the rest of the building is a grey-white indebted to the use of cement. The surfaces of the vertical elements that face the street are covered entirely in cast

![MOLDOVAGAZ building photograph]

concrete slabs with a repeating geometric pattern, similar to those of the ubiquitous 'PO-2M' cast concrete panels of the Soviet era. In the USSR, architects operated with budgets and technical resources that were much more austere than those of their colleagues in the West, and consequently, results were often more modest, exhibiting more restrained volumes and less complicated structures. Examples such as this building represent a sort of arte povera of Soviet brutalism.

D

The 'Toothed Wheel' Residential Block

22, Albisoara Street
Isaac Schvartzev
1987

069 D

This expressive block, notable for the staggered juxtaposition of its volumes, is located at the intersection of Ismail and Albisoara Streets. It is best viewed from the bridge connecting the industrial district and downtown area of the city. The Gutsulevka neighbourhood used to be located to the south of the area outlined by Ismail Street, Negruzzi Boulevard, and Albisoara Street. According to the architect, the first secretary of the MSSR CP, I. Bodiul himself, supported the accelerated construction of apartment buildings along Albisoara Street. The old houses in Gutsulevka, visible from the trains arriving at the main station, were the first thing visitors to Chisinau would see. As a result, the Gutsulevka neighbourhood was gradually demolished and replaced, according to a detailed plan, with apartment blocks made from prefabricated panels, which were built in several stages. The 1000-hectare area allotted at the time to the construction of the central part of the city was bordered by Mateevici Street down to the Bic River and by the railway station up to the intersection of Stefan cel Mare Boulevard and Calea Iesilor Street. Most of this area was designated for development for administrative and cultural purposes. Adjacent plots were reserved for such buildings along the entire length of Stefan cel Mare Boulevard (formerly V. Lenin Boulevard). The detailed plan mainly foresaw tall administrative and residential buildings. Other parts of the central area were used for housing development. The adjusted detailed plan was approved in 1971, having been developed

D

based on the consolidated proposals prepared by the Moldgiprostroy Institute and LenNIIP (the Leningrad Institute of Research and Engineering in the Development of Master Plans) as the result of a competition organised in 1966. One drawback of this plan was the layout of the controversial Cantemir Boulevard (originally M. Frunze Boulevard), which contributed to the destruction of the Gutsulevka neighbourhood, while the placement of the apartment blocks on Albisoara Street, together with the infrastructure serving them, resulted in the complete annihilation of this old district. This particular apartment block, with its curved layout, sits on a corner. Nearby running along these streets are nine-storey apartment blocks of a standard prefabricated panel construction, which form a continuous structure with the curved block. The curved façade is marked by five protruding vertical

volumes, the middle three of which stand out due to the way they extend beyond the roof of the curved volume. These vertical elements seem to form the expressive 'teeth' of a gear wheel and recall constructivist architecture. At the same time, the building, with its inwardly curved and shallow balconies, has a hermetic appearance, almost like a chain-mail surface cast in concrete. The narrow minimalist openings running the height of the five vertical volumes enhance the fortress-like appearance of the structure as well as its brutalist character. The load-bearing carcass of this structure is different from that of the neighbouring buildings, which were assembled entirely from precast elements and prefabricated modules. This apartment building was constructed using a combined method of assembly and jump forming, enabling the resulting structure to withstand earthquakes of greater magnitudes.

The Track and Field Arena

26, Andrei Doga Street
Stepan Homa
1985

 070 D

When looking at the range of buildings constructed throughout several decades, one notices a tendency in which important edifices were often finalised around an anniversary or other significant date. This is also the case of the sports arena designed by the Moldgiprostroy Institute and built for the 60th anniversary of the establishment of the MSSR and the Moldovan Communist Party. Classified as the country's principal sports arena, it was equipped with an indoor track and field facility with a 200-metre track and 3,000 seats. The sports arena was built quite late, given that sports and the fitness of the general population, especially that of the youth, had been a priority in the USSR from the very beginning. However, as an agrarian country, Moldova had limited resources that were often redirected towards more essential or important sites. At the time, the Republican and Dinamo stadiums built in the 1950s had become obsolete in terms of infrastructure and looked like relics of the past. The Tennis Arena had been built in 1975, and the Tineretea Swimming Pool belonging to the Moldova Sports Society had been commissioned in 1981, the year in which the first union-level swimming competition had taken place. The building of the Track and Field Arena has an elongated volume, with the main façade showcased by a convex surface with vertical ribs made of prefabricated concrete. Meanwhile, the rear façade, which faces an outdoor pitch, has broad windows with aluminium frames that are punctuated by massive casings made of

reinforced concrete. These are grouped in blocks, lending the building a brutalist air. Access is via the entrance on the main façade, where administrative offices are also located. The exit is through two prefabricated concrete parapets that run across the first-floor level and have stairs leading to the ground level. The solutions developed for the side façades are expressive. In addition to galleries, the side façades feature a row of vertical elements with narrow windows on the sides, which allow light in at an angle in order to avoid direct sunlight falling into the sports hall. The exit doors of the spectator stands are located under these windowed strips. Such sports infrastructure was self-sustainable and operated solely based on public funds. Therefore, over time, the arena has been used as a venue for concerts and private events. Beginning in 1987, many rock concerts by popular rock bands took place there. They have now been replaced by K-1 competitions and other commercial events in order to viably maintain the structure.

The Holy Trinity Christian Centre

13, Dacia Boulevard
Felix Shostak, Gennady Zhinkin
1989

Originally designed as a cinema with two auditoriums and a seating capacity of 1,000 people, the building, with its geometric volumes, is now a Christian house of worship. In keeping with the name of the boulevard, the name of the cinema was supposed to be Pacea ('peace'). Construction work started in 1988 but stopped in the early 1990s. The disintegration of the USSR posed a challenge to Lenin's thesis that cinematography was one of the most important arts, since film was a means of disseminating ideas, while religion was the opium of the people. In an ironic twist of fate, the would-be cinema ended up becoming a house of worship. This was not a miracle, as it was finished shortly after the Republic gained independence and during a whirlwind period of privatisations in which the authorities control over public spaces and buildings was weakened, and so the fate of the building was decided. There are several Neo-Baptist houses of worship in the city, one of which is active in the former Shipka cinema (G. Penbek) in the Rascani district. In this case, the building has been visibly altered, making the original volume hard to recognise now. Shostak specialised in the design of residential buildings; he had coordinated the project of the residential complex located at the intersection of Dacia and Hristo Botev Boulevards as well as that of the dormitory on Unirea Principatelor Square. The cinema was designed as a structure consisting of several interlaced volumes. Docked onto the main octagonal section of the building is a stepped front structure, which consists of a tall tower as the central entry, which repeats the shape

of the octagon and similarly shaped volumes set back on each side. The play of multi-sided geometric shapes continues on the grounds. Individual and interlaced hexagons serve as flowerbeds, providing green spaces between the cinema and the boulevard. Some are situated at the sides of the building where a lower level is accessed along stepped terraces planted with grass and flowering plants. The cinema façade is visible from the central axis of Teilor Street. The structure of the original design has been well preserved, but the interior has been adapted by the new owner in order to suit its new purpose.

D

Guguta Municipal Puppet Theatre

1, Maria Dragan Street
Victor Yavorski, Eduard Kim
1983

Located in the industrial area of the city, this building was originally designed to house the Youth Centre for the Ciocana district (the Octombrie raion). Youth centres were customarily established close to large factories, and their operation was overseen and coordinated by the Komsomol raion organisations. The detailed urban plan of the Ciocana district was developed in 1962 by Isaac Bubis. It included a range of factories and affiliated residential areas, which were to be constructed in stages. The housing complexes along Maria Dragan Street were built in the 1970s, while those on Mircea cel Batran Boulevard date from the late 1980s. However, construction work stopped once the political system collapsed. The undeveloped areas visible today at the end of Mircea cel Bătrân Road are a testimony to a process of modernisation that came to an abrupt halt. After the collapse of the USSR and the accompanying tide of changes that washed over all domains of life, the function of this particular building changed, and it was adapted in order to house a puppet theatre. The building has a core rectangular volume, around which smaller rectangular spaces are symmetrically positioned, which gives the building a fragmented appearance. The entry level is situated below street level, to which it is connected via an elongated walkway that provides its audiences with access to the building. Seen from above, the building's layout seems to have been based on that of an Aztec temple with a cruciform shape. Its relationship with its surroundings draws from the typology of organic

the stairway leading to the ground floor. Undoubtedly this is a design that developed from a great deal of creative inspiration. Its architectural shapes have a sculptural monumentality. If the builders had opted for exposed concrete without any surface finishings, the shapes and the surfaces would have been much more expressive as a result. While finding resources and using imported materials was not an issue in terms of the city's government buildings, the Youth Centre was finished during a period of austerity and shortages when the issue of quality was no longer a priority. The focus was simply on completing construction work and commissioning the building. As a consequence, the eaves of the roof were clad with zinc sheeting – a cheap and accessible material that now shows signs of wear. In addition, the monumental art included in the architectural programme lacks expression.

architecture. In terms of its details, the building bears similarities to the House of the Nations (Y. Tumanyan, V. Yavorski) in the flat outline of the roof and slanting eaves, the aesthetic of the supports for the walkway connecting the building to the street, and the walls supporting

D

The Business Centre
7, Miron Costin Street
Alexandr Boyarchuk
1987

073 D

Originally designed to house the industrial laboratories of the Moldselkhoztekhnika and Soyuzgortekhvodstroy Institutes, the Business Centre building is next to a 15-storey residential complex built in the 1980s. The complex consists of two volumes situated along Moscova Boulevard. The main structure is the taller of the two and is set back from the street with a slightly angled layout. The second L-shaped volume is positioned forward at the street corner and one side runs along Miron Costin Street. The latter consists of several low upper horizontal elements, which are staggered to create three stepped levels. The opposite side of this volume terminates in a rectangular structure with a flat façade, which connects the two volumes and forms the main entrance. Together these volumes have a stepped composition with an inner courtyard. The construction consists of precast elements assembled on a concrete framework. The façade of the main volume is partially covered with limestone. The main volume, nine storeys tall, consists of two wings that meet at an angle. A parapet of cast concrete panels runs along the top of the building. The terminal ends of this building have loggias, while front and back façades consist of rows of windows and vertically running lesenes made from profiles of anodised aluminium. The cornice of the taller building and those of the individual level elements of the stepped structure have a concave cantilevered shape, like a reversed waterspout, which accentuates the horizontal and ties the entire composition together. Currently, the lower structure is occupied by Victoria Bank. The rehabilitation of the building changed both its colours and the texture, causing the structures of the former institutes to appear more detached from each other. The main structure now houses various offices and businesses, but the exterior of the building has not been refurbished for years and shows signs of wear. The large

space in front of the complex at the intersection of Moscova Boulevard and Miron Costin Street was left untouched and remained vacant for several decades. In the Soviet era, it had been designated as the site for a building that would have corresponded with the institutes and housed a restaurant – Al saptelea cer ('Seventh Heaven') – with a spectacular architecture designed by G. Solominov. Plans indicate that it would have featured a tower with a dining room at the top, built in the shape of a flower. The restaurant complex would have also included a series of waterfalls, pools, and fountains. The waterfall would have flowed into an aqueduct spanning the boulevard and extending into the Memorial Complex Park (dedicated to soldiers killed in Afghanistan). This luxury restaurant with its organic architecture typology was never built. In recent years, the vacant plot was used to build a mammoth residential complex with 15 floors. This massive multi-structure development upsets the architectural balance of the entire neighbourhood.

D

Nicolai Gogol High School

074 D

90, Alexei Sciusev Street
Victor Zakharov, Mikhail Averbakh,
Ghita Goldschlag
1984

The high school building (original-ly Middle School No. 37), which includes three interconnected blocks, a sports area, and a square, was part of the complex plan to modernise the city centre, which was introduced in 1969. In order to carry out this plan, the housing quarter outlined by N. Iorga, M. Cibotari, A. Shchusev, and Bucuresti Streets had to be demolished. The location proved to be challenging and complex, requiring a customised approach in terms of design and also a judicious use of space, since the site was narrower than the architects liked. The complex solution adopted to meet the building's artistic and utilitarian objectives resulted in a balanced proportioning of the façades that faced the four surrounding streets. By placing the buildings along the perimeter of the site connecting them at the narrow ends, the architects were able to organise a generous atrium for festive events and internal activities and also provide a leisure and sports area in the adjoining space. In terms of their use of volume, the structures have a terraced layout and are organised in modules that have varying heights. The top level consists of classrooms for the middle school, which have access to the open terraces on the roofs of the one-storey modules. Special attention was paid to the parts of the complex intended for communal activities, the gymnasiums for the primary and middle school pupils, the indoor pool, the workshops, and the track and field area. The load-bearing structure consists of a framework of precast elements, with concrete panels on the exterior. The cornice of the top floor features an expressive cantilever element, which together with

D

the terraced modules gives the building its specific character. The façades have wide windows alternating with strips of narrow windows and are covered with white limestone. The main façade has a mosaic that extends the entire height of the building. It is executed in an abstract style and is extremely elaborate in terms of composition and colour. A remarkable combination of architecture and monumental art, the mosaic requires adequate maintenance and conservation.

The Municipal V. Ignatenco Clinical Hospital for Children

075 D

149, Grenoble Street
Liudmila Gofman, Gennady Zhinkin
1985

The hospital, built at the outskirts of the city, exhibits a dynamic use of volumes. It is set below street level, and patients enter via a wide stairway. The hospital handles up to 4,000 patients a month, of which approximately 1,000 are inpatients. Access for ambulances is through auxiliary entrances located on the hidden side of the lateral block, which is laid out in a zigzag on the ground floor. Before working on this project, the architect L. Gofman had collaborated with B. Zakharov for the Publishers' House. Collaborating architect G. Zhinkin went on to design the Russian Embassy in Chisinau. The configuration of the six-storey complex resembles a leaf of clover, with its three wings joined at the centre and a smaller wing forming the 'stem' and connected to the centre node through a narrow gallery. The latter single-storey block houses the main entrance, which consists of a combination of shapes. It is dominated by an overhanging portal, which supports a concrete incline in the shape of a waterspout pointing towards the top of the building. The top level of the lateral façades features three overhanging rectangular elements, each with two small windows. These apparent utility spaces seem to perch on the roof, thus animating the austerity of the block-like structure and suggesting a sci-fi aesthetic. On the roof, at the point where the 'leaves' meet, there are a few elements of a similar typology, marking the centre of the building. The terminal façades of the wings have a concave outline and at its outer terminus each wing rests on a pair of columns. The load-bearing structure consists of a framework assembled from precast

D

concrete elements, and the façades consist of rows of windows alternating with concrete panels. The node of the building is accented by a vertical row of balconies that extends out between the flat surfaces of the wings, which have windows but no balconies. Between the two wings opening towards Grenoble Street, there is a patio meant to create a relaxed atmosphere for the patients. The centre of the patio contains a hexagonal fountain surrounded by a network of footpaths. Originally the colour scheme of the building featured only two tones: it was predominantly white in tone with brick-red accents. The building looks different now though, having been altered in many ways on the exterior and in the interior. Over the years, the original flat roof began leaking. The management decided to solve the problem by installing traditional angled roofs throughout the complex, and even at the entrance. These alterations obliterated the novelty of the original architectural solutions and turned the ensemble into a bizarre combination of styles.

The County Government Building in the Botanica District

10, Teilor Street

Leonid Voronin, Nadezhda Maltseva
1987

076 D

All the County Government office buildings (originally the Party Raion Committees) in the various districts of Chisinau were built according to an identical design by B. Shpak, with some variations. An exception was made for the Botanica district building, which presented an opportunity for the architects. It served as a precedent for breaking the mould and bestowing a different kind of status on an administrative building. The design was developed by L. Voronin in collaboration with N. Maltseva, who approached the design from an experimental angle, creating a building based on the principle of an inverted pyramid, in which the volume decreases gradually towards the base. The building appears to be clasped in the middle on both sides by vertical volumes, like an immense vice, which camouflages the staircase. Thin pillars support the structure, elevating it above the ground. The overhanging top floor has a massive quality. In contrast, the ground floor is completely

D

transparent with a glazed front, which enhances the effect of a heavy body being suspended above the ground. Adding to this impression, the stacked volumes include horizontal strips of windows in an aluminium profile frame. As in the case of the Apa-Canal Chisinau building (L. Voronin), this inverted and stepped volume was the starting point for the design, which is typical of brutalist architecture. The plasticity of reinforced concrete and its 'sculptural' potential played a key role in the brutalist architectural vocabulary. The building consists of three independent sections with different purposes. The main volume houses offices; a second, smaller one hosts the conference hall; and a third serves the auxiliary functions. The three structures form a semi-open inner yard that creates correspondence with the lobby and the hallway of the main building, engendering a sense of open and interconnected space. The spaces around the building are organised as comfortable leisure areas and can be used by office workers during breaks as well as by people in the neighbourhood throughout the day. Situated on the outskirts of the city, the building is removed from everyday urban traffic. Without a doubt, this is an exceptional building, and it has a chance of surviving intact. Its location has kept it out of sight.

The State Hydrometeorology Service

193, Grenoble Street
Architects not identified
1983

077 D

The State Hydrometeorology Service building is a free-standing tower block overlooking the Botanica district from its highest point, not far from the intersection of Grenoble and Traian Streets. The service was established in 1983 based on the former Hydrometeorology Observatory (established in 1956) and the Meteorology Office. The building is adapted to its purpose – to efficiently and methodologically coordinate the state system of meteorological and agrometeorolgical observation. It belongs to the same type of buildings as the City Gates (Y. Skvortsova, A. Spasov, A. Markovich), but its concrete elements have a different configuration, forming a geometrised structure and lending the building a brutalist character. The load-bearing structure of the building is an 11-storey framework assembled from concrete elements and precast panels. This tower houses a range of departments – Weather Forecasting, Meteorology and Climatology, Agrometeorological Monitoring etc. The roof has a platform that extends beyond the body of the main block. Installed on this part of the roof are a number of antennae and emitters as well as a radar system enclosed in a protective spherical structure, which makes the building look like an enormous robot. This is enhanced by the shape of the white vertical structure running the height of the building and enclosing the stairs. In terms of its use of space and volume, the design of the building indicates the hand of a whimsical author. Here a building with a strictly utilitarian purpose takes on a personalised meaning; this is a typology influenced by the postmodernist tradition more commonly found in the works of Asian architects (such as Sumet Jumsai in Thailand or Arata Isozaki in Japan). Such designs belong to a postmodernist practice of drawing from anime-type characters in the design of high-rise buildings.

In the context of Soviet architecture, a comparable building is the Kaliningrad House of the Soviets (Y. Shvartzbreym), which was nicknamed 'the robot head'. Thin concrete lesenes are imposed over the rows of windows of the front and back façades of the building. A grid pattern dominates the dynamic of the entire block-like structure, which has a greenish hue. This contrasts with the pure white of the expressive 'robot', which seems to be grasping it with its arms.

The Pharmaceutical Storage Facility

145, Arheolog Ion Casian-Suruceanu Street

Vadim Klevensky

1985

Ordinarily, a utilitarian building such as a storage facility does not pose much of a challenge for a designer. However, this building is an exception. At first sight it appears to have a rectangular layout, in which a combination of elements forms a fragmented but hermitical structure, which raises the curiosity of the viewer. Four identical elements in the shape of tall pillars form the four corners of the building, creating the impression of interlaced volumes forming a compact and robust structure. The colour scheme of the building emphasises the composition: the corner elements are brick-red, echoing the base volume of the building. The core volume of the building is grey, and the manner in which this volume is set off from the corner structures almost seems as if the force of the four corner pillars is squeezing out the insides of the building. On the sides of the grey blocks, where they intersect with the corner volumes, there are strips of windows that run the height of the building and let light in. Additional vertical strips of windows are located on the front of the building and in the middle of each façade, but they are too narrow to allow much light inside. The austere lighting and ventilation design obviously corresponds to the purpose of the building, helping to preserve constant temperatures inside. In this building, the architect has found an intelligent solution for correlating function and form. The main entrance is a portal-like structure set onto the front of the building and highlighted by its white limestone cladding. White stone cladding is also used to accent the strips of narrow windows on the outer ends of the corner elements. Like other storage facilities, the building has been placed in a location removed from heavy traffic, towards the outskirts of the city at the intersection of Grenoble and Arheolog Ion Casian-Suruceanu Streets. It is located close to the hospitals and diagnosis centres on Nicolae Testimiteanu, which it supplies with pharmaceuticals. The storage facility also serves the neighbouring Municipal V. Ignatenco Clinical Hospital for Children (L. Gofman, G. Zhinkin) as well as an entire network of pharmacies throughout the city.

D

The ALFA Joint Stock Company 079 D

75, Alba Iulia Street
Architects not identified
1976

One of the largest industrial outfits in Chisinau was the ALFA television set factory, which went into operation in 1976. It was located on the outskirts of the city at the end of Alba Iulia (formerly F. Engels) Boulevard. ALFA was a 'hybrid' factory, like many other leading factories in the USSR: it not only produced television sets, but also manufactured classified military equipment. The product that brought it fame was the ALFA colour TV, which was remarkable due to its advanced design. Its technical components were based on parts supplied by Ukraine and the Baltic states. Once the USSR disintegrated, TV set production, as well as that of classified equipment, entered a decline, and the factory was liquidated in 2005. The factory is a multi-part structure consisting of three elongated horizontal volumes and one tower block facing Alba Iulia and Onisifor Ghibu Streets. It was built on a plinth, which surrounds an immense rectangular industrial complex connected to the blocks via narrow walkways with a band of windows on each side, visible from the inner courtyard. At one extremity of the complex there is a 15-storey tower block on Alba Iulia Street, which houses the administrative offices. It is also connected to testing laboratories in a third block that faces a street running parallel to Onisifor Ghibu. Like most industrial buildings, the load-bearing structure of the factory was built from precast concrete elements. The exterior façades feature rows of windows, punctuated vertically by precast concrete pilaster strips alternating with horizontally positioned concrete panels. The first two floors have a different treatment. Set in front of the main structure, they are laid out in a series of staggered spaces forming a zigzag façade, punctuated by windows. At the corner of the complex, where the entrance to the factory is located, these levels extend slightly beyond the upper levels toward the street. This portion of the building is accentuated by its curved shape and broad cornice, which lend a dynamic to the entire structure. A similar shape was used for the base

of the tower block on the opposite side of the complex. As a whole, the factory is a highly complicated yet also quite laconic structure in terms of its aesthetics. Today, the complex appears visually disintegrated. Most of the former industrial compound has been taken over by shops, restaurants, fitness centres, and offices belonging to commercial businesses. The small remaining portion of the factory still produces television sets, washing machines, refrigerators, and other household goods. The minimised production site bears witness to a detrimental loss of industry that has cost jobs and caused entire sectors of the country's economy to disappear. On the opposite end of the main structure from the entrance, the complex houses Perspectiva University. In 2017, part of the central building accessible via Alba Iulia Street was transformed into the Alfa City Shopping Mall, a retail outfit that not only took over an important part of the nine-storey building but also appropriated the former factory's logo. The top floor of the mall is designed as a leisure area with terraces and bars, and the roof features three indoor pools, open year-round.

D

The Ion Creanga State Pedagogical University
1/1, Ion Creanga Street
Nicolay Naumov
1978

080 D

Established in 1940, the Ion Creanga State Pedagogical University (the Ion Creanga State Pedagogical Institute prior to 1992) is the oldest higher education institution in the city. It comprises nine departments: IT and Computer Science, Foreign Languages, Psychology and Psychopedagogy, Visual Arts and Design, Philology, History and Ethnopedagogy, Pedagogy, Professional Training for Teachers, and Social Work. It has an enrolment of approximately 6,000 students. The university has six classroom buildings and seven student dormitories, a library with six reading rooms and computer rooms, and printing facilities. The main building is an eight-storey rectangular volume that sits on pillars. The entry level, framed by the building's pillars and thus narrower than the upper volume, has four distinct wings. These auditorium modules stand out with their uplifted brutalist forms. This use of volume is characteristic of a typology similar to that used for the building type that B. Shpak designed for the raion Party Committees (currently used by the administrative departments of each district); similar is the combination of an expressive volume (assembly hall) with a rectangular one (administrative offices). The university building demonstrates a more complex spatial approach. The classroom modules are attached to

a narrow gallery framed by pillars, and it is separated from the elevated body of the upper building by a strip of windows. These protruding auditoriums are also the most expressive elements of the design. The load-bearing structure of the building is a framework assembled from precast reinforced concrete elements. On the ground floor, the concrete pillars are visible from the side, positioned in pairs and thus forming 10 branching reinforced concrete supports. Visible at the outer ends of the building, the pillars are an integral part of the building's character. The façades consist of alternating rows of concrete panels and groups of windows. The repeating window patterns consist of four vertically aligned windows alternated by three narrower windows, which are outlined with deep profiles. These protruding frames lend the façade a dynamic rhythm. The upper floors are accessed through stairwells, the position of which is indicated by a windowless vertical stripe on one side of the façade and a glazed segment on the opposite side. These accents add a vertical movement to the horizontal volume of the structure. The copper bas-relief portrait of the writer Ion Creanga (1839–1889), executed in a realistic style (sculptor: V. Cuznetsov, architect: V. Cudinov), was installed on the façade of the university in 1982. Stylistically, the sculpture does not match the architecture; it is a decorative element that could readily be replaced. Following the refurbishment of the building after 2000, some façade elements were altered, reducing the overall appearance of the building to that of an ordinary housing block with thermopane windows.

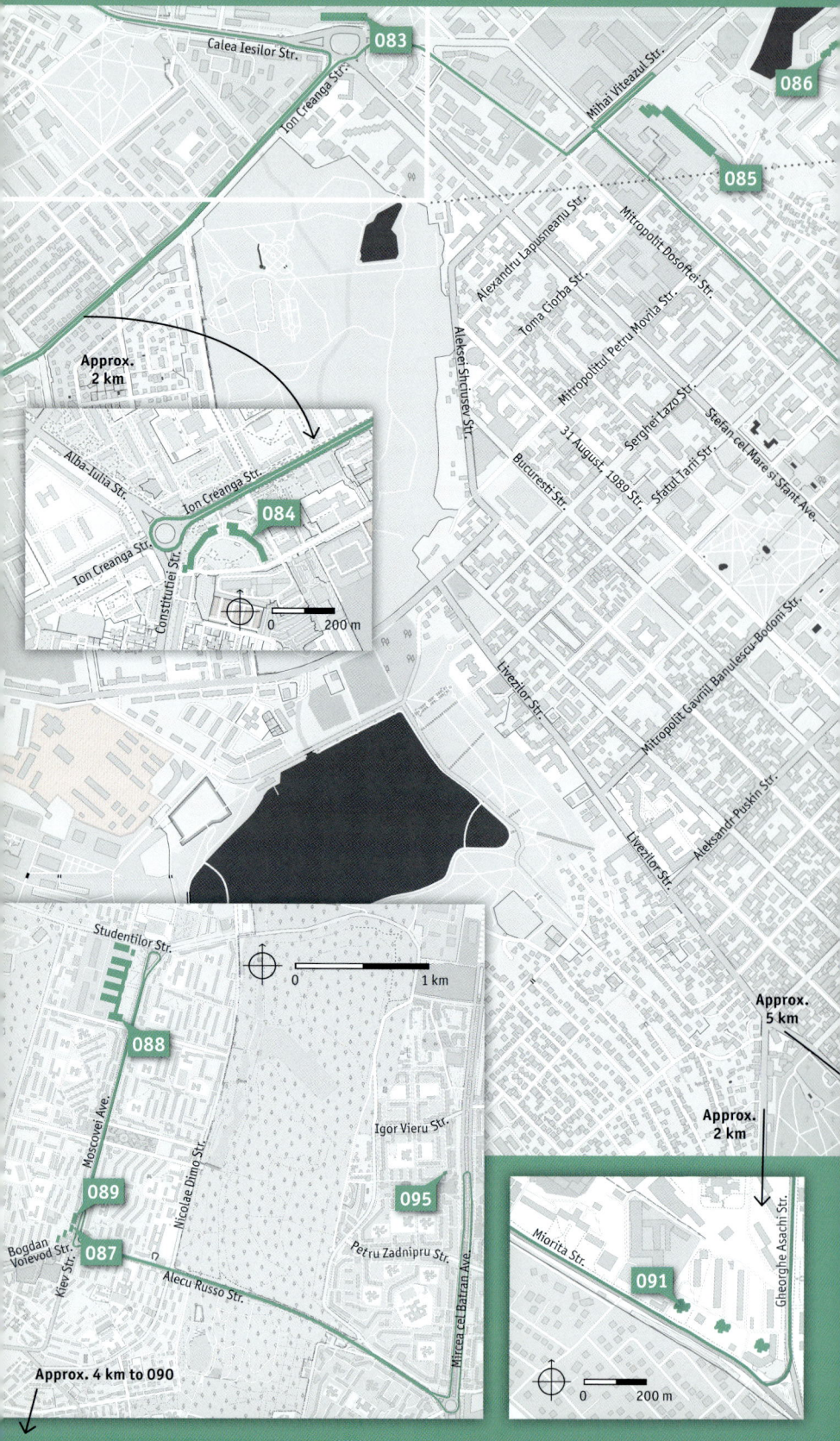

Calea Iesilor Str.

083

Ion Creanga Str.

Mihai Viteazul Str.

086

085

Alexandru Lapusneanu Str.

Toma Ciorba Str.

Mitropolit Dosoftei Str.

Aleksei Shciusev Str.

Mitropolitul Petru Movila Str.

Serghei Lazo Str.

Stefan cel Mare si Sfant Ave.

31 August, 1989 Str.

Bucuresti Str.

Sfatul Tarii Str.

Approx.
2 km

Alba-Iulia Str.

Ion Creanga Str.

Ion Creanga Str.

084

Constitutiei Str.

0   200 m

Livezilor Str.

Mitropolit Gavriil Banulescu-Bodoni Str.

Aleksandr Puskin Str.

Livezilor Str.

Studentilor Str.

088

0   1 km

Approx.
5 km

Moscovei Ave.

Igor Vieru Str.

Approx.
2 km

089

Nicolae Dimo Str.

095

087

Kiev Str.

Bogdan
Voievod Str.

Petru Zadnipru Str.

Alecu Russo Str.

Mircea cel Batran Ave.

Miorita Str.

091

Gheorghe Asachi Str.

Approx. 4 km to 090

0   200 m

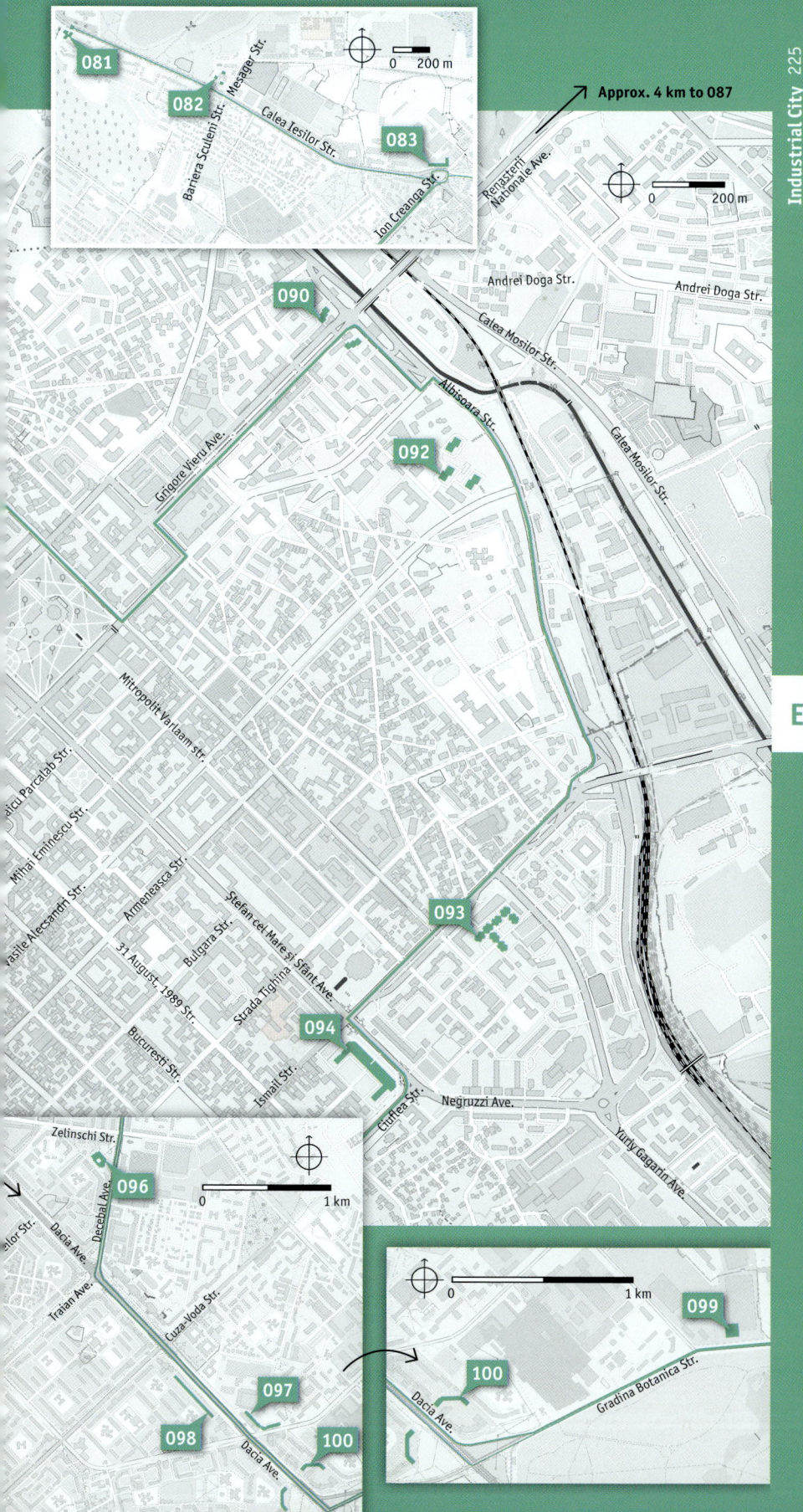

081

082

083

Bariera Sculeni Str.

Mesager Str.

Calea Iesilor Str.

Ion Creanga Str.

0 200 m

Approx. 4 km to 087

Renasterii Nationale Ave.

Andrei Doga Str.

Andrei Doga Str.

Calea Mosilor Str.

0 200 m

090

Albisoara Str.

Calea Mosilor Str.

092

Grigore Vieru Ave.

Mitropolit Varlaam str.

E

ălcu Parcalab Str.

Mihai Eminescu Str.

Vasile Alecsandri Str.

Armeneasca Str.

Bulgara Str.

31 August, 1989 Str.

Stefan cel Mare și Sfant Ave.

Strada Tighina

093

Bucuresti Str.

Ismail Str.

094

Ciuflea Str.

Negruzzi Ave.

Yuriy Gagarin Ave.

Zelinschi Str.

Decebal Ave.

096

0 1 km

Dacia Ave.

Traian Ave.

Cuza-Voda Str.

097

098

100

Dacia Ave.

0 1 km

099

100

Dacia Ave.

Gradina Botanica Str.

The Porumbeii Pacii ('Peace Doves') Towers

61/2, Calea Iesilor Street
Oleg Vronski
1982

081 E

The two tower blocks, located next to one another but slightly staggered, are oriented towards Calea Iesilor Street and visible to those entering the city from the northwest. The towers have the appearance of symbolic gates or watchtowers guarding the polis, as this intelligently planned complex of buildings stands out from its surroundings. Across the street is the leisure area of La Izvor Park (formerly Prietenia Popoarelor or 'Friendship of Peoples' Park), which includes a lake divided into two parts by a dike. There were plans for the leisure area in the Buiucanii de Jos ('Lower Buiucani') district to be connected to Buiucanii de Sus ('Upper Buiucani') by a cable car designed by the Gruzgiproshakht Institute in Tbilisi (architects: Manana Kariauli, Vidjen Abovyan, engineer: Vakhtang Lezhava). The cable car worked for a while, but it ceased operating after an accident. The concrete structures of the cable car have remained intact, and given sufficient initiative, the cable car could easily be refurbished and restarted. Built next to the lower station of the cable car line, the Butoiaș restaurant provided much-needed refuge nestled into the green area on Calea Iesilor Street. The tower blocks

themselves have a monolithic load-bearing structure made of reinforced concrete. Their rough surface resulted from the construction formwork for the concrete not having a convincing aesthetic quality, so it was coated with a white-greyish plaster. The façades feature balconies constructed from pre-cast elements; these are the only parts of the building that have retained the original concrete surface. The roof originally featured a metal structure assembled from a pipework skeleton covered with sheet metal shaped to form a silhouette of peace doves – part of the vocabulary of the era's visual propaganda. The doves' optical message corresponds with the name of the nearby park (the former 'Friendship of Peoples' Park) and indeed the name of Pacii Boulevard ('Peace' Boulevard) in the district of Botanica, the city's broadest boulevard, which forms a symbolic counterweight to the 'City Gate' residential complex located at the entrance to the city on the opposite side of town. These dove structures have decayed over the years and only the skeleton framework remains. Originally designed as a spatial and volumetric landmark on the outskirts of the city, the tower blocks are now surrounded by residential buildings that seem to have sprouted up at random. Furthermore, a portion of the green area between the blocks and the Butoiaș restaurant has been consumed by developers.

Dormitory Complex
16, Calea Iesilor Street Calea
Iesilor Street
David Palatnic, Alexei Chmikhov
1974

082 E

The slender towers, which the project architects likened to three birch trees due to their shape, are located in proximity to the greenery of La Izvor Park (formerly Prietenia Popoarelor or 'Friendship of Peoples' Park). The complex seems to be lifted straight from a 1970s minimalist handbook. Planned as dormitories for young workers, the buildings were a defining landmark of the area during a period of accelerated development in the city. When the Chisinaugorproiect Institute became its own entity in 1973, independent of the Moldgiprostroy Institute, its work exclusively specialised in the development of the capital. It was during this period that the construction of tall monolithic concrete residential buildings began in Chisinau. One of the first architects to implement this technology was David Palatnic. In 1971, one of Palatnic's designs was used for a residential block on Calea Ieșilor Street near Alunelul Park. A few years later, he designed this dormitory complex in collaboration with Alexei Chmikhov. The tower blocks of the complex were designed as distinct structures, which contained the same module of four three-room apartments on each floor. The shared loggias used during warm weather are covered with patterned grids made of precast concrete breeze blocks, which form a repetitive pattern running almost the full height of the building and lending it a modernist air. The narrower sides of the high-rises feature pairs of loggias that are set off from the façade at an angle and dovetail inward at the central vertical axis. This compositional pattern is replicated identically on the three blocks. The block farthest from the street is more slender and has a different grid pattern, breaking the monotony. The outline of the loggias and the matrix of the protective grid on the loggias of the side buildings lend individuality to the ensemble. In order to diversify its functions, the complex was equipped with a canteen, a cafe, and a concert hall, all interconnected by first-floor walkways set on columns,

which together form a semi-open courtyard. The inner courtyard was designed
as a green oasis hidden between the concrete blocks. Currently, the additional buildings opening onto the courtyard
host the Maria Biesu Music School. Due
to their new function, these structures
have been substantially altered, while the
high-rises look like the pieces of a defrag-
mented puzzle.

Topaz Factory

1, Dimitrie Cantemir Square
Architects not identified
1978

083 E

The plant is situated in the Sculeni industrial area and is one of the former Soviet military equipment enterprises that remains operational despite the precarious situation of the country's economy. While linked to the military and space programme developed by the USSR on the territories of several Soviet republics, factories like this generally also produced consumer goods (cassette players, computers, etc.). The structure of the building rests on a skeleton constructed from reinforced concrete elements, which is covered with precast concrete slabs and prefabricated panels. Consisting of horizontal strips of windows alternating with reinforced concrete slabs, the façade is accentuated by horizontally running strips of aluminium that serve the dual functions of sun protection (brise-soleil) and decoration. The building is positioned in D. Cantemir Square, which was designed by Isaac Bubis in 1959. It marks the tip of the triangle created by the axes of Stefan cel Mare Boulevard and I. Creanga Street. This building serves as a screen that masks the less sightly infrastructure of the industrial area, hence the increased care given to the elements of the protective aluminium grid of the façade. In order to increase the building's height, the façade extends an extra storey above the core and is formed by a grid of concrete slabs and aluminium – a transparent structure similar to the one used for the Gh. Asachi High School (S. Shoikhet, A. Kirichenko). The seven-storey building is visually divided into two parts. The section on the left was intended for administrative offices; it is set back from the rest of the building

and has a tighter pattern of windows. The larger section on the right has taller sets of double windows and was meant to house production spaces. The pattern of the windows is vertically punctuated by U-form aluminium profiles. In order to support Soviet-era companies that were in decline, between 1998 and 2001 a project funded by the World Bank provided training for managers in the EU, the US, and Japan. After the political changes of 2001 and the accompanying reorientation, the project ceased, and former industries' chances of survival diminished. A decade ago, the plant was bought by the Russian group Salyut, which specialises in the production of engines for military aircraft. A portion of the production spaces are sublet, while others on the ground floor are used as retails spaces.

Tractor Plant Dormitories

1, Unirii Principatelor Square
Felix Shostak
1985

084 E

An imposing presence on Principatele Unite Square (formerly Constitutiei Square) is the large complex that dominates the view from the axis of Alba Iulia Boulevard (formerly F. Engels Boulevard). The buildings were designed as dormitories for the nearby tractor plant. The size of this housing complex corresponds to the substantial assets managed by the plant and the investment made by management in attracting young specialists through decent living conditions. The two blocks of the complex, with a modular layout, each consist of three connected buildings, which together form a compact structure, whose volume forms an encircling wall. The details of the façades are kept to a minimum. The austerity of the design is characterised by the typology of the apartments. There are open loggias and shared kitchens and the common spaces lead to the staircase. The buildings are equipped with rubbish collection stations on the ground floor. The three blocks are divided into four protruding vertical sections, which are interconnected by the wider and taller vertical volumes of the stairwells. The blocks are marked in the middle by a row of balconies, forming an expressive structure. The carcass of the apartments is a monolithic structure, which was built using a mobile formwork method – one of the most economical and fastest technologies of its time, surpassing the sliding formwork method. The jump forming technology, developed by the Department of Construction

135 of the Ministry of Construction and the Moldgiprostroy Institute, was fundamentally different from the construction methods practiced at the time. The use of a mobile formwork in the planning and construction of residential buildings is indebted to the work of architect F. Shostak. It was under his supervision that the tall buildings on Hristo Botev Street, Roz Street, Calea Iesilor Street, and others were built. The austere appearance of the building is worth noting. The light horizontal bands indicate the joints between the floors, and precast concrete panels with a faceted surface pattern – an ornamentation that modernism borrowed from Renaissance architecture – majestically highlight the volumes of the stairwells. The plaza was decorated with a monument dedicated to the constitution of the USSR (sculptor: I. Canashin), which is currently in ruins. Only the red granite stele has been left standing as a testimony to the dismantled system.

E

Bucuria Joint Stock Company 085 E

162, Columna Street
Architects not identified
1964

Confectionery factory no. 1 in Chisinau was established in 1946, right after the Second World War. Out of this emerged the experimental confectionery factory Bucuria ('Joy') in 1962. The factory was built on the site of a former military barracks, and the Moldovan confectioners started producing sweets using machinery from Germany. Between 1956–1964, the factory was rebuilt and equipped with mechanised production lines manufactured locally and then later with imported technology. In 1982, its gross production already amounted to 61.45 million roubles, and production capacity reached 42,000 tonnes of confectionery per year by 1986. The factory was a habitual guest at farming and food processing exhibitions in the USSR and MSSR, and its products were displayed at international exhibitions and fairs in Eastern Europe, India, Colombia, Mexico, Brazil, etc. The production structure consisted of production spaces located inside the factory, with over 1,500 employees, and other facilities were located in departments equipped with specialised machinery. The load-bearing structure of the building is typical of industrial facilities and was made from prefabricated elements fixed on a casing assembled from reinforced concrete elements. Part of the concrete structure located on the ground floor is visible at the entrance to the administrative block

on Mihai Viteazul Street. The façade of the administrative block is marked by vertical ribbed elements of reinforced concrete, which alternate with vertical strips of windows. Another airy structure, a kind of curving pergola with reinforced concrete pillars, connects the administrative block and the company flagship store, thereby forming a spacious courtyard that welcomes visitors.

The production spaces are located in the elongated block, placed a few levels below the administrative portion of the building that runs along Columna Street and features a similar industrial design. In 2017, the company Arhi Terra published the designs for their reconstruction project, which foresees the complete reconfiguration of the existing spaces. Work has yet to begin.

Five-tower Residential Complex

82, Albisoara Street
Yulia Skvortsova, Yurii Tumanyan, Anatoly Spasov
1987

This residential complex, consisting of five adjacent high-rise buildings with a shopping centre on the ground level, is a symmetrical structure. It is one of the era's most successful residential ensembles in terms of the composition of its volumes. The complex is located on an artificial lake on Albisoara Street, which reflects the architecture in a flattering manner. Built facing Mihai Viteazul Street, the towers have a modular construction with repeating layouts. Their configuration resembles an enormous Lego display. The individual towers are

placed up against each other, corner to corner, each either in a parallel or perpendicular position to its neighbour. The complex forms a mass of interconnected, earthquake-resistant structures. The monolithic concrete shell was built using a jump forming method. The façades are covered with a layer of plaster to hide the uneven traces of the formwork. The exterior retail spaces on the ground floor are highlighted by a cladding of white limestone. When viewed from the front, the blocks have a similar silhouette. The design of the complex is based on an expressive staggering of vertical volumes and a stepped height, both due to varying apartment layouts, which differ from one floor to the next. This is accentuated by the different shapes and volumes of the balconies. In the period after the year 2000, a building was shoehorned into the open space between the towers and the lake. The building is practically identical in length with the complex and has an appearance typical of this period of uncontrolled construction and development. This structure obscures the view of the five-tower complex, almost as if a concrete fence has been placed in front of it. The original intended effect of the ensemble has been lost as a result.

E

Residential Complex
1, Moscova Boulevard
V. Shalaginov, T. Derkachenko
1975

087 E

This complex of three residential buildings, arranged in staggered succession and interconnected by open terraces on the ground floor, wase intensely publicised at the time it was built, becoming an iconic image of the city. Elevated on a terrace between the first and second buildings, there is a suite of rectangular umbrellas supported by concrete pillars with a fountain at the base, which provide much needed shade and coolness. A little further on towards the intersection, an alcove-like area used to serve as a parking area for taxis. In terms of layout, the complex strikes a balance between open spaces and solid block-like volumes. The head planner of the complex, Vladimir Shalaginov, was active in Chisinau from 1962 (after graduating from the Academy of Arts in Kyiv) until 2005. He participated in the development of the general plan aimed at improving the aesthetics of the republic's capital (1980) as well as in designing and organising visual propaganda within the city and the development of residential complexes in the Centru, Rascani, Botanica, and Ciocana districts. The architecture of the National Hotel, the apartment ensemble on Stefan cel Mare Boulevard, and this three-part complex in the Rascani district are definitive of his work as a refined professional. In this apartment project, the load-bearing structure was built as a framework assembled from reinforced concrete elements, and the configuration of the loggias and the forms of the precast components lend the structures a monumental aspect. The sides of the buildings were often used for advertising texts and slogans, visible from a great distance. A slogan for the airline Aeroflot used to mark the top of the building – '1 hour and 45 minutes to Moscow'. The retail spaces on the ground floor of the apartments (including the Miorita bookstore, a grocery store, a pharmacy, etc.) are interconnected by a continuous canopy, supported by the asymmetrical layout and dynamic volume of the loggias on the façades – a stylish and expressive design

solution. Nowadays these spaces, used by a range of businesses (banks, cafes, restaurants, etc.), have been altered so that they visually compete with the towers behind them, while the square, once open and spacious, has been taken over by a host of fast-food restaurants (KFC, McDonald's, Andy's Pizza) and parking spaces. Originally, V. Shalaginov, working in collaboration with D. Palatnic, had planned the open space between this apartment ensemble for the (now demolished) trade union house of culture according to a systematic concept, which made the site one of the most successful urban ensembles. Together they formed a generous outdoor area, intelligently conceived in terms of the use of space. Due to the chaotic agglomeration of businesses on the grounds of the housing complex and the disappearance of the house of culture, this ensemble has lost its balance and the quality of its public space has been diminished.

E

The MEZON Factory

21, Moscova Boulevard
Architects not identified
1969

088 E

MEZON was one of the five leading microelectronics companies in the former USSR, with a production volume of over 130 million integrated circuits per year. It was the first microelectronics company in the southwest of the former USSR and the Balkans. Established in 1969, it specialised in high-tech microelectronics for the production of integrated circuits for the military-industrial complex and the consumer market. Located on a plot of land bounded by Studentilor and Matei Basarab Streets, the plant consists of a vertical volume that housed administrative offices, five production blocks flanking the office spaces and laid out perpendicular to Moscow Boulevard, and the company's canteen and production halls. The company was under the direction of the Ministry of the Electronics Industry of the USSR and was part of the Scientific Centre located in the city of Zelenograd. (Zelenograd itself was based on a Finnish prototype – the Tapiola satellite of Helsinki. The modernist buildings in Finland impressed Khrushchev to such an extent that he decided to engage in an experiment and laid the foundations of the city, planned by I. Pokroyvski, F. Novikov et al., which would become the research centre of the USSR's electronics industry.) The design of MEZON in Chisinau is virtually identical to the MICRON complex in Zelenograd, just with a different layout. The skeleton structure of the 12-storey administrative high-rise is an earthquake-resistant reinforced concrete framework assembled from prefabricated panels and slabs, and the façades, featuring vertical window strips, are covered with limestone. The production buildings are typical industrial halls with a reinforced concrete framework

supplemented by a metal structure. The façades consist of an aluminium profile grid and horizontal bands of windows alternating with strips of blue polychrome plastic panels. The four blocks, looking somewhat like giant aquariums, are elevated from the ground on pillars. On the ground floor, a gallery runs underneath all these halls perpendicular to their main axis and connects all the buildings. This gallery extends the entire length of the boulevard, joining these buildings with the administrative tower. The other side of the administrative building has a lower rectangular structure with expressive ribs, which houses the company canteen along with a conference room. This block could easily have been made from reinforced concrete, which would have made it much more dynamic, but the limited budget reduced it to a prefabricated concrete framework covered with a metal framework and sheet metal panels. The factory has not been in operation for some 15 years, and it has now been privatised, having been purchased by a Singapore-based company trying to set up an industrial park. The canteen building has been transformed into a Fourchette supermarket.

The Tashkent Building
3/6, Moscova Boulevard
Tashgiprogor Institute
1978

Decorated with mosaics and oriental motifs, this building cuts a lonely figure on Moscow Boulevard. In terms of volume, it forms a natural counterpart to the complex of buildings on the corner (V. Shalaginov and T. Derkachenko) and the ensemble running along the boulevard (V. Kudinov). The building has its origins in the 7.0 magnitude earthquake of 1977, the epicentre of which was in Vrancea, Romania. A state commission was established to assess the damage caused in Chisinau, which found that 11,848 buildings had been damaged, 2,786 were completely destroyed, and the total damage amounted to some 16.3 million roubles (21.7 million US dollars in 1977). Most of the high-rises withstood this test, especially those with a monolithic reinforced concrete carcass. The city of Tashkent had had its own difficulties during the 1966 earthquake and was substantially rebuilt thanks to a consistent effort, to which all the Soviet republics contributed. The fact that the Tashkent building was placed on Moscow Boulevard is symbolic. This was a gesture of solidarity as well as a symbol of the pan-Soviet policies of the Communist Party in the USSR. Designed by the Tashgiprogor Institute in Uzbekistan, the structure is made of prefabricated concrete forms and panels (3 × 3 m). The panels, including the mosaic tiles designed by fine artist Nicolai Jarskii as well as those used for the ornamentation on the main façade, were transported by rail from Central Asia. The grid-like patterning was the result of collaboration between the architects from the Tashgiprogor Institute and Aleksandr Jarskii, brother of Nicolai, who introduced embossed decorative elements into the design of architectural buildings in Tashkent. The fretwork grid marked an important stage in the Jarskii brothers' architectural activities, which incorporated mosaics as well as traditional sunscreens, or pandjara, into the technical processes of the time, with both used in the façade decoration of apartment blocks. The layouts of the apartments are modest, and the rectangular volume of the building is straightforward. The main façade is set forward from the rest of the building and encloses the loggias. It bears the geometric lattice-like ornamentation described above and is flanked on the side by a vertical row of windows. The side façades are constructed from panels decorated with mosaics with oriental motifs, and the cornice of the building features a frieze with the same motif, which tops the composition of the building. Today, the building is literally swarmed by parasitic structures on the ground floor. These spaces originally had a social function. Now they are occupied by the Victoria Bank offices, which have been substantially expanded over time. Enveloping one side of the building is a double-glazed shopping centre that encompasses several levels. What is most unfortunate is the way that several parts of the build have been illegally clad with polystyrene, which has disfigured the external appearance of the building, making it a parody of its former self.

E

The Gates of the Centre District

26–29, Grigore Vieru Boulevard
Architects not identified
1984

090 E

The two groups of dormitory buildings positioned symmetrically across from each other at the end of Grigore Vieru Boulevard are symbolic gates marking the boundary between the Rascani and Centre districts. Mirroring each other, the two groups each consist of three identical volumes, which decrease gradually in height down the boulevard. This complex, built during the heyday of the Soviet state, added a new landmark and accent to a boulevard designed in the 1950s. The symbolism of the city gates reflects the imagination of the architects, being part of a common set of themes related to the image of the city-fortress, which, as a rule, has guard towers placed on the main thoroughfares. Historically a small city, Chisinau never had protective walls, and thus the gates symbolically lent the city a new status in keeping with Soviet typologies. In terms of design, the buildings have a nested appearance. The shorter structures dock onto their taller neighbours, encircling them in a way that leaves a narrow vertical space between the buildings, which is punctuated by the stairwell volume. The load-bearing structure of the buildings has a rectangular monolithic configuration. The sober façade treatment is quite modest compared to other tall buildings in the city, which stand out with elaborate shapes and more complex spatial configurations. Their simplicity and minimalist decor underscores their likeness to medieval towers and is indebted to the aesthetics of the PO-2M precast panels used in construction. A similar decoration was used on the building of the Apa-Canal Chisinau Company. Only the façades facing the boulevard have

a vertically aligned row of balconies. Otherwise, the blocks have windows organised in a regular pattern, resembling the ordered grid of graph paper. In the spirit of the times, the roofs of both blocks featured neon structures simulating unfurled flags, which turned the blocks into landmark beacons at night. Today they are merely lit up with the advertising of commercial brands.

Residential Towers
11, Miorita Street
David Palatnik, Alexei Chmikhov
1975

091 E

This residential complex, consisting of three towers, is situated in a prominent place in the city on Telecentru Hill close to the campus of the Science Academy. The 15-storey blocks are placed a certain distance from each other along Miorita Street. The designs show a spectacular use of volume based on a rectangular block surrounded by multiple rounded vertical elements. These curved corners with their corresponding sets of windows marked the living rooms of the apartments. This use of panoramic windows is unique in Chisinau and gives the building a somewhat futuristic look. Similarly curved loggias are inserted between the rounded corner structures. A curious incident occurred during the 1977 earthquake, which proved to be serious test of these towers and their sliding formwork construction. Two of the high-rises withstood the calamity, while the structure of the third was badly twisted. A lawsuit followed, and the designing architects were investigated. It was discovered that the building was damaged due to unauthorised alterations made inside the cooperative apartments by the tenants during the construction of the building. The striking aesthetic of these complexes was part of an effort to counter the perception that all attention and resources were being directed to the city centre and the wide thoroughfares of various districts. Special attention was therefore paid to the outskirts of the city. This striking complex of apartment blocks is visible from the highway that leads into the city from the south.

E

Residential Complex on Mazarache Hill

092 E

2/2, Romana Street
Y. Skvortsova, A. Kurovsky,
A. Spasov, G. Rodidyal, E. Fedchenko,
S. Nedler
1984

According to legend, the Mazarache Hill, with its nearby spring, is the point of origin of the city. A site with sacred significance yet insufficiently explored by scholars became a place where tradition collided with modernity. One of the objectives of the urban plan approved in 1969 – and one of the points in the feasibility study developed in 1983 for a new urban plan – was to develop the city vertically rather than horizontally in order to preserve the arable land on the outskirts. The designs proposed by the architects responsible for the building – including I. Schvartzev, G. Solominov, and F. Shostak, who had designed similar ensembles – focused on breaking the monotony of standardised towers and creating a new image of the city. The complex was meant to be an architectural landmark in relation to the nearby nine-storey buildings, while the prominence of the church, a seventeenth-century heritage site, was toned down by the construction of this complex. The monolith-type towers each have two core volumes with modified layouts on each floor, together forming a well-organised spatial-volumetric ensemble. The alternation of different vertical volumes energises the entire structure, which is punctuated by the oscillating patterns of the balconies with their varying formats. The complex was designed in a minimalist colour scheme. A reddish hue forms vertical stripes and also accentuates the jagged pattern of the balconies. Over time, the standards of apartment living evolved, and some of the residents improved their homes on their own by adding a layer of polystyrene on the exterior, disrupting the original colour scheme of the façade. Today, the spatial balance that the design team meticulously sought to achieve has been visibly altered by the recent addition of an expressionless and poorly constructed apartment block nearby.

E

Complex of High-rises 'On Stilts'

093 E

112, Ismail Street
Gennady Solominov, Valery Kapliy
1984

The tower blocks located at the intersection of Ismail Street and Cantemir Boulevard are a sign of the new typology of urban planning, which was implemented starting in 1973 based on the urban plan developed in the late 1960s. By the time he relocated to Chisinau, G. Solominov had already designed, together with O. Vronsky, an apartment building on Dacia Boulevard (formerly Pacii Boulevard) as well as a number of administrative buildings, which represented calculated interventions in the urban fabric. The project of the high-rises 'on stilts' foreshadowed a complex plan of radical change in the image and identity of the city. The buildings are strategically located at a stop highlighting their outlines, and they occupy the hub of several streets with intense vehicle and pedestrian traffic. The spatial design is founded on the contrast between the dominant vertical volumes that form the corpus of the building and the horizontally running stripes on the exterior, the austere pattern of which is modulated by the undulating rhythm of the balconies. The dramatic use of volumes in these designs stems from the combination of various vertical volumes of different heights resting on a base or 'trunk' in the shape of the letter T. The upper core of the building protrudes nine metres in a cantilever beyond this, thereby creating the image

of a building sitting 'on stilts'. The living rooms of the apartments have a trapezoidal shape, with the location of the window openings depending on the orientation of the tower. The 15-storey monolith structures were built using a jump forming technology, which enabled the construction of an extensive complex consisting of seven apartment blocks on one side of Cantemir Boulevard and another four on the other side. The colour scheme was a tepid attempt to visually energise the sometimes monotonous landscape of standard reinforced concrete constructions. A similar spatial solution and grouping of apartment buildings was planned for the upper part of the city, near the new University complex. G. Solominov contributed to this project, but it was never realised.

E

Residential Complex with Service Infrastructure

3, Stefan cel Mare și Sfant Boulevard

094 E

*Vladimir Bessonov, Vladimir Shalaginov
(with contributions by V. Gandabulov,
V. Papushin, N. Ossenei, V. Grishko)*
1987

The complex consisting of four interconnected towers (with two and three modules) is one of the few examples of this kind. It occupies an area flanked by two side streets and a central boulevard. The shorter sides of the complex face Ciuflea and Izmail Streets. The oriel-type windows of the façade resonate with the nearby residential complex designed by V. Voitsekhovski on the central boulevard. These structures were used to increase the amount of sunshine reaching the interiors of the apartments. At the same time, the configuration of these bay windows along with the built-in loggias lends the façade a distinctly brutalist expression. The interior layout was designed for two- and three-room apartments. It offers comfort with living rooms that face the courtyard, while bedrooms looking out onto the boulevard are quiet at night. The load-bearing structure consists of a reinforced concrete framework and standardised panels, slab construction walls, and entire concrete modules premanufactured at the JBI reinforced concrete plant. The façades of the apartment buildings are plastered, and the service spaces on the ground

floor are clad with white limestone. The inner courtyard is one of the strengths of this complex; it is well organised and shielded from street traffic. Vehicle access is through the middle of the complex from L. Tolstoy Street. On the other hand, the complex was designed in such a way that the street space between the blocks and the boulevard is also generous and comfortable for pedestrians, with trees and shaded paths. The long side of the complex has a network of retail spaces that service the apartments (music store, pharmacy, travel agency, etc.). Another side is occupied by the C. Brancusi exhibition hall of the Artists' Union (UAP). The entrance to the exhibition hall is in United Nations Square, and the façade is decorated with a number of aluminium sheet sculptures representing the muses, which signals a privileged status for the complex.

Administrative Centre in the Ciocana District

13/1–13/2, Mircea cel Batrin
Boulevard
*Vladimir Bessonov, Yuri Tumanyan, Vadim
Kharitonov*
1989–2011

The administrative centre was designed for microraion n3 in the Ciocana district (formerly the Budesti district) and was conceived as a highly ambitious architectural ensemble. It consists of several types of nine- and 20-storey buildings aligned along Mircea cel Batran Boulevard. The detailed plan of the Ciocana district was laid out by Isaac Bubis in 1962, and the plan foresaw building over 7,000 apartments on an area measuring 15 hectares. In addition to the residential area, this city district included an industrial zone located between Mesterul Manole Boulevard and Industriala Street. The industrial area was developed in 1972 by a team led by G. Leventali, for which he won an award from the Council of Ministers of the USSR. The whole administration

centre was designed following a competition in which Isaac Shvartsev also took part, as well as the team led by Y. Tumanyan. Shvartsev came up with another more visually ambitious layout, which proposed a unique building in the shape of a vertically placed fan (with a

rainbow colour scheme) to complete the ensemble. Ultimately the more pragmatic project by Tumanyan's team was chosen. The administrative centre surpassed other similar structures in the city in terms of size and spatial-volumetric solutions, such as the complex of four blocks with

service infrastructure on Dacia Boulevard (G. Solominov, O. Vronski). The project underwent changes in the final stages, and the group of three tower buildings on the hill and the buildings with semi-circular layouts aligned on Mircea cel Batran Boulevard did not materialise. Instead, rectangular monolithic-type buildings were built, and their appearance negatively affected the initial visual solution. Only parts of the standard apartment buildings (series 143), the social area aligned with the centre of the ensemble (now the Ciocana District Court), and a series of other elements were positioned according to the initial layout. In fact, the entire Ciocana district was only partially developed and nothing was built beyond I. Dumeniuc Street. Currently, the semi-circle in front of the rectangular structures, which was designed as green space, is occupied by entrepreneurs who have inserted a gas station, a supermarket, and a bank on the site, practically swallowing up any free space and depriving the viewer of the wide panorama of the ensemble.

Sigma Production Company

76, Decebal Boulevard
Architects not identified
1963–1980

096 **E**

The twin towers of the company's administrative buildings can be seen from the intersection of N. Zelinski Street and Decebal Boulevard, while the engineering spaces were located in the rectangular building on the opposite side of Decebal Boulevard, behind which stood the production halls. The exterior design of the towers is simple but very expressive. They are positioned in parallel but staggered to one another and connected by a narrow vertical overlap. The two towers sit on a broad plinth and are situated along the axis of Teilor Street, thereby making them local landmarks that can be seen from afar. It is possible to see metal scaffolding on tall pedestals on the roof of each of the towers, visible from the upper Botanica neighbourhood. These were part of a neon lighting installation developed by a team of architects as part of the city's visual and generally propagandistic programme. They are no longer functional today. When it was operational, the company specialised in the production of special-purpose computer technology, which was used for research institutions, spacecraft (including the Mir space station), and the production of military equipment. The company's main product was radio-electronic equipment, including components for on-board ballistic missile computers as well as other electronic products and consumer goods. Throughout its lifetime, the company changed its name several times. Beginning in 1963, it was called the 'Luch' factory ('Луч' is Russian for 'ray of light'). From 1972 onward it became known as the '50th Anniversary of the USSR' calculator factory, or 'Scetmash' (from the Russian word for calculator), and since 1995 the remnants of the former company have been known as the Sigma Joint Stock Company. The elongated building housing the engineering facilities was built in the 1960s. Its load-bearing structure was a classic framework made of prefabricated elements. The façade has a standardised design characteristic of industrial Soviet modernism, in which strips of windows alternate with prefabricated concrete slabs. The load-bearing structure of the towers has a similar framework, while the elements on the corners and the façades are made of vertically aligned prefabricated concrete slabs, which are interspersed with rows of narrow windows set in aluminium profiles. The former site of the industrial halls, now demolished, is currently occupied by a Kaufland superstore and the construction site of a mammoth residential complex. Most of the former engineering spaces are occupied by the Elat shopping centre and other retail businesses.

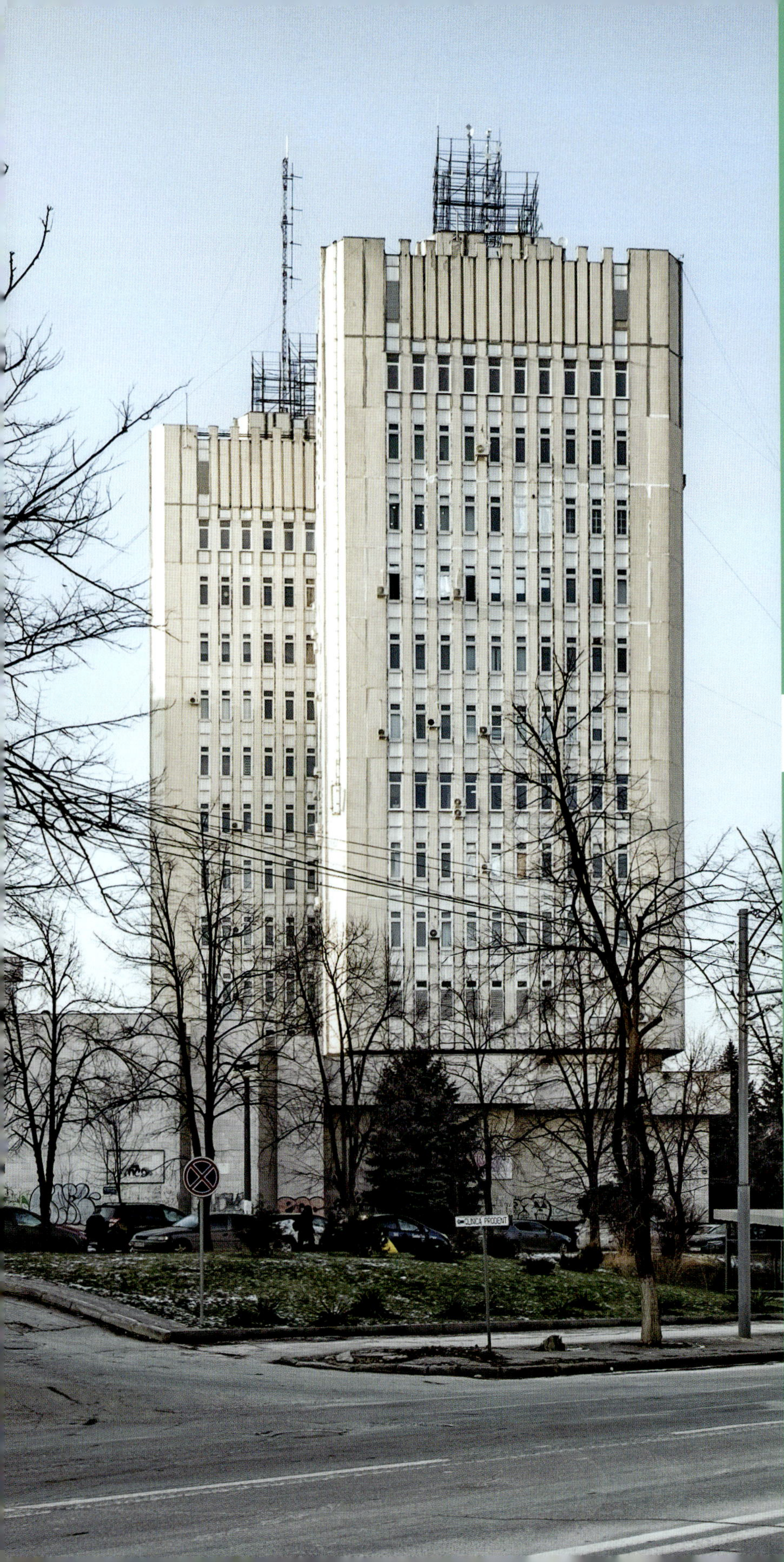

Experimental Residential Complex

47/2, Dacia Boulevard
Anatoly Gordeev, Alexandr Kireev,
Anatoly Kolotovkin, Semyon Shoikhet
1987

The Soviet KPD 143 series was another standardised series for residential housing successfully implemented in the Republic of Moldova. It was adapted for this site by the local architects (engineers P. Shibko and A. Snipelishsky). Experience gained in the field of design and construction of residential buildings through the use of large, prefabricated panels led to the introduction of new engineering and planning solutions. These led to a significant adjustment of the standardised designs produced by the construction

materials plant in Chisinau. The design of the KPD 143 series was developed by the Gosstroy Institute of the USSR. For this building, this series was taken as a starting point and then modified to increase the span of the transverse walls. This modification allowed the rectangular layout of the living room to be extended to optimal proportions. The hallways also became more spacious, allowing the incorporation of cabinets and summer spaces. In addition to these improvements, a version of a four-room apartment on two levels was also developed. This experimental 14-storey residential complex at the intersection of Dacia Boulevard and Burebista Street was built by a team of designers from the Moldgiprostroy Institute. The complex consists of two wings: the one facing Dacia Boulevard has four sections, while the

other one facing Burebista Street is made up of three sections connected by a central vertical volume. The residential building and the constructive elements of the 143 series have a signature appearance, which is not only characterised by the pattern of the decorative grid of the loggias but also by the modified configuration of the exterior walls. In addition, a concrete with a lighter composition was used for the production of the base panels. This was the first experiment in the construction of buildings like this in areas prone to earthquakes of a magnitude of seven. Decorative grids were used as ornamentation on exterior surfaces of the façades as well as on the reinforced concrete components of the loggias. The typology of the façade decoration was adjusted during the actual production process.

E

Residential Building Based on the 135 Series  098 E

38, Dacia Boulevard
Ivan Zagoretski
1974

The horizontal stretch of this building on Dacia (formerly Pacii) Boulevard is a unique presence in the urban landscape of Chisinau. This experimental building measures 300 metres in length and was assembled from six sections of 135-series blocks. It was developed by the Reinforced Concrete Engineering Bureau of the Gosstroy Institute of the Russian Federation (Irkutsk branch) and was then adapted to the local site by I. Zagoretsky. The unique scale of the apartment block, namely its unusual length, corresponds to the bordering boulevard and forms an appropriate counterweight to the two groups of monolithic tower buildings located to the side. The apartments in this block were designed with a functional layout, including the common rooms of kitchens and hallways and the personal spaces of the bedrooms and bathroom

facilities. The nine-storey buildings in this series have various technical furnishings, being equipped with elevators and waste collection devices. After multiple improvements to various constructive solutions and modifications to the façade, this series was widely applied in the construction of residential

E

buildings in other cities of the Republic of Moldova. In 1977, Chisinau's nine-storey, 135-series buildings withstood the strong earthquake that occurred in the Vrancea region of Romania without any notable damage, proving to be sufficiently strong and stable even in the face of a magnitude of seven-eight. The design of the 135 series for residential buildings with a prefabricated panel construction was developed in accordance with the decree of the Central Committee of the CPSU and the Council of Ministers of the USSR no. 382 dating from 28 May 1969, 'On measures to improve the quality of housing and civil construction'.

The Floare-Carpet Company
15, Gradina Botanica Street
Anatoly Kudla
1978

The administrative building of the carpet company stands out due to the flower bud shape made of sheet metal that seems to be sprouting from its roof. This highly visible motif refers to the name of the company (*floare* means 'flower') on the one hand, and to the floral elements that are omnipresent in the patterns of traditional Bessarabian carpets on the other. Founded in 1978, Floare-Carpet was the first carpet production factory in the Republic of Moldova. It was originally part of the manufacturing association known simply as Floare. It went

through several phases of changes to its product line, branding, and marketing. The Floare-Carpet brand was finally created in 1988. The company consists of an administrative building connected to the showroom area and a canteen for employees. Next to this are the production halls, which are covered by the typical sawtooth roofs of industrial buildings. The administrative tower consists of four vertical volumes, reminiscent of a stem or a cell in the process of division, an association enhanced by the floral element on the roof. The load-bearing structure is a framework made of prefabricated reinforced concrete elements and standardised panels. The façades are constructed from prefabricated slabs with individual designs. The entrance to the building

is accentuated by a cantilevered volume resting on two pillars. The administrative block sits on an extended stylobate. A gallery connects the ground floor of this building to a rectangular space covered with a semi-dome, which houses the showroom and the canteen. The ground floor gallery features a row of windows with vertical screen-like elements that have the dual function of providing security and decoration. The ribbed metal elements are continued on the façades of the administrative block and on the side façade of the semi-dome structure, taking this vegetal motif to the verge of kitsch. It is not clear whether this patterning was a deliberate design or simply a consequence of limited finances and time.

Portile Orasului ('City Gates') Residential Complex

100 E

50–51, Dacia Boulevard
Yulia Skvortsova, Anatoly Spasov,
Andrey Markovich
1980

With a shape reminiscent of open gates, this group of apartment building has become a symbol of the city as well as an indisputable landmark in terms of its architecture. The complex was designed by the Chisinauproiect Institute. During an initial development stage, the general plan for the districts on both sides of Dacia (formerly Pacii) Boulevard was drawn up, and then later the design and layout of the apartment blocks was finalised. The complex was designed by Y. Skvortsova, head of a creative workshop at the institute, in collaboration with A. Spasov and A. Markovich, and the project was coordinated by Y. Tumanyan, the chief architect of the city, together with the chief architect of the institute. The result was an ensemble that relates well to the adjacent eight- and 15-floor high-rises in terms of space and volume. Chisinau was a step ahead of other Soviet republic capitals in its testing of a range of standardised residential buildings – a process that was overseen by the State Committee on Construction (Gosstroy USSR). This complex consists of two symmetrically positioned 24-floor towers, which form the highest level in the stepped sequences of the building modules. The complex constituted a significant advancement in the quality of housing construction. The structure of the tower modules is a monolithic type, cast through movable formwork (jump forming), which was made of metal and had an adjustable configuration. The floors are made of large,

prefabricated panels the size of a room. In some instances, mixed-type floors with metal elements and reinforced concrete were also used. The reinforced concrete construction method made it possible to create a graduated volume, whose maximum increment was two floors due to earthquake safety regulations. Loggias cover the façade. They were built with prefabricated elements attached to the monolithic structure, and they form a geometric pattern reminiscent of traditional ornamentation, a pattern particularly prominent on the highest towers that face the boulevard. With their horizontal formats, the loggias form an expressive pattern that is repeated on all the façades, lending the volumetric structure an iconic monumentality. Both sides of the 'city gates', buildings 50 and 51/1, are owned by the municipality. According to the representative of the municipal company managing them, they are well maintained and do not require any major repairs.

E

Perspectives for the Future

Stefan Rusu

An article from the 1972 *Tinerimea Moldovei* newspaper, discovered on social media, makes detailed reference to the city of the future. A number of projects are mentioned, some standardised and adapted to the local context, others unique, with new boulevards and streets, an innovative social and cultural infrastructure, and green spaces and parks. All are deemed priority objectives. [1] The horizon of expectation conveyed by this plan coincided with the first year of the ninth five-year plan. Starting from this projection of the future, we shall try to visualise the city in two hypothetical states: from the perspective of the enthusiasts who were building the city and imagined it in the near future and from the perspective of the future that has materialised in the meantime.

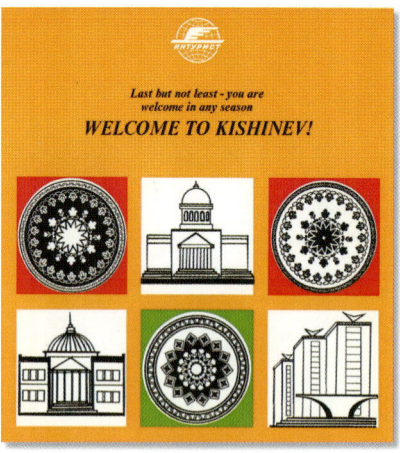

Welcome to Chisinau tourism booklet.
Vneshtorgizdat, USSR, 1970

The Future Seen from the Past

At the time of the article, a number of buildings (the Intourist Hotel, the Opera and Ballet Theatre, the State Circus, and the Trade Union Palace of Culture) had not yet been built, and the city was in a state in which a resident could imagine multiple scenarios for what Chisinau might look like in the future. A number of projects produced by the architects and creative teams of various design institutes (Moldgiprostroy, Chisinaugorproiect, etc.), which are available today in the form of drawings, sketches, copies, or altered photographs only, offer fascinating images of this extremely creative laboratory, which was mostly inaccessible to the general public. These designs and their unaltered visions of hotels, restaurants, and government buildings are testimonies to the process of materialisation. The image of the future is a cliché – part of the arsenal of romantic poets. The avatars of the future are usually associated with dreams, utopias, and ultimately, inaccessible horizons. In the case of Chisinau, the future was to be achieved at any cost. More than 60,000 young construction workers from all the enterprises and construction sites of the MSSR supported the architects' visions of building a new city, thus doubling the effort invested in the city's construction sites. Fuelled by the enthusiasm of the workers and the available resources of the republic, public buildings with social purposes – department stores, theatres,

The 'Al saptelea cer' restaurant on Moskova Boulevard designed by G. Solominov. Catalogue - Architect G. Solominov, Published by the Union of Architects of the Republic of Moldova

cinemas, public service houses, and research institutes – were already under construction. Professional expertise developed over time, and the teams of specialists from various design institutes were already conceiving architectural ensembles that would break the routine of the uniform streets and the standardised neighbourhoods. Creative methods and procedures for incorporating industrial prefabricated elements into residential blocks were being tested. A new type of city was emerging, both for residents and for potential visitors from other countries.

The architects of the 1950s and 1960s had been forced to work within the limits of strict regulations and standard constructions. They were unable to influence the appearance of the buildings, and they were focused exclusively on the configuration of the interior space of the apartments. Attempts to experiment with the volume and spatiality of the apartment blocks built from prefabricated panels, and later with the monolithic technology of the 1980s, did pay off. A few landmark structures were realised at the time are truly remarkable: the ensemble of the four tower blocks with social infrastructure on the ground floor on Pacii (now Dacia) Boulevard; the housing complexes on Moscova Boulevard; and the esplanade in front of the Trade Union Palace of Culture (since demolished), are just a few examples.

Other distinct examples are the plazas and squares on main thoroughfares,

such as the square at the end of the central boulevard, bound by the Intourist Hotel, the Chisinau Hotel, and the Academy of Sciences; the Square with its three-block complex (V. Shalaginov) and the Trade Union Palace of Culture (D. Palatnik) at the convergence of Kiev Street and Moscova Boulevard; and the G. Kotovsky Square (currently the C. Negruzzi Square), designed with several voluminous landmarks, where the Cosmos Hotel stands as a dominant marker of Y. Gagarin Boulevard. There are also the Ministry of Transport of the MSSR (currently the ATRIUM trade and leisure complex; V. Modarca, V. Shalaginov), which appears in the planned design in the shape of a clover leaf, and the building of the 'Moldovoschprom' industrial company, which was designed in the shape of a daisy (now the Uno shopping centre). Both landmarks shaped the square.

It is impossible to overlook Tineretului Boulevard (now G. Vieru Boulevard), which was designed and developed according to the highest standards of urban development and which strategically connects the central city with the Rascani district. The boulevard was designed in a compact and well-organised manner, and everything in it made sense: buildings, monuments, the cinema, green spaces, etc. The model of this boulevard was used as a prototype for other cities in the USSR (such as Gomeli, Belarus).

These are only a few landmarks, but it does not mean that other plazas, squares, and street intersections with their related infrastructure (pedestrian and underground crossings) were neglected. On the contrary, enormous resources were invested in every square metre of urban space, with the aim of creating comfort and meeting the needs of the inhabitants. Beyond all the rigours imposed by the planning system, one consistent aspect was the attention paid to the smallest detail and to the given context, whether the site was a public building or an apartment block.

At the same time, the development of the tourist industry was a priority on the agenda of the authorities, and the scale of the hotel networks (Tourist and Intourist) and the planned infrastructure

Reconversion of the Ministry of Transport of the MSSR (currently the ATRIUM trade and leisure complex), designed by V. Modirca and V. Shalaginov.
Photo: Vladan Jeremic & Rena Raedle

Mock-up of the building of the Russian drama theatre designed by G. Solominov.
Catalogue Architect G. Solominov, Published by the Union of Architects of the Republic of Moldova

(restaurants, cafes, tourist routes, etc.) in all the neighbourhoods of the city shows the attention increasingly paid to this area. Each architect had solutions and ideas for this type of site. In addition to the hotels that already existed and those under construction, in March 1978, the architect Gennady Solominov designed the Tourist Hotel, with a capacity of 924 guests (never built). A little later on in 1986, another hotel with nine floors and a capacity of 600 guests was designed (V. Bessonov, A. Neamtu) on Stefan cel Mare Boulevard at the intersection with Toma Ciorba Street (never built).

Another large hotel, which would have become a landmark on Pacii (Dacia) Boulevard, was designed by Y. Tumanyan and Y. Skvortsova. A unique project that would have rounded out the image of Moscova Boulevard was the 'Al saptelea cer' restaurant (G. Solominov) planned for the Rascani district, which is notable for its unique use of volume, both in terms of shape and the use of space. The central axis of the complex was marked by a tower offering a panoramic view and complemented by a suite of waterfalls and fountains. [2] The waterfall was to cross over the boulevard through an aqueduct and continue into B. Glavan Park (now the War Memorial To Sons of Motherland Park).

In the mid-1970s, the city was only beginning to take shape. The projects finished later on and those that existed as sketches, drawings, and paper models were an attempt at a fragmented reconstruction of the imagined city. Green spaces are an integral part of the image of the future city, as are places of leisure, which are attractive for residents as well as tourists coming from abroad. Valea Morilor Park, Cathedral Park, and Stefan cel Mare Park were rebuilt and redeveloped, and a new park was to be created in the Rascani district (called the 50th Anniversary of the Soviet Power). The Botanical Garden (the Dendrarium) of the MSSR Academy of Sciences was designated for the younger generation through the construction of a Pioneer Palace, a sports school, and a recreation area for children. In Prietenia Popoarelor Park (currently La izvor), where work started in 1972 in the Sculeni area, a theme park for children was planned and situated on the lake shore with an extension on one of the islands, which was populated with sculptures and fairy tale characters (the park was never finalised). [3]

Another important (but never realised) project was slated for the main boulevard. The four-storey Casa Cartii (House of the Book), developed by a team of architects from Georgia, was to have 10 reading rooms designed to hold over a million volumes and equipped with a digital catalogue and assisted book search. It was to simultaneously host over a thousand readers studying in the two halls, a lecture hall with 350 seats, and a cinema theatre. The complex of the Academy of Sciences of the MSSR (A. Kolotovkin, S. Shoikhet, V. Yavtukhovski, V. Tyayko) was projected at the end of Pacii (Dacia) Boulevard. It would have included a number of research institutes: the Institute of Ecologic Agriculture, the Institute of Genetics, Physiology, and Plant

The project of the residential complex of Budesti Hill in the Ciocana district. Designed by V. Bessonov, Y. Tumanyan, H. Kharitonov, 1989–2011

'Rainbow building' on Budeşti Hill in the shape of a semi-circle (chromatically representing a rainbow). I. Shvartsev. *Photo: I. Shvartsev Image source: forum oldchisinau.com*

Protection (V. Yavtukhovski, V. Kaplyi), and the Institute of Microbiology and Virology (designed between 1977 and 1980 by V. Sumishevsky). The Vine and Wine Research Institute (G. Bosenko, 1977–1978, unfinished) was supposed to be located at the entrance into Chisinau from the direction of Ialoveni. The institute was to be equipped with specialised laboratories, but the project was abandoned. [4] However, the most grandiose project planned was the State University complex (S. Shoikhet, V. Severinov, I. Vyhovanko, V. Khomenko), which would have utterly changed the landscape of the upper part of the historical city core. The headquarters of a scientific research institute (S. Shoikhet, B. Shpak, A. Esanu) housed in a 30-storey tower block positioned on the axis of Tineretului (G. Vieru) Boulevard was to have been a significant urban landmark of Rascani Hill. Furthermore, the Philharmonic complex (V. Sumishevsky) and the Museum of Arts were also in the process of being designed, and both were to complete the cultural area located in the city centre.

Such projects comprised the agenda for the new city, and most were developed by design institutes as part of national competitions. One planner, Isaac Shvartsev, stood out through numerous proposals for projects that were both unique and strategic in relation to social transformation: the main building of the Polytechnic Institute, the Sports Palace (similar to the Sports Palace in Minsk through its use of volume), the building of the telecommunications agency, and a complex of studios for animation films, among

other projects. The entire neighbourhood bounded by Bulgara, Kogalniceanu, and Shchusev Streets (except for the church in the area) was to be sacrificed for the construction of these studios. Another proposal, developed in collaboration, encompassed the entire civic centre of the Ciocana district, which culminated with a building on Budesti Hill, whose main façade was shaped in a semicircle (chromatically representing a rainbow) and aligned with the main axis of the complex. [5] In the end, the solution proposed by V. Bessonov, Y. Tumanyan, and H. Haritonov was preferred, completing the ensemble with three tower blocks (never built). [6]

For another competition, I. Shvartsev, in collaboration with A. Zaltsman, proposed a unique project for the building of the Russian Drama Theatre, the façade of which was based on a structure with geometric elements inspired by the aesthetics of Central Asian architecture. G. Solominov also took part in the competition; his idea was a building in the shape of a stone flower with petal elements that unfolded around a piece in the shape of an elongated ship. This proposal would have resulted in a postmodernist building with slanted and expressive surfaces, with a motif carved by the folk craftsmen from Cosauti as its striking feature. These bold visions of architecture landmarks did not materialise because they either embodied utopian ideas and did not fit ideologically into the urban context or they involved technical solutions that were too costly at that time.

Sketch of Chisinau 2000 according to the 'Cascadogrot' system
Image source: S. Lebedev doctoral dissertation, LISI, 1983

Sergey Lebedev, chief architect of Chisinau (1970–1986), seems more radical but also more complex in his visions, which sketched a futuristic image of the capital similar to the utopian visions of the Metabolists of the 1960s. [7] As an official rooted in the mechanisms of power, Lebedev, as a pragmatist, had insisted on the development of the capital on the vertical scale. At that time, Chisinau was surrounded by fertile lands and their importance to the country's economy was enormous. According to a decree of the Council of Ministers of the MSSR, construction on agricultural land was prohibited. The city was supposed to develop in the form of a homogeneous urban agglomeration within the confines of the existing urban area. However, this perspective and the principles that have underpinned urban development for decades were only partially implemented by Lebedev and his 'successors'.

A fascinating concept for the structure of the city for a somewhat more distant future is visible in the sketches of Lebedev, in the role of the visionary, made for his doctoral dissertation. The seven hills surrounding Chisinau form a rhizomatic system with viaduct roads that connect them with the city centre through concentric and multi-level belts. In his vision, the central part of the city is dominated by tall buildings, and thus the city of the future rises far above the historic core, and traffic flows high above it. Viewed in section, the seven hills have a densely populated internal structure that extends deep

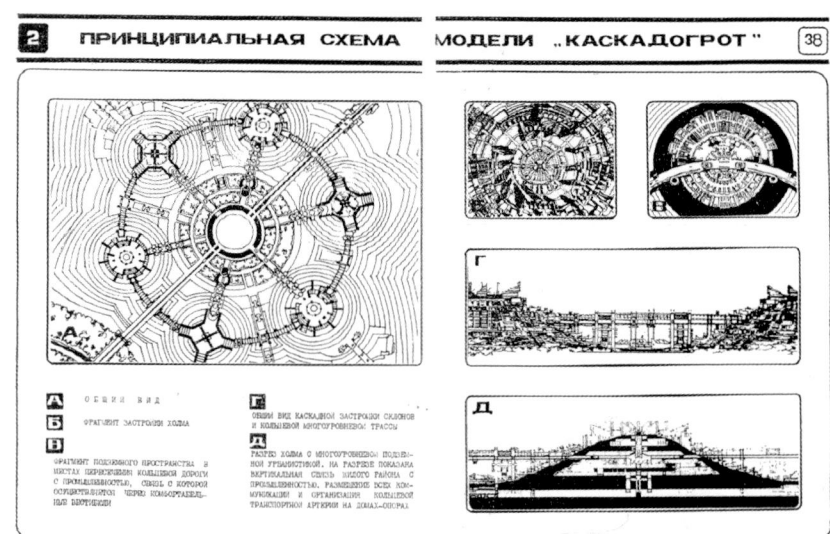

The scheme of the 'Cascadogrot' ('cascade' + 'grotto') system - Chisinau 2000
Image source: S. Lebedev doctoral dissertation, LISI, 1983

underground and are habitable both on the surface and below. The key elements of the project are the residential complexes that support the viaducts and thus form a single body. Other residential complexes cascade down the hills to the valleys, resulting in a modular and complex structure of gigantic proportions. Thus, the whole city becomes a huge organism, and the essence of what Lebedev proposed is called the 'Cascadogrot' ('cascade' + 'grotto') system – Chisinau 2000.

This is a utopian vision of a socialist city, which in some respects is similar to that of the founder of the Russian Social Democratic Party, philosopher A. Bogdanov, whose science fiction novels describe a communist utopia realised on Mars (*Red Star*, 1908; *The Engineer Manni*, 1913). This vision is even more similar in structure to Sergey Pavlov's novel *The Lunar Rainbow* (1977–1983), which describes the underground city of Arkad on Mercury – a bizarre combination of architecture and nature with flowing shapes and spaces that cascade into each other. [8]

The Future Seen from the Present

I have outlined the city imagined by the architects of the 1970s and 1980s, but what does the city of the future look like in the future that society found itself after 1992, and especially after 2000? How did those visions and projects materialise? One of the architects of the 1970s said that organisation and order disappeared as soon as the USSR was dismembered, and the ensuing shock did not help the city prosper or promote tourism. In fact, since the 1990s, the political spectrum has diversified, and so have real estate interests. A number of public buildings have fallen into the hands of individuals and groups exclusively guided by profit. In the absence of a functional mechanism for regulating and managing development, the architectural heritage remained exposed and was left to deteriorate. Without the political agenda of an authoritarian system and a lack of strict regulations and norms in design and construction, the development of the city was left uncontrolled. Existing land

and buildings have, for all practical purposes, ended up in the hands of real estate companies and interest groups. The whole mechanism, from designer to executor (construction trusts) has become entirely dependent on the investor, who can pull all the levers and is able to influence the decision-making process on all levels.

Since 1992, architects from the Soviet school of architecture and with solid experience have produced examples of architecture without being conditioned by a political programme or ideological pressure (V. Modarca, V. Shalaginov, for example). Later, other projects and other authors with individual visions and agendas (G. Telipiz, G. Zhinkin, for example) depended on a different type of relationship between investors and the architects, one that took many different manifestations. This is a different stage in the city's development and this period of transitional architecture has yet to be evaluated. The first investment projects in the central area of the city were owned by banks. Here we should mention the Moldindconbank building (V. Modarca, 1995), which heralded a series of new buildings that appeared in the strictly protected historical area of the city. It signalled that the era of a new architecture for a new political class had arrived.

Turbo-Architecture in the Period of Wild Capitalism

At first glance, post-Soviet architecture appears to be based on a trend of using a diverse range of shapes, finishings, and advanced technologies, all of which are disconnected from the spirit of a place. The phenomena of ignoring a site's relationship with the urban environment was worsened by the typological discrepancy of the new administrative buildings, which were perceived as if they were private buildings custom designed for VIP clients. In the end, when compared to the existing buildings, the projects for the business sector in the city centre recall in every aspect – from the colour scheme to the scale and the style of the new constructions – a kind of dental work that leaves the street with an expensive but

Moldindconbank designed by V. Modirca, 1995

nevertheless foreign implant. Most of the new buildings (offices, shopping centres, etc.) have façades that are made with a minimalist but strident choice of materials, while other cases use diverse materials and sophisticated combinations (bank headquarters, business centres, etc.), but with bizarre design solutions.

The result of all of the above taken together is a style that can be associated with turbo-architecture, a term that migrated from the 'breaking culture' of 1990s Serbia, where it was identified with an attitude of 'rule-breaking', including organised crime, intelligence services, the media, commercial architecture, and 'turbo-folk' music – an amalgam resulting from wars and recession. [9] Rambo Amadeus, a self-taught rock musician from Belgrade, was the one who coined the term 'turbo folk', which was later readapted by Srdjan Jovanović Weiss and introduced as 'turbo-architecture' in his book *Almost Architecture* (2005). He states: 'The heart of turbo culture is victory, but not under the flag of a single art form. Turbo must win. Not only to succeed, but to humiliate others at the same time.'

The slogan is also perfectly valid in the case of the architecture of the transition period in Moldova. The lack of a party or politicians with vision that would promote urban policies and regulations has enabled the development of an architecture built by an invisible authority, associated with the traffic of influence, bribery, and string-pulling.

A construction boom occurred in the mid-2000s after the country emerged from the financial crisis of the late 1990s. Then, after a period of stagnation, it picked up again after 2009 when the Democratic Coalition came to power. On several occasions, injections of cash were used in the construction of business centres, bank offices, and commercial and leisure complexes (malls), as well as residential complexes, which are practically dominating the market in the design sector.

The residential blocks, which quickly became a favourite area for real estate developers, are not notable for their diversity, except for a few residential complexes. The Coliseum Palace residential complex (Georgy Telpiz, 2011) was built on the site of the Gradina Moldovei store, which was privatised and later demolished. It is majestically placed on the axis of the park and the Memorial Complex dedicated to the victims of the 1979–1989 war in Afghanistan (the War Memorial to the Sons of Motherland Park). Consisting of two blocks assembled from several elements placed in a semi-circle and

The Coliseum Palace residential complex, 'ARD' GROUP, designed by G. Telpiz et al, 2011

resulting in a round-shape structure, the complex vaguely suggests an amphitheatre. The title of the complex celebrates an idea anchored in the mythology of the national discourse of the 1990s and of the Unionists (the presence of the Roman Empire in the Romanian space) in order to make it attractive to the locals. Here, the designers relied on the image resulting from the circular placement of the apartments and the layout of the apartments, which was freed from the rigours of Soviet regulations and thus constitutes an offer targeting the national elite.

An exception, at least in terms of the use of volume, is the residential complex consisting of three adjacent blocks with a three-angle profile, forming a dynamic pattern. It is named after the author: the 'Sailing Ship' (Vladimir Shalaginov).

The 'Sailing Ship' Residential complex designed by V. Shalaginov

Sun City shopping centre designed by V. Shalaginov

The residential complex is masterfully situated. It is oriented on one side towards Valea Trandafirilor Park, a green area with several lakes and another elitist destination accessible mostly to VIP clients. It is a terraced building with a decreasing number of floors in the direction of the sloping profile. The housing block designed by E. Prodan (Gorgona Architecture & Design) is a somewhat unique presence, partly the result of exceeding the mandated building height in a strictly protected area. The huge volume of the block is propped on leg elements, and the geometrically embossed shapes on the body of the building outline

ATRIUM trade and leisure complex designed by V. Modirca and V. Shalaginov

The housing block designed by E. Prodan of Gorgona Architecture & Design

the profile of a mammoth that strayed into the middle of a neighbourhood with nineteenth century houses.

After that came the Sun City shopping centre (V. Shalaginov). This project made use of the structure of a restaurant complex that had been abandoned for a long time, with investments made during the period of economic growth in the 2000s. In the business centre category, there are several notable buildings, most of which ignore the existing urban structure. There are, however, some exceptions. For example, the Eximbank headquarters (G. Telpiz) was placed at the northern end of the central boulevard between

Eximbank Headquarters, 'ARD' GROUP, designed by G. Telpiz et al

the ARTICO children's and youth centre and the pedagogical university, somehow removed from the critical area of the historic centre. [10] The Eximbank building contains an unusual combination of volumes, representing the most explicit expression of the turbo aesthetic.

We can also include the new headquarters of Gaz Natural Fenoza (Mihai Eremciuc), which was refurbished, like all other government funded buildings, using affordable materials and not much else. The strategy consisted of providing a more modern look for the old, Soviet-style building. The architects who worked on the new project deserve credit for preserving and showcasing the existing mosaic mural on the façade. This

The head office of Gaz Natural Fenoza designed by M. Eremciuc

demolished), anticipating another 'vacant lot' for the next big schemes in real estate. The Skytower Business Centre (G. Telpiz, 2007), located near the Post Office (V. Mednek, 1962), followed the same logic as Moldindconbank, only in a much more limited space. The image of the building recalls a slice of giant Swiss cheese, clad in metal and glass and sneaked in among the surrounding neo-Stalinist buildings. An awkward situation was speculated, as the demolition of the surrounding buildings was not allowed, but the new construction eclipses them through its height (which exceeds the mandated height of the area) and its position – semi-turned towards the central boulevard – which disregards the classic alignment on Vlaicu Parcalab Street. Several other projects that try to breathe fresh life into the city are worth mentioning, such as the 'Le Roi' International Business Centre (G. Telpiz, 2008) and the ARTCOR Centre for Creative Industries (M. Calujac et al, 2019), yet they do not change the general trend. Also, they are both located in a strictly protected area and do not demonstrate any affinity to the urban context – looking like pretentious stakes driven into the heart of the historical heritage of the city.

The dominant trend of turbo-architecture has nothing to do with the styles practiced in the MSSR during the socialist period, despite the fact that colossal experience has been accumulated. Chisinau had been designed as a unique architectural ensemble with the distinct specialisation of individual urban planning areas, with independent subgroupings, and a centre that was structured in accordance with the classical principles of urban planning. How could we return to normal and balanced planning for the city?

A possible path was suggested by the pragmatic Lebedev some time before he died. Once upon a time, the 'Moldgiprostroy' Institute had specialised departments in charge of all the areas of the city, and an entire department was dedicated to the 'city master plan'. Nothing remains. [11] Today, part of the city is in ruins, appearing as a desolate, sometimes apocalyptic landscape.

subjective inventory could continue with Energobank, an eclectic building, with pseudo-columns on the ground floor and a sequence of stairs, with a vertical insert that springs from level three and accentuates the façades. The building, crowned with a grill crown that marks the convergence of the façades, is located directly next to the Republican stadium (currently

We have become accustomed to seeing abandoned buildings in the city centre. The wind-blown skeleton of the National (Intourist) Hotel has become a structure associated with the period of transition and illicit privatisation methods. The fate of the hotel is currently uncertain, but there are signs that the current owner is planning to demolish it and build a new mega-hotel complex. After the transition, the hospitality industry did not become less profitable, on the contrary, but difficulties persist. The outdated standards and the tired infrastructure need modernisation. The hotels built in the 1970s cannot meet current needs. They require investment, but new owners try to solve the problems the easy way by demolishing and building something else instead. Ironically, the hotel that was renamed the 'National' during the changes brought about by the national movement that swept Moldova in the 1990s became privately owned and was subsequently

ARTCOR Centre for Creative Industries designed by M. Calujac et al, 2018

abandoned. The derelict Yuri Gagarin Youth Centre, which has been waiting for more than 20 years to be demolished, is in the same situation, while the Trade Union Palace of Culture was recently demolished only to be replaced by a Kaufland shopping complex. Some of the architects of the generation that contributed to the materialisation of today's city see the current cityscape as a chaotic, corrupt agglomeration, while they behave like Talibanic intellectuals who wish its instant annihilation as a bad dream, as an urban nightmare.

Despite multiple crises, whether financial or, more recently, related to the pandemic, Chisinau continues to experience a 'construction boom'. Office complexes, commercial centres, hotels, and restaurants are popping up like mushrooms after the rain. Meanwhile, the cost of living space keeps growing, and new apartments are increasingly harder to sell. Looking at the urban landscape today, we wonder what would have been if the utopian city densely populated on the vertical and horizontal that was proposed by the visionary Lebedev would have materialised? Would we have a happier and more responsible society due to this compact form of cohabitation?

Bibliography:

[1] I. Semenov. Chisinau orasul viitorului. Tinerimea Moldovei daily newspaper, 1972. Published on 15 February 2016. Source: <www.locals.md>

[2] Catalog - Arhitect Gennady Solominov, Published by the Union of Architects of the Republic of Moldova.

[3] A. Kolotovkin, S. Shoichet, I. Eltman, Arhitectura Sovetskoi Moldavii, Moskva: Izdatelstvo Stroyizdat, 1987, pp274.

[4] The Vine and Wine Research Institute (G. Bosenko). Журнал Архитектура СССР, N 8, 1977.

[5] The failed projects of the architect Isaak Shvartsev. Source: forum oldchisinau.com

[6] A. Kolotovkin, S. Shoichet, I. Eltman, Arhitectura Sovetskoi Moldavii, Moskva: Izdatelstvo Stroyizdat, 1987, pp296.

[7] Sergey Lebedev. Formirovaniye arkhitekturno – prostranstvennoy sredy krupnogo goroda v usloviyakh slozhnogo relyefa. Avtoreferat na soiskaniye uchenoy stepeni kandidata arkhitektury, LISI, Leningrad, 1983.

[8] Loren R. Graham & Richard Stites (ed.), Alexander Bogdanov. Red Star: The First Bolshevik Utopia. Bloomington: Indiana UP, 1984.

[9] Almost Architecture, Srđan Jovanović Weiss, published by Akademie Schloss Solitude, Jean-Baptiste Joly, Printed by Daniel Print, Novi Sad, 2006.

[10] Svetalana Platon, Luchshiye arkhitektory Kishineva, Published in Aquarelle magazine on September, 2005.

[11] Why Chisinau is included in the list of the worst cities in the world? Interview with S. Lebedev. Published on 13 April 2017. Source: <noi.today.ru>

The Skytower Business Centre, 'ARD' GROUP, designed by G. Telpiz et al, 2007

Index of buildings

Sorted by project number

Index of architects

Sorted by project number

Bibliography

A. Kolotovkin, S. Shoichet, I. Eltman,
Arhitectura Sovetskoi Moldavii, Moskva:
Izdatelistvo Stroyizdat, 1987

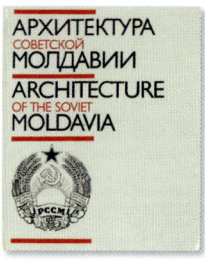

V. Smirnov, Gradostroitelistvo
Moldavii XIX-XX vekov. Editura Kartea
Moldoveneasca, Kishinev, 1975.

A. Kolotovkin, I. Eltman, G. Peldash.
Arhitectura Sovetskoi Moldavii, Moskva:
Izdatelistvo Stroyizdat, 1973

Y. Taras, Pamyatniki Arkhitektury
Moldavii (XIV - nachalo XX veka),
Izdatelistvo 'Timpul', Kishinev, 1986

K. Rodnin, Pamyatniki Moldavskoy
Arhitektury XIV-XIX VV. – K. :
Izdatelistvo Kartya Moldoveneaska,
Kishinev, 1960

Zadaci arhitectorov Moldavskoi SSR v 4-i
stalinskoi piatiletke. 1947. Soiuz sovetskih
arhitektorov Moldavskoi SSR. Upravlenie
po delam arhitectury pri Sovete Ministrov
MSSR. Biuleteni.

Haralambie Corbu (presedinte).
Enciclopedia 'Literatura si arta'.
RSSM: Editura: Redactia principala a
Enchiclopediei Sovetice Moldovenesti,
1986.

K. Afanasyev, 'A. V. Shchusev', Moskva:
Izdatelistvo Stroyizdat, 1978

I. Smolyar. Novyie goroda. Moskva:
Izdatelistvo Stroyizdat, 1972.

G. Gradov. Gorod i byt. Izdatelstvo
Stroyizdat, 1968

Nauchnyie prognozy razvitiya i
formirovaniya sovetskikh gorodov na baze
sotsialinogo i tekhnicheskogo progressa.
Vypusk 1 – 3. TSNTI po grazhdanskomu
stroitelistvu i arkhitekture, 1968 – 69.

A. Ikonnikov, G. Stepanov. Estetika
sotsialisticheskogo goroda.
M. Izdatelistvo Akademii Khudozhestv
SSR. 1963

N. Milyutin, Problema stroitelistva
sotsialisticheskikh gorodov. Osnovnyie
voprosy ratsionalinoy planirovki i
stroitelistva naselennykh mest SSSR,
Gosudarstvennoye izdatelistvo, 1930

M. Ginzburg, Stili i epokha. Problemy
sovremennoy arkhitektury, Moskva, 1924

Image credits:
Stefan Rusu (14 (a,b), 17 (a,b), 18, 19, 24, 39 (a,b), 45, 51, 54, 55, 58, 59, 60, 61, 62, 63, 64, 67, 70–71 (a, b), 72–73 (a, b), 74–75, 78 (a,b), 79, 80, 82, 83 (a, b), 84–85 (a,b), 86–87, 88–89, 90–91, 92–93, 96 (a, b), 100 (a, b), 101, 102, 105, 106–107, 108–109, 110–111, 112, 114–115, 116–117, 119 (a, b), 122–123, 124–125, 126 (a, b)–127, 128–129, 130–131, 132–133, 134 (a, b)–135 (c), 136 (a)–137 (b, c), 138 (a, b)–139 (c), 142–143, 144–145, 146–147, 148 (a, b)–149 (c), 150 (a, b)–151 (c), 152, 154–155, 156–157, 158–159, 160–161, 162–163, 164 (a, b)–165 (c), 166, 167, 168, 169, 170 (a,b)–171 (c), 172 (a)–173 (b, c), 174–175, 176 (a, b)–177 (c), 179, 180–181, 184 (a)–185 (b, c), 187, 188–189, 190–191, 192, 194–195(a, b), 196–197, 198–199 (a, b), 200–201, 202–203 (a, b), 204–205, 206–207, 208–209, 210 (a, b)–211, 212 (a, b)–213, 214–215, 216, 217, 218–219, 220–221, 222–223, 226–227, 228–229 (a, b), 230, 232 (a, b)–233, 234, 235 (a, b), 236 (a, b)–237, 238–239, 240–241, 243, 244–245, 246, 247, 248, 249, 250–251, 252–253, 254–255, 256, 257, 258–259, 260–261, 262–263, 264–265, 272, 273 (a, b), 274 (a, b), 275 (a, b), 276 (a, b), 277, 278 (a, b), 279), Philipp Meuser (4, 6–7 (a, b), 104, 118, 120–121(a, b), 153, 167, 186 (a), 231, 287), Max Kuzmenko (66, 68–69, 77, 94–95 (a, b), 97, Vlada Ciobanu (26), G. Solominov (267, 268 (b)), Vladan Jeremic& Rena Raedle (268 (a)), V. Smirnov (11 (a), 25, 28 (b), 29), S. Lebedev (270 (a,b)), B. Krutsko (20 (b)), A. Beloconi (269 (a), I. Shvartev (269 (b)), Forum Oldchisinau.com (9 (b),

10 (a), 40, 76 (a), 103), National Archive of Republic of Moldova (8, 11 (a), 18 (b), 43, 52, 113), Archive of A. Shchusev Museum, Chisinau (9 (a), 10 (b)), Archive Vladimir Jakushewitsch (53), Archive of A. Vatamaniuc (9 (c)), Archive of N. Velichko (12, 13), Vneshtorgizdat (11 (b), 266), Wikimedia Commons (19 (a), 20 (a), 28, 32 (a, b), 37, 40, 50, 55 (b), 266, 269 (a))

The author would like to express his gratitude to Andrei Ichim, Sorana Lupu, Lilia Dragneva, Max Kuzmenko, Anatoly Gordeev, Ovidiu Tichindeleanu and Aliona Niculita for their support and contributions to this publication. Special thanks to the team of oldchisinau.com for keeping the forum alive and preserving an open-source archive on the history of the city and its development.

Author and Co-authors

Stefan RUSU (born 1964) is a freelance curator and urban researcher currently based in Islamabad, Pakistan. Through his projects, he contextualised in a critical manner the political transformation processes and the changes occurring in post-socialist societies after 1989 that influenced the way people and communities relate to the use of public space. His recent initiative, Insular Modernities, investigates how the socialist architecture designed and built in Eastern Europe is maintained and perceived today at the peripheries of the former empire and explores modernist architectural heritage in various formats (exhibitions, publications, documentaries, social media platforms, etc.).

Vlada CIOBANU (born 1988) is an activist, blogger, and project coordinator within the organisations Primăria Mea and the Centre for Policies and Reforms, based in Chisinau. Ciobanu is a trainer in community organisation, advocacy campaigns, fundraising, and crowdfunding. Her research interests are related to the way the city of Chisinau was built and is being built.

Irina DUBINSCHI (born 1984) is an urban and socioeconomic researcher based in Chisinau. She achieved a master's degree in social philosophy in 2008. She currently works in an architectural studio, where the main duties are the analysis of urban development, social needs, and landscape projects. Her major research interest remains on the issue of inter-confluence between urbanisation and social progress.

Anastasia FELCHER (born 1986) specialises in the cultural history of East European borderlands. She holds a PhD in cultural heritage management and development from the Scuola IMT Alti Studii Lucca (2016). She has published works on the heritage of minorities in pluralistic societies, dilemmas of Jewish heritage in the post-Holocaust age, and literature and politics in Eastern Europe. Currently, she is employed as the Slavic Archives Specialist at the Vera and Donald Blinken Open Society Archives at Central European University in Budapest.

Vitalie SPRINCEANA (born 1982) is a sociologist, blogger, journalist, and urban activist based in Chisinau, Moldova. He has a BA in political sciences from Sveti Kliment Ohridski University in Sofia, Bulgaria, and a Magister Philosophiae from the State University of the Republic of Moldova, where he has also worked as a university lecturer. He is co-editor at platzforma.md, a web platform for social, economic, and political critique. He is interested in and argues for inclusive democratic public spaces, social justice, free knowledge, and plurality of worldviews and practices.

View from the city center of the ATRIUM trade and leisure complex designed by V. Modirca and V. Shalaginov.

The *Deutsche Nationalbibliothek* lists this publication in the *Deutsche National-bibliografie*; detailed bibliographic data are available at *http://dnb.d-nb.de*

ISBN 978-3-86922-548-7

Layout and Maps
Andrei Ichim

Translation
Sorana Lupu

Proofreading
Laura Schleussner
Sandie Kestell

QR codes
Masako Tomokiyo

Printing
Tiger Printing (Hong Kong) Co., Ltd.
www.tigerprinting.hk